Old Age Abuse

A new perspective

Second edition

Edited by
Mervyn Eastman

Social Services Department
Enfield, Middlesex, UK

Co-published with Age Concern England

CHAPMAN & HALL

London · Glasgow · Weinheim · New York · Tokyo · Melbourne · Madras

362. 6042
EAS

84487

Published by Chapman & Hall, 2–6 Boundary Row, London SE1 8HN, UK

Chapman & Hall, 2–6 Boundary Row, London SE1 8HN, UK

Blackie Academic & Professional, Wester Cleddens Road, Bishopbriggs, Glasgow G64 2NZ, UK

Chapman & Hall GmbH, Pappelallee 3, 69469 Weinheim, Germany

Chapman & Hall USA, One Penn Plaza, 41st Floor, New York NY 10119, USA

Chapman & Hall Japan, ITP-Japan, Kyowa Building, 3F, 2-2-1 Hirakawacho, Chiyoda-ku, Tokyo 102, Japan

Chapman & Hall Australia, Thomas Nelson Australia, 102 Dodds Street, South Melbourne, Victoria 3205, Australia

Chapman & Hall India, R. Seshadri, 32 Second Main Road, CIT East, Madras 600 035, India

Distributed in the USA and Canada by Singular Publishing Group Inc., 4284 41st Street, San Diego, California 92105

First edition 1984
Second edition 1994

© 1984 Age Concern, England, 1994 Chapman & Hall

Typeset in 10/12pt Palatino by Mews Photosetting, Beckenham, Kent
Printed in Great Britain by St Edmundsbury Press,
Bury St Edmunds, Suffolk

ISBN 0 412 48420 X   1 56593 291 9 (USA)

A catalogue record for this book is available from the British Library

Library of Congress Catalog Card Number: 94-70927

∞ Printed on permanent acid-free text paper, manufactured in accordance with ANSI/NISO Z39.48–1992 and ANSI/NISO Z39.48–1984 (Permanence of Paper).

This book is dedicated to the memory of my father-in-law, Ted Levett, whom I miss greatly

' ... I pushed her down the stairs and killed her ... '

Anonymous telephone call following item in
The Guardian, *17.3.82*

' ... I would honestly not have thought that I could ever have felt like I did, and still think "granny battering" is abhorrent. If there is an answer I hope society will find it quickly.'

Mrs N. (Gwent)

Contents

Contributors

Drew Alcott Chartered Clinical Psychologist, Unsted Park Rehabilitation Hospital, Surrey.

Dr Gerald Bennett Senior Lecturer in Health Care of the Elderly, London Hospital Medical College; Honorary Consultant, Royal Hopsital Trust; Consultant in Care of the Elderly, City and East London Family and Community Health Services.

Dr Simon Biggs Programme Co-ordinator, Central Council for Education and Training in Social Work, London.

Mervyn Eastman Deputy Director of Social Services, London Borough of Enfield, Middlesex.

Dr James George Consultant in Medicine for the Elderly, Cumberland Infirmary, Carlisle.

Dr Chris Gilleard Top Grade Clinical Psychologist, Springfield University Hospital, and Senior Lecturer in the Psychology of Old Age, St George's Hospital Medical School, London.

Fiona Goudie Chartered Clinical Psychologist, Nether Edge Hospital, Sheffield.

Dr Elizabeth Hocking Consultant Geriatrician (retired), St Margaret's Hospital (Skatton), Wiltshire.

Dr Ann Homer Consultant Physician, Department of Medicine for the Elderly, Edgware General Hospital, Middlesex.

Dr Raymond Jack Director of Post-Qualifying Studies in Social Work, Anglia Polytechnic University, Cambridge.

Professor Bernard Knight Professor of Forensic Pathology, Institute of Pathology, Royal Infirmary, Cardiff.

Claudine McCreadie Age Concern Institute of Gerontology, King's College London.

Bridget Penhale Social Work Team Leader, St Michael's Hospital, Norfolk.

Chris Phillipson Professor in Applied Social Studies and Social Gerontology, University of Keele, Staffordshire.

Jacki Pritchard Locality Manager in the Sheffield Family and Community Services Department, Sheffield.

Dr Phil Slater Principal Lecturer in Social Work, Middlesex University and Enfield Social Services Department, Middlesex.

Jim Traynor Community Care Manager, Leeds City Council, Leeds.

Foreword

Age Concern always seeks to be at the forefront in raising issues of importance as part of our continuing fight to improve the quality of life of older people. To this end we are privileged in being able to draw on the skills of people with the commitment, expertise and enthusiasm to press for much needed change. When, some years ago, we published a book by Mervyn Eastman on old age abuse, the subject was largely unrecognized. He played a pioneering role in drawing attention to this difficult and sensitive topic, classifying the various types of abuse, analysing their causes, their tragic effects and the different contexts in which they were likely to occur.

Earlier, when I joined Age Concern, I had been struck by the paucity of knowledge of old age abuse. My previous work with children and young people provided me with stark reminders of how much more developed both policy and practice were in dealing with the abuse of children. Even in that field there was still much to learn, and subsequent legislation, policy guidelines and codes of practice have taken us further down the road by constructing clear lines of accountability and by protecting and representing children at risk, by helping potential abusers and developing practice that avoids punishing victims through removing them from their homes. Such progress was made from a position of strength when compared with the situation of elderly people, whose vulnerability to abuse was often denied, misunderstood or discounted. In a subsequent book, published in 1986, Age Concern drew up a range of recommendations for changes in the law. Some of those appear to have influenced the comprehensive proposals recently drawn up by the Law Commission. Recent guidelines

produced by the Social Services Inspectorate will also, hopefully, improve practice in this delicate and sensitive area of
work.

Another welcome initiative is the recent establishment of
a new specialist organization, Action on Elder Abuse, which
Age Concern has been able to support in its initial stages of
development. Through it, we hope that people in different
disciplines and professions will be able to come together,
drawn by their determination to eradicate a most pernicious
and tragic form of ill treatment affecting one of the most
vulnerable groups in our society.

There has certainly been some progress since the early days
when our attention was first drawn to old age abuse, and this
new book, with which Age Concern England is delighted to
be associated, is both a major step forward in its own right
and a pointer to the future. Through it we can better appreciate
the complicated relationships from which explosive situations
may well erupt. We should be better equipped to prevent abuse
by understanding the underlying power relationships frequently involved and the dilemmas and stresses affecting professional care staff and carers alike.

The book underlines the need for training to help us grasp
this difficult issue with sensitivity and strength, so that if we
cannot totally eradicate old age abuse we can at least hope to
reduce its occurrence and mitigate some of its worst effects.
Some questions, however, remain. How much is this form of
abuse a human response by a tiny minority to society's neglect
and to the fact that collectively we hold an unrealistic assumption about people's capacity to care, whether for a relative or
for a patient or client, with little support, for a period that may
extend to many years? Most people enter a caring relationship through devotion and love, but some will face an intract-
able situation in which individual choice, dignity and a degree
of autonomy for vulnerable elderly people or those who care
for them are unrealistic options talked about by people who
often have little understanding of what is really involved.

Through all these years Mervyn Eastman's commitment to
this subject has remained unparalleled. In this book he has
been able to complement his own very particular insights with
those of experts in many areas of specialist interest. It is most
fitting that he has taken on this role in a publication that marks

an important step in our quest to improve the lives of the many people who need our help and whose voices must be heard. They are, by definition, frail and extremely vulnerable. It is easy to ignore them. This book is important as one way of ensuring that they are **not** ignored and that their voice **is** heard before it is too late.

Sally Greengross
Director
Age Concern England

Preface

Much has changed since the mid-1980s in how we view violence against older people by family members, and new 'experts' have come to the fore. Baker, Bursten and myself have been joined, even eclipsed, by the likes of Bennett, McCreadie, Homer and Pritchard, and this is how it should be. Their contributions to the field since the publication of the first edition of this book, *Old Age Abuse*, in 1984 have enhanced our knowledge, broadened our understanding and raised more questions.

It is therefore the intention of this book to provide an overview of the current thinking on the causes and consequences of, and possible interventions in, old age abuse by some of those who are committed to increasing our awareness of the problem.

Two issues in particular have grown in importance for me since 1984. Firstly, is 'dependency' a factor in abuse or simply a function of the sampling done by researchers? And second is the matter of violence in the residential setting.

With regard to the former, I am still of a mind to consider dependency (whatever this may mean) to be a key factor. But dependency cannot be separated from 'power'! The use and abuse of power in relationships, whether intimate or casual, formal or informal, paid or unpaid, perhaps offers a key to increasing our understanding. This area needs further work and will, perhaps take several years: even in child protection work we skirt the edges of the pool – or is it a sea – in coming to terms with 'dependency' and the power of an adult over the life of a child.

It is a matter of deep regret to me that I have paid so little attention over the past decade or so to the second important issue, that of the links between elder abuse in the domestic setting and institutional abuse. From Barbara Robb's *Sans Everything* published in 1967 (Thomas Nelson & Sons) to the *Inquiry into Nye Bevan Lodge* (Gibbs, Evans and Rodway, see References to Chapter 5) in 1987 and beyond, one is forced to ask: what are the differences between an adult daughter or son caught in the carer's trap and a care assistant or officer caught in the mindless routine of residential provision?

Taking the concept of power, I have often been asked by audiences of professional workers to comment on the notion that older people contribute to their own abuse. While I accept that the behaviour of some older people does act as a trigger for their carers to abuse, this should not justify, but rather explain, the reason(s) people abuse. Whatever the causal factors, to harm another person, especially when vulnerable, remains an offence both in legal and human rights terms. 'They asked for it, didn't they?' was a prevalent notion in the late 1970s. It is still around today, and can easily lead to the further disempowerment of older people. Victims can easily be turned into 'persecutors' especially if the power rests with those who care for vulnerable adults.

I hope that this edition will plug many of the unintentional gaps of the 1984 book, although I am aware that as some gaps are filled, others open up. No reader should approach this edition expecting the definitive update on abuse. It is not a handbook, a study text or a manual, it is simply reflections brought together in the form of contributions from leading experts. It is intended to complement the growing literature on elder abuse, an issue that I am convinced is set to explode over the next five or so years.

One significant gap, soon to be filled by the work of Malcolm Holt, a social worker with Northumberland social services, is in the area of elder sexual abuse in the UK. I recently met Malcolm at a conference where he outlined his findings. These were published in 1993 by King's College Age Concern Institute of Gerontology as part of the Ageing Update Conference proceedings – *Elder Abuse: New Findings and Policy Guidelines*.

Sexual abuse, he argues, needs to be specifically included in definitions of elder abuse and in practice guidelines. His work is extremely challenging and I am convinced that, as a result, he will find many enemies within social work, research result, he will find many enemies within social work, research and management as he bravely seeks to break through what is, perhaps, the final taboo. I was unable to invite him to contribute, and hope this acknowledgement will in some way give Malcolm support and encouragement in his pioneering work so reminiscent of my own experiences between 1980 and the publication in 1984 of *Old Age Abuse*.

There is inevitably some overlap in material between chapters, but I follow Jordon Kosberg's reasoning in *Abuse and Maltreatment of the Elderly* (John Wright, PSG Inc., 1985), that such overlapping 'underscores certain commonalities'. I have, nevertheless, attempted to edit out repetitiveness so as not to bore readers who prefer to read the book as a whole, rather than dipping in and selecting areas of particular interest.

The book is divided into sections. Part One examines the nature of abuse and Claudine McCreadie has given an excellent general introduction to the issues, practice and policy. Dr Ann Homer examines the prevention of abuse by drawing on a study she conducted in south London during the late 1980s, and Dr Elizabeth Hocking, a longstanding friend and co-worker of mine, considers the process that leads to abuse from the point of view of the carers.

Part Two continues the carers' theme, firstly by examining the notion of 'dependant abuse'. Dr Ray Jack then looks at dependence, power and violation as 'the currency of relationships rather than the property of individuals' and Dr Chris Gilleard looks at residential and hospital settings. The two thus address a significant gap in my first publication.

Dr Gerald Bennett begins Part Three, which looks at dealing with old age abuse, with a chapter on clinical diagnosis and treatment. Dr Bennett has become one of the UK's most fervent and prolific contributors to our understanding of old age abuse, and I am proud to have his name associated with this publication.

Jacki Pritchard is yet another whose name I am happy to include, and her chapter considers how local authority social services departments are currently addressing the issue of old age abuse, their methods and practices. Bridget Penhale continues the consideration of practice, examining the similarities and differences between old age abuse and other forms of domestic violence.

I make no apology for the emphasis in this section of the book on social work practice, as it continues to play a central and crucial role in assessment and prevention as we move towards the full implementation of the NHS and Community Care Act, 1990.

Part Four looks at various aspects of abuse. First, Dr James George considers the racial and ethnic dimension (a chapter which proved extremely difficult to obtain a contribution for) and then follows Professor Bernard Knight's fascinating, but disturbing, work on geriatric homicide. He writes, 'the killing of an elderly person by his or her spouse should not be too unexpected . . . ' and gives the reader a valuable insight into an often neglected aspect of elder abuse.

Part Four concludes with Jim Traynor 'Lifting the lid on elder abuse'. Traynor and I have been sparring partners for a number of years: I find his scepticism as disturbing as he finds my compulsion! Traynor offers readers a haven of balance.

Training issues provide the focus for the final section of the book. Dr Simon Biggs and Professor Chris Phillipson concentrate on the development of training programmes and Fiona Goudie and Drew Alcott consider assessment and intervention from a training perspective. Since we are moving increasingly towards multi-agency needs assessment and joint training initiatives, their contribution is greatly appreciated.

By having this book 'topped' and 'tailed' by McCreadie and Dr Biggs and Professor Phillipson, I consider I have brought together writers whose combined scholarship and experience (added to that of all the contributors who so willingly accepted the challenge and gave their time) make this book clear, understandable and, above all, unequalled and unique in the literature of old age abuse.

As the editor of this book I would particularly like to acknowledge the contribution of Sally Greengross. She supported and encouraged my interest in old age abuse when I was a young social worker and as I now enter middle-age she continues to pioneer this area of investigation and research. Her own contribution cannot be underestimated and her commitment knows no limits.

Chapman & Hall have, over nearly two years, offered encouragement, support, skill and determination. The patience of Lisa Fraley (editor) was remarkable and she was a constant source of help and support as I doubted my ability to draw the book together. I am also grateful to Lynne Maddock (sub-editor) whose work was always underpinned by professionalism and determination. My thanks also to Chapman & Hall's production department, and last, but by no means least, my thanks go to Fiona Toms (copy-editor), who demonstrated a skill and ability that were awesome. Without doubt, Fiona turned a rough and contradictory manuscript into a product of good quality. To her I owe a debt I can never repay.

Finally, attempting to produce a book that is up-to-date is like trying to catch a moving train. By the time it is published, well-informed readers may complain that it does not include the latest findings. This, I argue, cannot be avoided, and I would simply ask well-informed readers to bear in mind that their knowledge surpasses that of the majority, who will hopefully value the contribution this publication makes to understanding elder abuse.

The mission of this book is to encourage the opening of closed doors; to encourage care professionals and their managers to consider abuse of older people to be an aspect of their work that can no longer be denied or ignored.

Mervyn Eastman
July 1993

Part One

The Nature of Abuse

Introduction: the issues, practice and policy

Claudine McCreadie

Human beings, both at an individual and a social level, behave in ways that can readily be termed abusive.

INTRODUCTION

Two critical questions stand out in a general overview of the policy and practice issues associated with abuse of elderly people: what are we talking about and what is known about it?

To answer these questions we must turn to research. Research has important implications for policy and practice. An accurate understanding of the reality of abuse of elderly people is essential both for the necessary alleviation of suffering, preferably through prevention, and for the proper allocation of resources. Unless that understanding is present, scarce resources could be wasted.

What, then, can we learn from research? This chapter will focus on what is – or is not – known about four areas: the definition of abuse; how much abuse there is; who is abused and by whom; and what explanations are being offered for the problem.

Until 1989 relatively little had been written about abuse of elderly people in the UK apart from the pioneering efforts of Eastman (1984) and one or two others (McCreadie, 1993b). Since then, publications about elder abuse have increased significantly, and much needed research has begun (McCreadie, 1991; McCreadie, 1993a). However, this chapter relies heavily on research done in Canada and the USA, not least because it has informed recent thinking in the UK (Bennett and Kingston, 1993; Decalmer and Glendenning, 1993; McCreadie and Tinker, 1993). One general implication of the research is that elder abuse is a complex subject and one where we should be wary of stereotypes and simplistic explanations.

WHAT ARE WE TALKING ABOUT?
QUESTIONS OF DEFINITION

It seems unlikely that there will ever be agreement on a single all-embracing 'authentic' definition of abuse. The main reason for this is that a definition serves a purpose, and definitions for legal purposes or for guiding policy and practice may need to be different from those used for research. At a recent gathering in the USA of 10 of the top experts in the field of elder abuse, no single definition could be agreed (Stein, 1991). On the other hand, a large measure of agreement was reached in a poll of 63 experts from different professional backgrounds, suggesting that it is possible to gain precision in talking about abuse. However, within the current literature there are many different definitions (McCreadie, 1991; Decalmer and Glendenning, 1993; Bennett and Kingston, 1993).

Health and local authorities in the UK are developing definitions in the course of producing guidelines (Pritchard, 1992; Penhale, 1993). After extensive consultations, the Social Services Inspectorate of the Department of Health has published practice guidelines recommending that social services departments should adopt an inter-agency approach to definition (Social Services Inspectorate, 1993).

It would seem unlikely that there is a right answer to the problem of defining abuse, but a basic requirement of any definition is clarity, so that at least people know what they are talking about with some degree of precision (McCreadie, 1991). Clarity demands consideration of a number of different components in a definition: relevant age; the setting of abuse; the abuser; the abused person; the type of abuse; and increasingly recognized as important, the dimensions of abuse.

In the USA, there is a lively debate on whether self-abuse and self-neglect should be included, mainly because these constitute the majority of cases referred to protective service agencies, which are the legally mandated bodies for

investigating suspected abuse (Stein, 1991). While recogniz-
ing that the effect on a person may be the same, whether
inflicted by him- or herself or another (as would be equally
true of criminal acts by strangers), and that as a result the
person may require help, it would seem that clarity is best
served by making a distinction between self-abuse and
self-neglect, and abuse and neglect inflicted by others, so
that the meaning of abuse carries with it an interactional
connotation:

> The elderly are abused when others *in relationship to them* use them
> to their disadvantage
>
> *Cassell, 1989* (my italics)

This emphasis on the relational context of abuse is important
for two reasons. Firstly, a definition based on relationship
draws attention to the fact that both the behaviour of the abuser
and the effects of that behaviour on the abused person are relevant, although it is important, from the point of view of
clarity, to distinguish between them. Secondly, research has
uncovered a number of different scenarios for abuse – it may
be a pathological response, it may be provoked, it may be
mutual, it may have existed for a very long time; all these
suggest different relational contexts and therefore perhaps
different explanations of abuse.

Age

Elder abuse is something that happens to people over
a certain age. This may be 65, or 60 or 70; there is no right
answer but most research studies have taken 65 as a cut-off
point.

Setting

Abuse is abuse wherever it occurs. However, from the point
of view of policy and practice, as well as of research, it would
appear possible, and sensible, to draw a line between abuse
in an institutional setting and abuse of people in their own
homes. The main reasons for doing so are related to the reasons
for abuse, the responsibilities of hospital, nursing home
and residential care providers to certain quality standards

and the nature of the interventions required to deal with the abuse. Research suggests that there may be links between the abuse of individuals and the quality of care in institutions (McCreadie, 1991). However, the Social Services Inspectorate suggests there can be overlaps, as when a relative or friend abuses a person in institutional care, and that this is an area in need of further research (Social Services Inspectorate, 1992).

The abuser/perpetrator

Abuse occurs in the context of a relationship, and therefore excludes actions by strangers, e.g. someone mugging an elderly person in his or her own home, or extracting money by false pretences at the front door. However, research shows that abuse can be perpetrated by friends, neighbours and lodgers, as well as by family members (Podnieks, 1990; Pritchard, 1992). It would therefore seem important not to specify in the definition of an abuser a term such as relative, family member or carer. In particular, the introduction of the word 'carer' into the definition carries a danger of confusion. It may well be that the majority of instances of elder abuse take place when one person is caring for another, dependent person, but that is an empirical issue. Research from North America suggests the assumption that the relationship always involves care-giving is not supported by the evidence (Pillemer and Wolf, 1989; Podnieks, 1990).

The abused/victim

In the same way that the abuser can become the carer in the definition, so the abused person may be defined as the dependant. Again, dependency, which itself needs definition, is a factor to be investigated empirically and cannot be assumed to be present (Hudson, 1989).

A number of people doubt the utility of distinguishing abuse of elderly people from that of adult abuse in general on the grounds that it is not age *per se* that is relevant, but vulnerability, which comes about through illness, frailty, disability or any other condition that results in one person being dependent for care on another person (Pugh, 1990; Crystal, 1986).

From a research point of view, it would be very difficult to limit the concept of abuse to situations where the abused party is vulnerable in this sense. It is arguable whether older people, defined in strictly numeric terms as people over the age of 65, are vulnerable by virtue of their age in the way that adults with learning disabilities are vulnerable by virtue of their disability. However, as older people, they may be victims of physical violence, intense bullying or financial exploitation. If vulnerability is taken as intrinsic to the idea of abuse, it would follow that, for example, physical violence towards an older person who is fit and independent would not be defined as abuse. Yet a not uncommon scenario for physical abuse appears to be a relationship involving an adult child who is dependent on an elderly parent (Pillemer and Finkelhor, 1989), and research in the USA and Canada has found that abuse between spouses accounts for a significant amount of the physical and psychological abuse among elderly people (Wolf and Bergman, 1989; Podnieks, 1990). The extent to which these relationships incorporate 'vulnerability' – and indeed which of the parties in the relationship is vulnerable – are, from a research point of view, empirical questions. It seems ageist to define all those over 65 as vulnerable, but confusing to call certain behaviours abuse if the older person is frail or dependent in some way, and something else if they are not. On this basis, it would seem clearer to distinguish elder abuse from adult abuse, and decide separately if the definition of adult abuse should incorporate vulnerability.

Categories of abuse

There are different kinds of abuse. Although seemingly a statement of the obvious, it is of the greatest importance in relation to why abuse occurs, what the risk factors are and the nature of the intervention required. Increasingly, this is being recognized in the research literature (Gebotys, O'Connor and Mair, 1992; Hudson, 1991). There is a reasonable degree of consensus over the following five categories of abuse:

Physical abuse

Physical abuse is 'the non-accidental infliction of physical force that results in bodily injury, pain or impairment' (Stein, 1991).

Psychological abuse

Psychological abuse consists of 'the wilful infliction of mental or emotional anguish by threat, humiliation or other non-verbal abusive conduct' (Stein, 1991). Researchers have frequently used verbal abuse as a measure of psychological abuse (Homer and Gilleard, 1990; Podnieks, 1990; Pillemer and Finkelhor, 1988).

Sexual abuse

Sexual abuse is coercion to sexual activity.

Financial abuse

Financial abuse is 'the unauthorised and improper use of funds, property or any resources of an older person' (Stein, 1991).

Neglect

Neglect is 'the wilful or non-wilful failure by the caregiver to fulfil his/her caretaking obligations or duties' (Stein, 1991). Leaving aside the semantic problem of whether neglect can be seen as a kind of abuse – Johnson (1991), for example, prefers the term 'elder mistreatment' for this reason – the notion of neglect is that of omission or carelessness in the provision of necessary care (Hudson, 1989).

Dimensions of abuse

Researchers are beginning to pay more attention to the dimensions of abuse in reaching a definition (Fisk, 1991; Stein, 1991). Human beings, both at an individual and a social level, behave in ways that can readily be termed abusive. The problem, for policy and practice purposes, is to decide on the situations that call for intervention, and the best guide for this can be found by a consideration of the dimensions of abuse. The most important of these would seem to be the severity of effect, perhaps measured by the distress caused to the individual and the frequency and duration of abuse (Fisk, 1991; Hudson, 1989; Johnson, 1986; Stein, 1991). The effects of abuse may range from a general level of unhappiness to injuries requiring hospital care. The latter case requires intervention in a way the former may not. Although one single episode of abuse, if sufficiently severe, may merit intervention, it **may** be the repeated nature of the abuse that is of most concern. The intention of the abuser may also be a relevant dimension. First is the question of whether harm is intended, or whether, as in some cases of neglect, it is a question of unintentional failure to provide necessary care. The second important question is whether the intention was malign or benign (Gebotys, O'Connor and Mair, 1992). A simple chart, with spaces to fill in with relevant adjectives may be helpful. Table 1.1 shows an example.

THE SCALE OF THE PROBLEM

There has only been one attempt to measure the prevalence of elder abuse in the UK (Ogg and Bennett, 1992). Use was made of a routine government social survey of 2130 people. The sample included 593 adults over pensionable age and was nationally representative of the population of the UK. This means that an estimate can be given of the national prevalence of elder abuse, although the small sample on which it is based means that the estimates cover a wide range.

Adults over pensionable age were asked whether a close family member or relative had recently **frightened** them by shouting, insulting them or speaking roughly to them (verbal abuse); pushed, slapped, shoved or been physically rough with them in any other way (physical abuse); or taken money or property from them without their consent (financial abuse). Of the 593 people surveyed, 32 (5%) reported having been recently verbally abused by a close family member or relative, 9 (2%) reported physical abuse and the same number financial abuse. The resulting national estimates can be seen in Table 1.2.

Ogg and Bennett also used the survey to ask adults if they had abused a person over the age of 60. The same definitions were used, but rather higher levels of abuse reported.

The most important non-UK study to date is the national study undertaken in Canada in 1989, which was financed by

Table 1.1 An example of a completed chart to assess abuse by type, behaviour, effect and dimension

Type of abuse suspected	Behaviour	Effect	Severity measured by client distress	Frequency	Duration
Physical	Assault	Bruising	Apparently mild	Once, so far as is known	Once, so far as is known
Sexual	Vaginal rape	Vaginal infections; fear	Severe	Repeated	Unknown
Psychological	Bullying	Depression	Severe	Constant	Goes back years
Financial	Taking pension	No money of own	Negligible	Every week	Six months
Neglect	Negligence	Poor hygiene	Mild	Intermittent	Recent

Table 1.2 Estimated number of adults aged
65+ experiencing abuse in the UK in 1992

Type of abuse	Numbers affected
Physical abuse	94 000–505 000
Verbal abuse	561 000–1 123 000
Financial abuse	94 000–505 000

(Source: Ogg and Bennett, 1992)

the federal government (Podnieks, 1990). People over the age of 65 and living in the community (i.e. not in institutional care) were asked over the telephone about their experience of four types of serious abuse and maltreatment: physical abuse, neglect, psychological abuse and financial exploitation. The sample size of just over 2000 people was large enough to allow generalizations to be extrapolated to the Canadian elderly population; the response rate was 85–90%.

The reported rates of abuse were rather lower than Ogg and Bennett found and were as follows:

• physical violence – 5 per 1000 elderly people;
• psychological abuse (measured by chronic verbal aggression) – 11 per 1000;
• financial abuse – 25 per 1000;
• neglect – 4 per 1000.

Nearly 19% of respondents were victims of more than one kind of abuse. Based on a total elderly population of nearly 2.5 million people in private dwellings, this would give an overall estimate of 98 000 people who had experienced at least one form of abuse (Podnieks, 1990). The authors regard these estimates as the probable **minimum** level of actual abuse.

A further random sample survey of prevalence was undertaken in Boston (USA) in 1985/6 (Pillemer and Finkelhor, 1988). People over the age of 65 living in the community were asked over the telephone about their experience of physical and psychological abuse and neglect. Reported rates were:

• physical violence – 20 per 1000 elderly;

- psychological abuse (again measured by chronic verbal aggression) – 11 per 1000;
- neglect – 4 per 1000.

The higher rate of physical violence reported in the USA survey is attributed by the Canadian authors to the generally higher level of physical violence in American society (Podnieks, 1990).
None of the prevalence studies has included the sexual abuse of elderly people, and it is only recently that professional awareness of this problem has been explored (Ramsey-Klawsnik, 1991; Holt, 1993a; Holt, 1993b).

Who is abused and by whom?

In analysing the research that forms the basis of the next sections it is helpful to bear two points of discrimination in mind. The first concerns the type of abuse under consideration. Much of the research bears out Homer and Gilleard's view that 'different types of abuse arise for different reasons' (1990). It is therefore important to be clear which kind of abuse is being referred to, although not all the research enables us to do this. The second point of discrimination concerns the basis of the research sample. It is now generally recognized that the picture of who abuses whom that is produced by professional workers on the basis of their workload may well present a biased picture of abuse. Because of the nature of their work, professionals are more likely to see those elderly people most in need – as a result of frailty, disability or illness, factors that invariably increase with age (Social Services Inspectorate, 1992). The extent to which these elderly people are representative of all those abused is still unknown.

Physical abuse

Firstly, and perhaps obviously, this occurs when people are living together (Podnieks, 1990; Pillemer and Finkelhor, 1988). The majority of abusers are spouses and adult children. Their age range is variable. They tend to be male. The research consistently points to **their** problems: alcohol abuse, a history of mental illness and ongoing physical or emotional problems appear in a large number of studies (Homer and Gilleard, 1990; Pillemer and Wolf, 1989; Greenberg, McKibben and Raymond, 1990; Pillemer and Finkelhor, 1988; Podnieks, 1990; Bristowe and Collins, 1989; Anetzberger, 1987; Wolf and Bergman, 1989). They are not always care-givers but are involved in a variety of relationships with those whom they abuse. Some research suggests that those who abuse may well be dependent in various ways on the person they abuse (Pillemer, 1986; Pillemer and Finkelhor, 1989; Greenberg, McKibben and Raymond, 1990; Podnieks, 1990). In their study of care-givers, Homer and Gilleard (1990) found that abuse was invariably mutual, supporting research on the carers of patients with dementia (Levin, Sinclair and Gorbach, 1989).

What about those whom they abuse? Perhaps the one consistent, and not very surprising, finding is that they are in poor **emotional** health. They are of varying ages. Both the random surveys in Canada (Podnieks, 1990) and the USA (Pillemer and Finkelhor, 1988) found significant numbers of men among the abused, and this would appear to be related to the fact that men are more likely than women to live with other people. In the Canadian study, married people constituted 91% of those who were physically abused; physical abuse appeared frequently 'to occur in the context of considerable marital conflict and dissatisfaction' (Podnieks, 1990).

Agency-based samples tend to show abused people as being older and female, but this could be related to the constituency they serve or perhaps to the severity of abuse. In the Boston random survey this latter was greater for women (Pillemer and Finkelhor, 1988). It does not appear to be the case that physically abused people are necessarily more frail or dependent physically (Korbin *et al.*, 1991; Pillemer and Wolf, 1989; Pillemer, 1986; Pillemer and Finkelhor, 1989; Homer and Gilleard, 1990; Podnieks, 1990).

Findings are sensitive to the basis of the research. In the Social Services Inspectorate (1992) study, where all the cases were selected by social workers, 43 of the 64 reported cases of abuse involved physical violence; approximately the same number (42 of the 64 abused people) were 'highly dependent', commonly as a result of strokes and dementia.

Psychological abuse

Many of the same conclusions apply to psychological abuse, which has usually been defined by researchers in terms of chronic verbal aggression. Psychological and physical abuse frequently coincide, and both the Canadian survey (Podnieks, 1990) and the SSI research (Social Services Inspectorate, 1992) suggest that verbal abuse may signal physical abuse. The same characteristics in the abuser – alcohol abuse, a history of mental illness, recent health problems – appear in the profiles of psychological abuse (Wolf and Bergman, 1989; Godkin, Wolf and Pillemer, 1989; Podnieks, 1990; Bristowe and Collins, 1989). Homer and Gilleard (1990) found that verbal abuse was significantly related to relationships that had been poor for some time before the onset of disability in the abused person, an association that was not found for physical abuse.

In the Canadian survey, most verbal abuse took place in the context of marriage, and about 30% of those abused felt it was their own fault (Podnieks, 1990). In this survey stress was found to be 'the dominant characteristic of the abuser. Nearly one half of abusive spouses were described by their victims as being under a great deal of stress in the past year, compared to less than 20% of the spouses of the rest of the respondents' (Podnieks, 1990).

Sexual abuse

It is only recently that sexual abuse of elderly people has been identified and recognized (Holt, 1993a; Holt, 1993b). The first published study was based on suspected cases picked out by social workers in Massachusetts (Ramsey-Klawsnik, 1991). Twenty-eight cases were reported; all victims were female and the majority were totally dependent on a close relation for care. Their abuser was either a husband or son with whom they were living. The author suggests that the vulnerability of the abused person is a crucial factor in sexual abuse. Holt (1993a; 1993b) analysed 90 reported cases. Both sex (females predominated among victims and males among abusers) and mental and physical frailty were key variables. However, the cases were selected by professionals and may therefore be subject to consequent bias (Holt, 1993b).

Financial abuse

The two main sources of information about financial abuse as a form of abuse in its own right are the Model Projects research (Pillemer and Wolf, 1989) and the Canadian national survey (Podnieks, 1990). In the Canadian survey, financial abuse was the most commonly reported type of abuse, constituting five times as many cases as physical abuse (Podnieks, 1990). However, the definition covered a wide variety of behaviour; respondents were asked if, at any time since they turned 65, anyone they knew had taken any one of six actions toward them: 'tried to persuade you to give them money; tried to cheat or trick you into giving them money; tried to persuade you to relinquish control over your finances; tried to influence you to change your will; tried to make you give up something of value; tried to persuade you to sign over your house to them'.

Both pieces of research lead to the conclusion that it is important to distinguish financial abuse from other kinds of abuse. Those who were financially abused were more likely to live on their own, be socially isolated and have health problems. The Canadian survey found no difference between victims of abuse and the rest of the respondents with respect to sex, education, income or employment status, but victims were a good deal more unhappy in a number of ways (Podnieks, 1990).

Both pieces of research agree that the perpetrators of financial abuse tend **not** to be close relatives (Podnieks, 1990; Wolf, 1990). The Canadian study found only a very small percentage (7%) of abusers were financially dependent on their victims (Podnieks, 1990). On the other hand, the Model Projects research found that abusers were likely to have financial problems and/or to have experienced a recent change in their financial or employment status (Pillemer and Wolf, 1989). Both studies found that alcohol consumption by perpetrators was a relevant factor, but are inconsistent over their mental health status.

The first piece of systematic research in the UK focused on 25 elderly people suffering from dementia. The research concluded that the financial affairs of only one of these had been administered appropriately (Rowe *et al.*, 1993).

Neglect

Although research suggests that neglect is the least prevalent of the different types of abuse, it is the type, apart from sexual abuse, that most nearly fits what has been the popular picture of abuse. Neglected elderly people are invariably in poor health and dependent on a care-giver, particularly for help with activities requiring physical mobility (Podnieks, 1990; Pillemer and Wolf, 1989). In the Model Projects research they were more likely to suffer from loss of memory or other cognitive handicaps associated with dementia. Those who neglected them were likely to find them a source of stress and to be socially isolated (Pillemer and Wolf, 1989). Homer and Gilleard (1990) found that neglect, like verbal abuse, was related to a long-standing poor relationship between the two parties, and also to carers who rated as socially dysfunctional on the general health questionnaire.

EXPLANATIONS FOR ABUSE

There is no single, straightforward explanation for elder abuse; indeed, researchers are increasingly aware that different kinds of abuse have different explanations (Hudson, 1991). Currently, there would seem to be three distinct profiles of the abuser and the abused: with regard to physical and psychological abuse, to financial abuse and to situations of neglect.

Underlying current research are two distinct, although not alternative, approaches. On the one hand is an approach that locates abuse principally in the context of care-giving. On the other is an approach that construes it as a form of family violence.

The first approach is represented in the USA by the work of Steinmetz (1987), Phillips (1988) and Fulmer and O'Malley (1987) among others. Phillips (1988) argues that the family violence paradigm does not take into account the care-giving dimension of elder abuse, which features so predominantly in the cases encountered by community nurses. From their standpoint, it is more appropriate to view abuse: 'as a function of a care-giving relationship gone awry rather than strictly as the act of a perpetrator against a victim' (Phillips, 1988).

This point has been taken up in the UK by Bennett (1990a; 1990b), who follows Fulmer and O'Malley (1987) in favouring the term 'inadequate care', and by Phillipson (1992).

The other approach, presented in the work of Pillemer and Wolf (1989), has been based on general theories of family violence, which have emphasized the following five factors:

1. The pathology of the individual.
2. The 'cycle of violence' in which violent behaviour is transmitted from one generation to another.
3. The pattern of dependency in the relationship between the abused person and the abuser.
4. The social isolation of families.
5. The amount of **external** stress, i.e. stress arising from factors outside the family such as unemployment.

Pillemer and Wolf's research has generally validated these explanations, apart from number 2, particularly with regard to physical and verbal abuse.

The role of individually-based stress in triggering physical abuse is still uncertain. The Canadian national survey, based on interviews with those that had been abused, reported that these victims felt that stress in their abuser had been an important factor (Podnieks, 1990). In a study of grown-up children care-givers, (Steinmetz (1987) suggests that it is the **perception** of stress that is important in explaining both physical and psychological abuse. A study of the potential to abuse of carers of dementia sufferers found that the potential to abuse was related to mood disturbance in the carer, not to the perception of stress (Bendik, 1992).

The Social Services Inspectorate report (1992) points out: 'It seems most useful to see the abuse not simply in terms of victim and perpetrator but as taking place within the changing context of family or social relationships'. This stress on relationships is emphasized by a number of researchers (Pillemer and Suitor, 1988; Godkin, Wolf and Pillemer, 1989; Podnieks, 1990). Research has begun to identify the different relational contexts of abuse – care-giving situations, marriage, the network of the elderly person who is living alone and relationships between competent elderly people and grown-up children (Gelles, 1991). Now research needs to be more discriminating in analysing the nature of these relationships, the circumstances that give rise to the different types of abuse and the responses of those involved to their situations. This is particularly critical in relation to caring. In a review of research on caring and its relationship to the problem of abuse, Nolan (1993) emphasizes that so-called 'caring' relationships embrace a very wide range of situations. He argues cogently: 'If we are ever to be proactive in addressing the area of abuse, it is [important] that we extend the way we think about caring'.

IMPLICATIONS OF THESE FINDINGS FOR POLICY AND PRACTICE

In terms of individual suffering, which is sometimes very severe, there is an urgent need to recognize a problem that, it would appear, is often hidden, and to direct policy and resources coherently towards it. There is a particular urgency in the context of the UK Government's community care policy and the estimated growth in numbers of elderly people. Prevalence figures from Canada suggest that financial abuse is a more important problem than has sometimes been thought and that it too requires a policy response (Greene and Anderson, 1993).

Research clearly suggests that it is unrealistic to look for a single theory to explain elder abuse; rather, it is necessary to be able to handle its essentially multidimensional nature (Sellers, Folts and Logan, 1992). Although there is some evidence of multiple abuse, particularly of physical and verbal abuse coinciding, it would appear that the characteristics of abuser and abused vary with the type of abuse. The explanations for abuse will vary accordingly. Consequently, it is important to beware of generalizations.

A crucial implication is that different kinds of prevention and intervention strategies are called for with corresponding discrimination in the allocation of resources (Marin and Morycz, 1990; Podnieks, 1990). The resources appropriate to support the stressed care-giver to an elderly person are unlikely to be the same as those needed to protect an elderly person from a spouse who is drinking too much. A study of physical abuse in the USA, for example, found that around a third of abusers were reported to have alcohol problems, yet only 1 in 10 of these were referred for treatment (Vinton, 1992). Recent research in Canada cautions against 'rushing in' with ill-thought out interventions. The study showed the **strengths** of many abused elderly people, their strategies for coping and their fierce desire to remain independent (Podnieks, 1992). The Social Services Inspectorate report (1992) on elder abuse in two London boroughs reached four very important conclusions as far as policy development is concerned. They are:

1. Although assessment was recognized as an element of good practice, a significant number of cases were not assessed.
2. There was little evidence of 'extensive inter-agency co-operation'.
3. Policies for the management of elder abuse had not been developed.
4. There were no guidelines for work on elder abuse and therefore 'the quality of intervention was dependent upon the good practice and personal initiative of respondents.

The Inspectorate has now contributed to the explicit recognition of elder abuse as a problem to be addressed (Social Services Inspectorate, 1993), but it is crucial to recognize the very considerable limitations of knowledge at present (Bennett and Kingston, 1993). In a review of a recent Canadian monograph (McDonald *et al.*, 1991), McCullough (1992) writes:

The recurring finding throughout is that policies, programs and practices related to elder abuse and neglect in Canada are being erected on inadequate theoretical and research foundations.

This is an argument for research to support policy, not for denial of the problem.

I hope the overview of issues presented in this introduction will suggest to readers that research can contribute to the development of these key constituents of good practice – assessment, inter-agency collaboration, policies and guidelines – to which the Social Services Inspectorate drew attention. Given our present slender knowledge, it would be an enormous advantage if professionals recorded basic facts about cases in a way that enabled their experience in dealing with elder abuse to be used as research data. This is one way it might be possible to promote the interplay of practice and research that results in a better understanding of, and better service to, our fellow humans in distress.

REFERENCES

Anetzberger, G. (1987) *The etiology of elder abuse by adult offspring*, Charles C. Thomas, Springfield, IL.

Bendik, M. (1992) Reaching the breaking point: dangers of mistreatment in elder caregiving situations. *Journal of Elder Abuse and Neglect*, **4**(3), 35–59.

Bennett, G. (1990a) Action on elder abuse in the 90s: new definitions will help. *Geriatric Medicine*, **20**(4), 53–4.

Bennett, G. (1990b) Elder abuse. *Current Medical Literature*, Royal Society of Medicine, October, 99–102.

Bennett, G. and Kingston, P. (1993) *Elder abuse: concepts, theories and interventions*, Chapman & Hall, London.

Bristowe, E. and Collins, J.B. (1989) Family mediated abuse. *Journal of Elder Abuse and Neglect*, **1**(1), 45–64.

Cassell, E.J. (1989) Abuse of the elderly: misuses of power. *New York State Journal of Medicine*, March, 159–62.

Crystal, S. (1986) Social policy and elder abuse, in *Helping Elderly Victims* (eds R. Wolf and K. Pillemer), Columbia, New York.

Decalmer, P. and Glendenning, F. (eds) (1993) *The mistreatment of elderly people*, Sage, London.

Eastman, M.L. (1984) *Old Age Abuse*, Age Concern, Mitcham.

Fisk, J. (1991) Abuse of the elderly, in *Psychiatry in the elderly* (eds R. Jacoby and C. Oppenheimer), Oxford University Press.

Fulmer, T. and O'Malley, T. (1987) *Inadequate care of the elderly*, Springer, New York.

Gebotys, R.J., O'Connor, D. and Mair, K.J. (1992) Public perceptions of elder mistreatment. *Journal of Elder Abuse and Neglect*, **4**(1/2), 151–71.

Gelles, R.J. (1991) *Theoretical models in family violence and their implications for the study of elder abuse*, Family Violence Research Program, University of Rhode Island.

Godkin, M.A., Wolf, R.S. and Pillemer, K.A. (1989) A case comparison analysis of elder abuse and neglect. *International Journal of Aging and Human Development*, **28**(3), 207–25.

Greenberg, J.R., McKibben, M. and Raymond, J.A. (1990) Dependent adult children and elder abuse. *Journal of Elder Abuse and Neglect*, **2**(1/2), 73–86.

Greene, B. and Anderson, E. (1993) *Breaking the silence on the abuse of older Canadians: everyone's concern*. Report of the standing committee on health, welfare, social affairs, seniors and the status of women. House of Commons Issue No. 21. Canada Communication Group, Ottawa.

Holt, M. (1993a) Elder sexual abuse in Britain, in *Elder abuse: new findings and policy guidelines* (ed. C. McCreadie), Age Concern Institute of Gerontology, Kings College London.

Holt, M. (1993b) Elder sexual abuse in Britain, preliminary findings. *Journal of Elder Abuse and Neglect*, **5**(2), 63–71.

Homer, A. and Gilleard, C. (1990) Abuse of elderly people by their carers. *British Medical Journal*, **301**, 1359–62.

Hudson, M.F. (1989) Analysis of the concepts of elder mistreatment, abuse and neglect. *Journal of Elder Abuse and Neglect*, **1**(1), 5–25.

Hudson, M.F. (1991) Elder mistreatment: a taxonomy with definitions by Delphi. *Journal of Elder Abuse and Neglect*, **3**(2), 1–20.

Johnson, T.F. (1986) Critical issues in the definition of elder abuse, in *Elder Abuse: Conflict in the Family* (eds K. Pillemer and R. Wolf), Auburn House, Dover, MA.

Johnson, T.F. (1991) *Elder Mistreatment: deciding who is at risk*, Greenwood, New York.

Korbin, J.E., Anetzberger, G., Thomasson, R. and Austin, C. (1991) Abused elders who seek legal recourse against their adult offspring. *Journal of Elder Abuse and Neglect*, **3**(3), 1–18.

Levin, E., Sinclair, I. and Gorbach, P. (1989) *Families, services and confusion in old age*, Avebury, Gower Publishing Group, Aldershot.

Marin, R.S. and Morycz, R.K. (1990) Victims of elder abuse, in *Treatment of Family Violence* (eds R.T. Ammerman and M. Hersen), Wiley, New York.

McCreadie, C. (1991) *Elder abuse: an exploratory study*. Age Concern Institute of Gerontology, King's College London.

McCreadie, C. (ed.) (1993a) *Elder abuse: new findings and policy guidelines*. Age Concern Institute of Gerontology, King's College London.

McCreadie, C. (1993b) From granny battering to elder abuse: a critique of U.K. writing, 1975 to 1992. *Journal of Elder Abuse and Neglect*, **5**(2), 5–23.

McCreadie, C. and Tinker, A. (1993) Review: abuse of elderly people in the domestic setting: a UK perspective. *Age and Ageing*, **22**, 65–9.

McCullough, A. (1992) Review of *Elder Abuse and Neglect in Canada* (McDonald, P.L., Hornick, J.P., Robertson, G.B. and Wallace, J.E. (1991) *Elder Abuse and Neglect in Canada*, Butterworths Canada Ltd, Toronto). *Journal of Elder Abuse and Neglect*, **4**(2), 198–202.

Nolan, M. (1993) Carer-dependant relationships and the prevention of elder abuse, in *The mistreatment of elderly people* (eds P. Decalmer and F. Glendenning), Sage, London.

Ogg, J. and Bennett, G. (1992) Elder abuse in Britain. *British Medical Journal*, **305**, 998–9.

Penhale, B. (1993) Local authority guidelines and procedures, in *Elder abuse: new findings and policy guidelines* (ed. C. McCreadie) Age Concern Institute of Gerontology, King's College London.

Phillips, L.R. (1988) The fit of elder abuse with the family violence paradigm and the implications of a paradigm shift for clinical practice. *Public Health Nursing*, **5**(4), 22–9.

Phillipson, C. (1992) Confronting elder abuse: fact and fiction. *Generations Review*, **2**(3).

Pillemer, K.A. (1986) Risk factors in elder abuse, in *Elder abuse: conflict in the family* (eds K. Pillemer and R. Wolf), Auburn House, Dover, MA.

Pillemer, K. and Finkelhor, D. (1988) The prevalence of elder abuse. *The Gerontologist*, **28**, 51–7.

Pillemer, K.A. and Finkelhor, D. (1989) Causes of elder abuse: caregiver stress versus problem relatives. *American Journal of Orthopsychiatry*, **59**(2), 179–87.

Pillemer, K.A. and Suitor, J. (1988) Elder Abuse, in *Handbook of Family Violence* (eds V. Van Hasselt *et al.*), Plenum, New York.

Pillemer, K.A. and Wolf, R.S. (1989) *Helping Elderly Victims*, Columbia, New York.

Podnieks, E. (1990) *National Survey on Abuse of the Elderly in Canada. The Ryerson Study*, Ryerson Polytechnical Institute, Toronto.

Podnieks, E. (1992) Emerging themes from a follow-up study of Canadian victims of elder abuse. *Journal of Elder Abuse and Neglect*, **4**(1/2), 59–111.

Pritchard, J. (1992) *The abuse of elderly people: a handbook for professionals.* Jessica Kingsley, London.

Pugh, S. (1990) Adult abuse, decision making, Tameside MBC (unpublished).

Ramsey-Klawsnik, H. (1991) Elder sexual abuse: preliminary findings. *Journal of Elder Abuse and Neglect*, **3**(3), 73–90.

Rowe, J., Davies, K., Baburaj, V. and Sinha, R. (1993) F.A.D.E. A.W.A.Y. The financial affairs of dementing elders and who is the attorney? *Journal of Elder Abuse and Neglect*, **5**(2), 73–9.

Sellers, C.S., Folts, W.E. and Logan, K.M. (1992) Elder mistreatment: a multi-dimensional problem. *Journal of Elder Abuse and Neglect*, **4**(4), 5–23.

Social Services Inspectorate (1992) *Confronting Elder Abuse*, a Social Services Inspectorate London Region Survey, Department of Health, HMSO, London.

Social Services Inspectorate (1993) *No longer afraid: the safeguard of older people in domestic settings*, Department of Health, HMSO, London.

Stein, K.F. (1991) A national agenda for elder abuse and neglect research: issues and recommendations. *Journal of Elder Abuse and Neglect*, **3**(3), 91–108.

Steinmetz, S. (1987) *Duty bound: family care and elder abuse*, Sage, London.

Vinton, L. (1992) Services planned in abusive elder care situations. *Journal of Elder Abuse and Neglect*, **4**(3), 85–99.

Wolf, R.S. (1990) Perpetrators of Elder Abuse, in *Treatment of Family Violence* (eds R.T. Ammerman and M. Hersen), Wiley, New York.

Wolf, R.S. and Bergman, S. (1989) *Stress, conflict and abuse of the elderly*, Brookdale Institute, Jerusalem.

2

The victims: older people and their carers in a domestic setting

Mervyn Eastman

So what is the profile of an abused person? Is there one?
Ten years ago I was more certain than now, but I do think
we can still be confident of certain characteristics.

For many years I have been propounding the concept of there
being two victims in any domestic setting where violence is
an everyday occurrence. To my mind, the terms 'abuser' and
'abused' suggest a judgemental view of the older person and
the relative that is physically abusive. People are different and
their responses to various situations can change over time.

A relative identified in *Old Age Abuse* (Eastman, 1984) later
stopped physically abusing her mother and since then has
experienced the trauma of having to watch her slowly
deteriorate from being an active, articulate woman. Finally,
the mother reached the stage where the daughter felt unable
to continue caring for her and she is now coping with the guilt
of having to put her dependent mother into either a hospital
or a nursing home.

Between 1980 and 1983 two-thirds of the hundreds of letters
I received on the topic of elder abuse indicated that the writer's
elderly relative was dependent as a result of physical or mental
ill health. Conditions highlighted were: incontinence; arthritis;
dementia; sensory disability; and poor communication. To
these physical problems were added emotional factors such
as resentment, contempt and isolation.

Mrs M.C. from Hertfordshire wrote: 'Why do the Browns keep granny in an expensive home, which she hates and they can ill-afford, when they have an empty room? . . . Face up to it, you are old. You are dependent on the grown-ups for running the world and looking after you. Resign yourself to being useless. Just be a good child, do as you are told, and give us as little trouble as possible.'

Contained in these few lines are, perhaps, certain clues: an expectation that the family will offer the older relative accommodation, and a resignation to the position of older people in society as being passive, roleless and childlike.

So what is the profile of an abused person or an abuser? Is there one? Ten years ago I was more certain than now, but I do think we can still be confident of certain characteristics:

- The abused person is severely physically or mentally impaired.
- The abused is very old (75 +) and, not surprisingly, usually female.
- The abused tends to be victimized by relatives, lives with those relatives, and experiences repeated incidents of abuse.
- Stress is still, in my opinion, a factor in abuse of elderly people, whether that stress be associated with alcohol, long-term medical problems (of the carer) or financial difficulties.

These characteristics have been consistently supported by American research (Block and Sinott, 1979; Legal Resources and Service for the Elderly, 1979; House of Representatives, 1981), but one problem with them is whether disability is independently correlated with abuse. Apart from one study (Godkin, Worth and Pillemer, 1989) there has been no research into the differences between abusing and non-abusing families; it may well be an area worthy of future investigation. Why is it that one family supporting an older relative abuses, while another, in otherwise similar circumstances, does not?

However, even comparing families that abuse with each other is difficult because of the lack of a consistent definition of abuse. A survey of 35 cases chosen at random from over 100 where physical abuse was indicated (Eastman, 1984) is illustrated in Table 2.1.

Table 2.1 Characteristics of 35 cases of suspected physical abuse

Male	Female	Age range				Disability	Chronic* illness	Mentally* infirm
		60+	70+	80+	90+			
4	31	2	14	17	2	11	15	19

*Numbers include those suffering from more than one condition; 5 of the cases were not suffering any of these conditions.

Five of the cases were chronically sick and suffering from mental infirmity as well as being over 80 years old, while a further nine of these two highly dependent groups were aged between 70 and 80.

Only five of the cases being abused by relatives were not suffering from any condition leading to dependency. Here, however, we touch on the concept of abuse motivated by power rather than dependency, an issue taken up by Raymond Jack in Chapter 6.

Although there is a clear correlation between dependency and abuse, those five cases illustrate an extremely important aspect about victims: they need not be suffering from mental or physical infirmity. It is frequently said that one of the tragedies of abuse is that anybody can become a victim. The thought that your son or daughter (or other relative) could, in later years, physically assault or even kill you is an uncomfortable one for most people, and may account for the fact that this remains the area of abuse that professionals find the most difficult to accept.

When lecturing on old age abuse I am often asked if abuse is more prevalent in some ethnic or socio-economic groups than others. This is virtually impossible to answer with our present knowledge. Nevertheless, I would suggest that as further information becomes available we can be increasingly confident that abuse is not restricted to any particular ethnic group, but research has shown that those on lower incomes are more likely to become victims (Chen *et al.*, 1981). I disagree with these findings, believing that abuse takes place across all the social groups and that greater dependency, rather than lower income, increases the risk of abuse. Furthermore, a person's ability to cope with ageing and a family's ability to cope with stress are also important factors irrespective of the level of dependency.

What, then, are the elements common to older people being abused in the domestic setting (although it is important to stress that abuse also takes place in other situations, such as residential care homes)? The majority are female, over 80 and dependent as a result of physical or mental incapacity. They are not confined to any particular social group, but are found in all social classes. Likewise, their abusers are not necessarily living in substandard accommodation or suffering from so-called inadequate personalities. Abuse can be a multigenerational part of a syndrome of family violence, or simply the result of living with a relative suffering from a personality disorder or psychological or behavioural problems. Lastly, violent situations can be triggered by the older person's own personality and behaviour, particularly emotional dependence and/or longstanding difficulties in the relationship with the carer.

Once, after I had been discussing the problems of abuse of elderly people on a radio phone-in programme, I was contacted by several relatives who believed that I was insensitive to the carers. Quite understandably they took exception to the term 'abuser' and pointed out that they were ordinary people, often in ordinary situations, who found themselves abusing their elderly dependents. For the most part they had no clear understanding of why they abused, except that on occasions their elderly parents provoked them. I am not sure if it is as simple as that, especially now that the increased power-base of carers' organizations has further disempowered elderly people. What is clear, is that carers who abuse do so for multifaceted and complex reasons. I am now less sure than I was what those reasons are.

So what sort of people become abusers of elderly relatives? In the survey mentioned above, of 35 cases where abuse had been substantiated, the breakdown was as follows:

Daughter	15
Son	6
Brother	3
Sister	3
Husband	2
Daughter-in-law	2

Grandson	1
Nephew	1
Son-in-law	1
Niece	1

These figures should not surprise us given that the care of older people, other than by spouses, falls in the main on the shoulders of female relatives. However, given the proportion of female carers to male it is surprising that the number of male abusers should be as great as it is.

There seems to be some disagreement among researchers about the incidence of family violence in general among black, Asian and ethnic minority groups. Some believe that because of racial prejudice and their increased likelihood of economic problems, black people and other minorities are more prone to abuse their children and, indeed, their spouses (Cazenave, 1983). On the other hand, professionals generally assume that older people in the black and Asian communities are less likely to be physically assaulted by their children because of their cultural heritage, which teaches that older people should be honoured and respected. In my experience, however, and after talking to those working with black and ethnic communities, I am led to conclude that stress and tension among such families is as high as among whites.

Thus, the first conclusions we can draw are that abusing relatives are more likely to be female, and are no more likely to come from one ethnic group than another.

Research from the USA shows that abuse is likely to come from a close family member, and the same trend was found in a study carried out in two London boroughs (Sutton, 1992). It showed that:

- of the 29 abused people living with a family member, 20 were abused by a son or a daughter;
- of the 18 people living alone, 9 were abused by their adult child;
- in 51 of the 64 cases examined, the abuser was seen as a principal carer of the elderly person;
- 32 of the abusers were men, 27 were women.

The study found that social workers considered stress to be an important factor leading to abuse. However, the report cautions against accepting stress as the major factor; attention must also be paid to the health – mental and physical – of the abuser and the context in which abuse happens.

The types of stress identified were:

- increased physical dependence of the abused;
- deterioration in mental health of the abuser;
- personal problems of the abuser;
- poor mental health of the abused.

Significantly, the abuse was not triggered by any one event, but came about as a result of a deterioration in the relationship between an increasingly dependent elderly person and a 'carer' who was, in many cases, unequal to, or unprepared for, the work (Sutton, 1992).

My own profile of an abuser, drawn from the letters I have received from hundreds of carers, would include the following factors:

- female;
- middle-aged (45–55);
- responsible for the care of another dependant;
- having a low self-image;
- feeling trapped.

In my model, factors such as occupation, socio-economic status and ethnic background are only relevant if they play a significant role in the carer's self-image or self-esteem.

REFERENCES

Block, R. and Sinnott, J. (eds) (1979) *The Battered Elder Syndrome: an exploratory study*, US Center on Aging, Maryland.

Cazenave, N.A. (1983) Elder Abuse and Black Americans: Incidence, Correlates, Treatment and Prevention, in *Abuse and Maltreatment of the Elderly – Causes and Interventions* (ed.J. Kosberg), John Wright, Boston, Bristol and London, section II, chapter II.

Chen, P.N., Bell, S., Dolinsky, D. *et al.* (1981) Elderly abuse in domestic settings: a pilot study. *The Journal of Gerontological Social Work*, **4**(1).

Eastman, M.L. (1984) *Old Age Abuse*, Age Concern, Mitcham.

Godkin, M.A., Worth, R.S. and Pillemer, K.D.(1989) A case comparison analysis of elder abuse and neglect. *International*

Journal of Ageing and Human Development, **28**(3), 207–25.

House of Representatives (1981) *Report of the Hearing of the Select Committee on Aging*, House of Representatives, Washington, DC.

Legal Resources and Service for the Elderly (1979) *Elder Abuse in Massachusetts: A Summary of Professionals and Para-professionals*, Boston.

Sutton, C. (1992) *Confronting Elder Abuse*, HMSO, London, pp. 5–6.

3

Prevalence and prevention of abuse

Ann Homer

We wanted to discover how much abuse there might be in a community-based sample of old people, and whether the characteristics of these people and their carers would be the same as in previously published qualitative accounts and case reports on abuse.

There are three widely held misconceptions about elder abuse. The first is the concept of 'the elderly' as being only frail defenceless victims, never aggressive, belligerent perpetrators of violence themselves. The second is that the type and number of services that can be provided by social services departments will alleviate the tensions in an already abusive situation. The third is the idea, which is unproved and frequently being refuted by research in the USA, that the stress and strain of caring is inevitably linked with abuse and vice versa.

It was with these preconceptions that I attended a multidisciplinary conference on elder abuse in 1988 (Tomlin, 1989), and then set out to do a small study on elder abuse in south London.

This chapter is in two sections. The first describes the study, the practical problems involved in such work and the results. The second section builds on the insight gained from the first to suggest ways that elder abuse could be prevented.

A STUDY OF ABUSE OF ELDERLY PEOPLE BY THEIR CARERS

We wanted to discover how much abuse there might be in a community-based sample of old people, and whether the characteristics of these people and their carers would be the same as in previously published qualitative accounts and case reports on abuse (Eastman, 1984).

Subjects and methods

In many health districts hospitals offer in-patient respite care on the geriatric wards to patients that are usually cared for at home, so that their carer can have a break. These elderly people are usually quite stable but suffer from a range of debilitating chronic conditions that make them too dependent to be cared for in a local authority residential home. All patients known to be receiving respite care in the geriatric hospitals in the south London boroughs of Putney and Barnes, and all new referrals over a six-month period were eligible for inclusion in the study. This amounted to 71 carer–patient pairs, of whom 51 carers and 43 patients were interviewed. Reasons for exclusions are shown in Table 3.1.

The commonest conditions suffered by the patients were stroke and dementia, with over half having more than one other condition as well, such as blindness, Parkinson's disease

Table 3.1 Reasons for patients and carers not being interviewed

Number of patients not interviewed (by cause)	
Died before admission	8
Not admitted for respite care during study period	8
Moved out of area	3
Admitted acutely to hospital (1 died, 1 stayed on limb-fitting unit)	2
Inappropriate referrals (under 60 years)	2
Total patients excluded from study	23

Number of carers not interviewed (by cause)	
Refused to be seen	3
Patient died before admission	8
Patient died during first respite admission	2
Moved out of area	3
Patient admitted acutely to hospital	2
Inappropriate referrals	2
Total numbers of carers excluded	20

(Source: Homer and Gilleard, 1990)

or severe arthritis. Nearly half the patients interviewed had dementia (21 out of 43) and they had a mean abbreviated mental test score of 6.7 (Hodgkinson, 1972). This made data obtained from the patients largely unreliable and so only that collected from the carers was used further. However, if patients knew who their carers were, recognized their surroundings and were generally felt to be able to express some meaningful response, they were asked about abuse, and the results are shown for comparison in Figure 3.1.

Three categories of abuse were considered using the consensus definitions described by Karl Pillemer in his research in the USA (Pillemar and Finkelhor, 1988). These were: physical abuse, being pushed, grabbed, slapped, hit with a weapon, etc.; verbal abuse, chronic verbal aggression, repeated

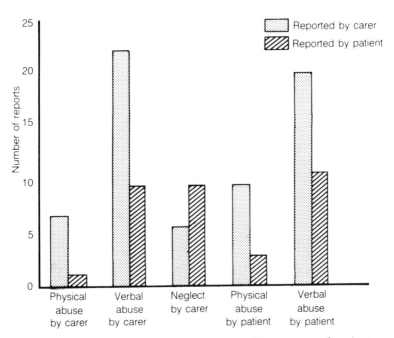

Figure 3.1 The prevalence of abuse as reported by carers and patients. (Reproduced with permission from A. Homer and C. Gilleard, Abuse of elderly people by their carers; published by the *British Medical Journal*, **301**, 15-12-1990, pp. 1359-62.)

insults, being sworn at, threats at least 10 times in the preceding year; and neglect, deprivation of some assistance that the elderly person needed for important activities of daily living such as meals, dressing, toileting, at least 10 times in the preceding year, or to a degree termed somewhat or very serious by the respondent.

There has been a lot written on the subject of definitions of abuse, (Hudson, 1989) and for comparability of research findings it is crucial that operational definitions exist. However, it is important that a preoccupation with definitions of abuse does not hamper attempts to help abusive situations where they exist on a practical level. There will inevitably be many 'grey areas' where workers may disagree about what is and is not abuse, and these can be particularly difficult when dealing with situations occurring in cultural or ethnic settings that are different from one's own background. But there are other, unequivocal cases of abuse when the abuse is unanimously recognized, and it is important that these are dealt with, irrespective of whether they fit into a particular definition.

Carers were interviewed at home and, wherever possible, alone. They completed a structured interview asking about many of the risk factors that have been proposed as signals of abuse (Figure 3.2).

In addition, the carer was asked what they found to be the main problem in caring for the elderly person, why they carried on doing it and about abuse. This subject was gradually

- Relationship of carer to patient.
- Occupation of carer, whether he or she stopped work to care.
- Type of accommodation, who owns it, who lives in it.
- Amount and satisfaction with number of services received, visits by friends and neighbours, respite care.
- Length of time spent caring.
- Opportunity to socialize.
- Disturbed nights.
- Receipt of allowances.
- Alcohol consumption, general health, visits to GP.
- Anger towards old people and triggers.

Figure 3.2 Content areas of the structured interview with carers. (Reproduced with permission from A. Homer and C. Gilleard, Abuse of elderly people by their carers; published by the *British Medical Journal*, **301**, 15–12–1990, pp. 1359–62.)

introduced towards the end of the interview in a non-judgemental way, using questions such as, 'Do you ever find yourself thinking about shouting at him/her? Many people would in your situation.'

During the interview carers also completed the pre-morbid relationship rating scale (Gilleard, 1986) as an index of the closeness of the previous relationship, the Clifton assessment procedures for the elderly behaviour rating scale (Pattie and Gilleard, 1979) as a measure of patient dependency and behavioural disturbance, and the general health questionnaire 28 (Goldberg and Williams, 1988) to assess the mental health of the carers.

All patients were routinely examined on the day of admission for respite care. Note was taken of any skin markings or injuries and the overall condition and appearance of the patient. The patient's mental state was assessed using the abbreviated mental test score.

Carers who admitted to some form of abuse were then compared with those who did not. They were then subdivided into those who admitted to physical abuse, verbal abuse or neglect, and each group was compared with the rest. Associations were sought between the factors mentioned above and the presence or absence of abuse.

Results

Table 3.2 shows that abuse was reported by more carers than patients, except for neglect. More carers reported abuse both by themselves and by the person they cared for. Four carers reported mutual physical abuse and 13 carers reported a mutually verbally abusive relationship. Overall, 23 (45%) carers admitted to some form of abuse, 14 (27%) admitted to one type, seven (14%) to two types, and two (3%) to all three types of abuse.

It may appear surprising that so much abuse was admitted by carers, even when the patients themselves did not complain. After much debate, the ethical committee that approved this study felt carers would be furtive and unwilling to talk about their feelings. It was even suggested that carers who had not thought of abusing the person they cared for might take up the idea and do it. The actuality was that most carers were

Table 3.2 Prevalence of abuse

(a) Numbers of carers reporting abuse (total numbers of carers = 51)

	Committed by carer	*Committed by patient*
Physical	7	9
Verbal	21	17
Neglect	6	N/A

(b) Number of patients reporting abuse (total number of patients = 48)

	Committed by carer	*Committed by patient*
Physical	1	3
Verbal	9	10
Neglect	9	N/A

(Source: Homer and Gilleard, 1990)

very relieved to be able to discuss their difficulties; some had tried to tell and had told other people before. This finding has been supported in other studies where carers have been sympathetically approached in their own homes (Levin, Sinclair and Gorback, 1983; Pillemer and Finkelhor, 1988).

Characteristics of the carers

Most of the carers were female (15 were male) and had a mean age of 66 years (range 37–87). There were 27 spouses, 22 children, one child by marriage, three siblings, one sibling by marriage, and two not related in any way. Seven carers did not live with the relative, but all the abusive carers did. Details of the statistical analyses have been published elsewhere (Homer and Gilleard, 1990).

The factors most significantly associated with abuse were the amount of alcohol drunk by the carer and abusive behaviour **by** the dependant. Physical violence by the carer was often triggered by physical abuse or threats of violence by the patient (five out of seven cases). Abusive carers were more likely to have stopped work to care for the old person (nine out of 23 abusive carers compared with three out of 28 non-abusive ones).

Twenty-four carers (48%) scored as 'cases' on the general health questionnaire. Normal population scores for elderly people living in the community are 29% for those aged 65–74 and 41% for those aged 75+ (Cox *et al.*, 1987).

Carers who admitted to physical and verbal abuse seemed significantly more depressed (Table 3.3). When asked what they saw as the main problem in caring, the abusive carers considered it to be the behaviour of the person they cared for significantly more often than the non-abusive carers. This finding was repeated in the Clifton assessment procedure for elderly people where the abused patients were rated as more socially disturbed and as presenting greater communication problems than the non-abused patients (Table 3.4).

Table 3.3 Carer abuse and general health questionnaire scores

GHQ-28 subscales mean scores	Physically abusive $n=7$	Not physically abusive $n=44$	Verbally abusive $n=21$	Not verbally abusive $n=30$	Neglect $n=6$	No neglect $n=45$
Somatic (A) complaints	1.9	1.5	1.9	1.4	0.8	1.7
Anxiety (B)	2.4	2.4	2.7	2.2	1.5	2.5
Social dysfunction (C)	2.2	1.4	1.8	1.4	0.3	1.7*
Severe depression (D)	1.9	0.8†	1.6	0.5‡	1.3	0.9

(Source: Homer and Gilleard, 1990)
* Mann-Whitney $U=58.5$, $p=0.01$
† Mann-Whitney $U=85.5$, $p=0.02$
‡ Mann-Whitney $U=195$, $p=0.01$

Table 3.4 Carer abuse and patient dependency ratings

CAPE subscales mean scores	Physically abusive $n=7$	Not physically abusive $n=44$	Verbally abusive $n=21$	Not verbally abusive $n=30$	Neglect $n=6$	No neglect $n=45$
Physical disability	8.4	7.4	7.8	7.3	8.5	7.4
Apathy	6.7	6.6	6.6	6.7	6.3	6.7
Communication difficulties	1.4	0.6*	0.9	0.6	1.5	0.6
Social disturbance	3.6	2.2	3.0	1.9†	4.7	2.1

(Source: Homer and Gilleard, 1990)
* Mann-Whitney $U=77.5$, $p<0.05$
† Mann-Whitney $U=214$, $p<0.05$

There was no difference in the level of physical dependency between the two groups, which suggests that the number or frequency of physical care tasks that have to be performed for a person do not indicate the likelihood of abuse. This is supported by other studies (McCreadie, 1991). Other problems concerning physical difficulties, social isolation, financial hardship and emotional strain in seeing the cared-for change were not reported any more often among abusive or non-abusive carers.

Characteristics of the care-giving relationship

Many of the couples had a longstanding mutually abusive relationship that preceded the onset of disability in the one and the assumption of the caring role in the other. Seven out of 21 verbally abusive carers reported a previously verbally abusive relationship compared with two out of the non-abusive group. Two of the seven physically abusive group and two of the 44 others reported a previous relationship with the dependant involving physical abuse. Abusive carers rated their pre-morbid relationship as poorer than did the non-abusive ones.

Between husbands and wives, the abuse often went back to near the beginning of the marriage and these couples had 'graduated' after 50 or 60 years into the realm of elder abuse, coming to the attention of the health care professionals at times of illnesses often associated with ageing. For example, one man who frequently used to come home drunk from the pub and beat his wife, or throw her and their children out for the night, had a stroke in his late 70s. His aggression remained undiminished, fuelled by his frustration and disinhibited by his stroke he lashed out at anyone who went near or tried to help him, especially his wife.

Parents and children who had never had a very close relationship also proved to have problems. There was support for the model of transgenerational transmission of abuse. Suzanne Steinmetz, in her book on family care (Steinmetz, 1990), talks about the 'negative controlling techniques learnt in childhood' being expressed by adult offspring trying to control their elderly parents, making the victim and the perpetrator indistinguishable. One middle-aged man in our study said, referring to his father: 'He was always a sadistic bastard. He used to beat me a lot as a child. Now I can get my own back. I feel physically sick clearing up his mess. He's driving me to drink. I think about strangling him a lot'.

Characteristics of the patient

It is an important negative finding that there was no significant correlation between physical signs and the presence or absence of abuse in these patients. There certainly were marks and bruises on their skin, urine rashes and so on, but these were equally distributed between the abused and the non-abused group. When patients have had strokes and/or are suffering from dementia, they lose their normal protective reflexes on falling and can get some strange-looking injuries. Some elderly skin is very thin and fragile and even normal handling will result in marks. If an abused old person is thoroughly examined there may well be signs of injury, but, although constant vigilance is needed, signs do not necessarily represent abuse and the absence of any physical signs does not exclude it.

Conclusion

This is a small study on a very dependent group of people and results should not be extrapolated to the general population. In this study there seemed to be, on the one hand, the 'normal exasperation' that anyone would feel caring for an elderly relative under difficult circumstances and which has been well described by researchers such as Enid Levin in her community-based study (Levin, Sinclair and Gorback, 1983) and carers alike. On the other hand, there is verbal abuse, which is often an integral part of a relationship, predates the caring role of one partner, and is associated with depression and anxiety in the carer. The distinction may seem blurred, but the carers seemed to know and acknowledge when exasperation becomes abuse.

Altogether separate from this is physical abuse, which depends on carer characteristics rather than the abused, as has been noted elsewhere (Bennett, 1990) and represents people with disturbed and disorganized personalities, often dependent on alcohol or other drugs.

PREVENTION

In this section I will consider the opportunities for preventing abuse in the domestic setting. Some of the strategies for helping carers in the community are also applicable to care assistants in residential or nursing homes. There are three stages at which abuse can be prevented:

1. To prevent an elderly person potentially at risk from abuse from being put with a high risk carer in the first place.
2. To detect established potentially abusive situations and try to prevent actual abuse from occurring.
3. To prevent repeated episodes of abuse once an abusive situation is recognized.

As with so much in health care, the situation is easier to prevent than resolve, and any action is likely to be easier, and more effective, the earlier it is taken.

Prevention of the establishment of potentially abusive situations

Becoming the full-time carer of an elderly relative is an enormous undertaking requiring reserves of stamina, endurance and a willingness to compromise, preferably on both sides. This arduous task is carried out willingly and well by millions of carers, often with little support (Jones and Vetter, 1984). It is not to be entered into lightly or without consideration, yet unfortunately it is often a crisis of some sort, causing a drastic change in circumstances, that leads to its being necessary. Death of a father or mother may reveal the frailty of the remaining parent; the GP may say he or she 'should not be left alone' so a grown-up child takes the parent to live with him or her. A temporary arrangement while one parent is hospitalized may become entrenched. Loss of employment or, increasingly these days, divorce of a child, may result in him or her being homeless and moving back in 'to care for' an aged parent. Care may be reluctantly given because the full implications had not been realized before the task was undertaken. The old person and the carer should be given the opportunity to make a fully informed decision before their living arrangements are changed (often irreversibly).

A variety of people may be in a position to help with the decision. The GP is the most obvious, as, knowing the family circumstances, he or she may be privy to family discussions. Community and hospital social workers are in a similar situation and may be able to act as advocates for an old person whose interests are not being well served. Health visitors for the elderly or community psychiatric nurses may also be involved. The practice nurse who carries out screening for those aged 75 and over is in a crucial position to be able to identify elderly people not known to any other services, and to ask questions to stimulate thought and discussion about future arrangements in the event of someone no longer being able to cope at home alone.

It is therefore self evident that all these professionals must, at the very least, be aware of the risk factors associated with abuse and have access to a trained senior social worker with a special interest in elderly people who can evaluate the situation and help clients to make an informed decision.

There are two questionnaires that could be used in these situations. The high risk placement worksheet was developed by Kosberg in the USA (Kosberg, 1988) for use by trained professionals (such as social workers) to assess systematically the characteristics of the elderly person, the main care-giver and the family system prior to placement decisions (Figure 3.3). It is recommended that it be completed separately by the carer and the old person so that any areas of incongruity may then be further explored. It signals potential problems rather than giving a risk rating.

Figure 3.4 shows the Cost of Care Index, also developed by Kosberg (Kosberg and Cairl, 1986), which can be used by anyone involved with carers, such as practice nurses on their screening visits, community psychiatric nurses and so on. This questionnaire helps the carer to consider the anticipated cost of caring for their impaired relative and is scored up to a maximum of four points for each response. A total maximum score of 80 is possible, and this would suggest very real problems and risks within that relationship. Exploration of alternatives might be encouraged. If the Cost of Care Index reflects this it

Name of Client/Patient _____

A.   Characteristics of older person   **Existence of risks**

    1. Female   _____

    2. Advanced age   _____

    3. Dependent   _____

    4. Problem drinker   _____

    5. Intergenerational conflict   _____

    6. Internalizer   _____

    7. Excessive loyalty   _____

    8. Past abuse   _____

    9. Stoicism   _____

  10. Isolation   _____

  11. Impairment   _____

  12. Provocative behaviour   _____

B.   Characteristics of care-giver   **Existence of risks**

    1. Problem drinker   _____

    2. Medication/drug abuser   _____

    3. Senile dementia/confusion   _____

    4. Mental/emotional illness   _____

    5. Care-giving inexperience   _____

    6. Economically troubled   _____

    7. Abused as child   _____

    8. Stressed   _____

    9. Unengaged outside the home   _____

  10. Blamer   _____

  11. Unsympathetic   _____

  12. Lacks understanding   _____

  13. Unrealistic expectations   _____

  14. Economically dependent   _____

  15. Hypercritical   _____

C. **Characteristics of family system**   **Existence of risks**

    1. Lack of family support _____

    2. Care-giving reluctance _____

    3. Overcrowding _____

    4. Isolation _____

    5. Marital conflict _____

    6. Economic pressures _____

    7. Intra-family problems _____

    8. Desire for institutionalization _____

    9. Disharmony in shared
responsibility _____

D. **Congruity of perceptions
between older person and
(potential) care-giver**   **Existence of risks**

    1. Quality of past relationship.

      a. Perception of older person

      b. Perception of care-giver _____

    2. Quality of present relationship

      a. Perception of older person

      b. Perception of care-giver _____

    3. Preferred placement location

      a. Perception of older person

      b. Perception of care-giver _____

    4. Ideal placement location

      a. Perception of older person

      b. Perception of care-giver _____

Figure 3.3 The high risk placement worksheet. (Reproduced with permission from J. Kosberg, Preventing elder abuse: identification of high risk factors prior to placement decisions; published by *The Gerontologist*, **28**(1), 1988, p. 48.)

	Strongly disagree	Disagree	Agree	Strongly agree
1. I feel that meeting the psychological needs of my elderly relative to feel wanted and important is not (will not be) worth the effort.	1	2	3	4
2. I feel that my elderly relative is (will be) worth the effort.	1	2	3	4
3. I feel that caring for my elderly relative has negatively affected (will negatively affect) my family's or my physical health.	1	2	3	4
4. I feel that as a result of caring for my elderly relative I do not (will not) have enough time for myself.	1	2	3	4
5. I feel that caring for my elderly relative is causing me (will cause me) to dip into savings meant for other things.	1	2	3	4
6. I feel that meeting the health needs of my elderly relative is not (will not be) worth the effort.	1	2	3	4
7. I feel that my elderly relative tries (will try) to manipulate me.	1	2	3	4
8. I feel that caring for my elderly relative has negatively affected (will affect) my appetite.	1	2	3	4
9. I feel that caring for my elderly relative puts (will put) a strain on family relationships.	1	2	3	4
10. I feel that my family and I must give up (will have to give up) necessities because of the expense of caring for my elderly relative.	1	2	3	4
11. I feel that caring for my elderly relative disrupts (will disrupt) my routine in my home.	1	2	3	4

	Strongly disagree	Disagree	Agree	Strongly agree
12. I feel that caring for my elderly relative has caused (will cause) my family and me much aggravation.	1	2	3	4
13. I feel that meeting the daily needs of my elderly relative is not (will not be) worth the effort.	1	2	3	4
14. I feel that caring for my elderly relative has caused me (will cause me) to be physically fatigued.	1	2	3	4
15. I feel that my family and I cannot (will not be able to) afford those little extras because of the expense of caring for my elderly relative.	1	2	3	4
16. I feel that my elderly relative makes (will make) unnecessary requests of me for care.	1	2	3	4
17. I feel that meeting the social needs of my elderly relative for companionship is not (will not be) worth the effort.	1	2	3	4
18. I feel that caring for my elderly relative has caused me (will cause me) to become anxious.	1	2	3	4
19. I feel that caring for my elderly relative interferes (will interfere) with my friends or friends of my family coming to my home.	1	2	3	4
20. I feel that caring for my elderly relative is (will be) too expensive.	1	2	3	4

Figure 3.4 The Cost of Care Index. (Reproduced with permission from J. Kosberg and R. Cairl, The Cost of Care Index: a case management tool for screening informal care providers; published by *The Gerontologist*, **26**(3), 1986, p. 276.)

is helpful to have the information recorded for future reference, in case the situation changes. Counselling and training may be appropriate for the 'in-between' cases (Bennett and Kingston, 1993).

Prevention of abuse in an 'at risk' situation

'At risk' situations may be clearly apparent to people visiting the house, or, if there is a good 'social front' maintained for visitors, may become apparent if a screening instrument such as the Cost of Care Index is used by the practice nurse at her yearly check. A change in the Cost of Care Index score over time would highlight deterioration in an established situation. Carers and their dependants may well be able to suggest what they would find helpful to make the situation more tolerable; whether such help is available locally, if at all, is another matter.

Training in anger and stress management are available in some areas, but getting care-cover for carers to attend may be a problem. Counselling and information have been shown to reduce carer stress (Sutcliffe and Larner, 1988). Helping the carer and the patient to understand the nature of the disability the patient suffers from is beneficial and questions should be encouraged. Listening should be accurate ('What is the worst thing? ... ').

Strengths and achievements within the relationship should be recognized as well as acknowledging the difficulties. Marriage guidance for the elderly is extremely difficult to find and there have been few evaluations of its effectiveness in the very old. Carers' support groups, such as that provided by the Alzheimer's Disease Society, can be helpful. The Carers' National Association (Useful addresses) certainly understands the needs of carers working within poor quality relationships (Pitkeathley, 1992) and joining the association reduces the sense of isolation that many carers feel.

Arrangements for carers to have professional help with their own psychiatric or alcohol dependency problems may be appropriate. Day care for the elderly may be helpful, so long as the journey can be tolerated and getting them ready to go in the morning is not seen by the carers as an extra strain. In an ideal world the option of financial and housing independence would be available to the carer. Not all carers would wish this, but many are trapped in an unalterable situation, dependent on care allowances and the elderly person's house for their home. Further research to quantify the importance of this factor is urgently needed (McCreadie, 1991).

Prevention of recurrent abuse in an identified abusive situation

The Office of Population Census and Surveys asked a community sample about abuse and found up to 3% of the elderly people interviewed admitted to having been physically or financially abused, and up to 7% to having been verbally abused (Ogg and Bennett, 1992). Studies abroad have suggested that about 3–4% of the elderly in the community are abused (Pillemer and Finkelhor, 1988, Podnieks, 1992).

Simply talking about the problem seems to reduce the chances of it reoccurring. A recent survey confirmed our findings that the abused are extremely reluctant to complain themselves, but the carer may find it a relief (Sutton, 1992). It is important that such interviews are conducted by someone who has set aside at least an hour, preferably more, to allow an opportunity for the carer to express him or herself fully. The carer should be seen alone in an undisturbed and comfortable environment of his or her own choosing to give him or her more confidence. The interviewer should know about elder abuse and have some idea of the phrasing of certain questions so as to be able to modify them to suit different situations. When differences of racial or ethnic background are involved the interview is best done by a professional who speaks the same language. The interviewer should not be offended or judgemental, but reassure the carer that this happens with other carers too.

I found it best to make detailed notes after the interview rather than during. Details of any circumstances that trigger a violent outburst may be helpful when thinking of ways to reduce further episodes. If the elderly person being cared for has a repetitive behaviour which the carer finds particularly trying the psychogeriatrician or clinical psychologist may be able to help. If incontinence is a major trigger, treatment or better containment of the problem may be obtained by consulting a geriatrician or continence adviser.

Guidelines have been published on how to approach the gathering of information in a suspected case of elder abuse (Age Concern, 1990). Many health districts have developed their own detailed guidelines to be used by social services and health authorities in their area, such as Tower Hamlets in London.

Professionals working with elder abuse often encounter powerful emotions in their clients and these may provoke similarly strong feelings in themselves. This has been recognized in other highly emotionally charged areas of work, such as hospices, and those involved have found that a chance to discuss these feelings with another professional, and time spent with others who do the same sort of work, discussing different ways of resolving problems is crucial to the maintenance of high quality care.

Most people who are abused are already known to the social services department and often to the health service as well. This was certainly the case in the study we carried out, and often abuse had already been suspected by either the home help or the district nurse but they had been unsure what to do next and had received little guidance. It is important that each district has its own guidelines, agreed by all agencies, freely available and known about, with contact numbers, for all professionals working with elderly people.

The services abused people receive reflect what is available rather than what they would like and are not correlated with the type or frequency of abuse. It is not household chores or personal care tasks that determine whether an old person will be abused, so help with these activities does not relieve abuse. Services are often provided as a way of monitoring the situation rather than alleviating it.

Services that are inappropriate (or even appropriate ones in some cases) may be refused. This does not mean the case should be closed or that other help would not be accepted (Sutton, 1992). These are always difficult situations, often very resistant to change, and it is important not to 'give up' on a couple or condemn them for refusing what is available if it is not what they think they need.

There is still much to learn about abuse of elderly people in the UK. Further public debate and co-ordinated research is needed (Bennett and Kingston, 1993) and it is to be hoped that the establishment of Action on Elder Abuse will add impetus to this (useful addresses). Much greater effort and time is needed to help an established abusive situation than to prevent abuse. The interdependence of the carer and the cared for can be difficult to unravel. The greater chance of success must lie in preventing these situations from arising in the first place, and for this we need greater public and professional awareness of the difficulties inherent in a caring relationship and all it entails.

REFERENCES

Age Concern (1990) *Abuse of elderly people: Guidelines for Action*. Available from The Distribution Services Department, Age Concern (England), 1268 London Road, London, SW16 4EJ.

Bennett, G. (1990) Shifting emphasis from abused to abuser. *Geriatric Medicine*, **20**(5), 45–8.

Bennett, G. and Kingston, P. (1993) *Elder Abuse: Concepts, theories and interventions*, Chapman & Hall, London, Chapter 4, Intervention and Chapter 7, Prevention.

Cox, B., Blaxter, M., Buckle, A. *et al.* (1987) *The Health and Lifestyle Survey*, Health Promotion Research Trust, Cambridge.

Eastman, M. (1984) *Old Age Abuse*, Age Concern (England), Mitcham.

Gilleard, C.J. (1986) Family attitudes to caring for the elderly mentally infirm at home. *Family Practice*, **3**, 31–6.

Goldberg, D. and Williams, P. (1988) *A user's guide to the general health questionnaire*, NFER Nelson, Windsor.

Hodgkinson, H.M. (1972) Evaluation of a mental test score for assessment of impairment in the elderly. *Age and Ageing*, **1**, 223–8.

Homer, A.C. and Gilleard, C.J. (1990) Abuse of elderly people by their carers. *British Medical Journal*, **301**, 1359–62.

Hudson, M.F. (1989) Analyses of the concepts of elder mistreatment: abuse and neglect. *Journal of Elder Abuse and Neglect*, **1**(1), 5–25.

Jones, D.A. and Vetter, N.J. (1984) A survey of those who care for the elderly at home: their problems and their needs. *Social Science and Medicine*, **19**(5) 511–14.

Kosberg, J.I. and Cairl, R.E. (1986) The Cost of Care Index: a case management tool for screening informal care providers. *The Gerontologist*, **26**(3), 273–8.

Kosberg, J.I. (1988) Preventing elder abuse: identification of high risk factors prior to placement decisions. *The Gerontologist*, **28**(1), 43–50.

Levin, E., Sinclair, I. and Gorback, P. (1983) *The Supporters of Confused Elderly Persons at Home*. National Institute for Social Work, Mary Ward House, 5–7 Tavistock Place, London, WC1H 9SS.

McCreadie, C. (1991) *Elder Abuse: an exploratory study*. Age Concern Institute of Gerontology, King's College (London), Cornwall House Annexe, Waterloo Road, London, SE1 8TX.

Ogg, J. and Bennett, G. (1992) Elder abuse in Britain. *British Medical Journal*, **305**, 998–9.

Pattie, A.H. and Gilleard, C.J. (1979) *Clifton Assessment Procedures for the Elderly – Manual*, NFER Nelson, Windsor.

Pillemer, K. and Finkelhor, D. (1988) The prevalence of elder abuse: a random sample survey. *The Gerontologist*, **28**(1), 51–7.

Pitkeathley, J. (1992) Letter in *Geriatric Medicine*, March, 36.

Podnieks, E. (1992) National survey on abuse of the elderly in Canada. *Journal of Elder Abuse and Neglect*, **4**(1/2), 5–8.

Steinmetz, S.K. (1990) *Duty Bound Elder Abuse and Family Care*, Sage Publications, California, Chapter 7.

Sutcliffe, C. and Larner, S. (1988) Counselling carers of the elderly at home: a preliminary study. *British Journal of Clinical Psychology*, **27**, 177–8.

Sutton, C. (1992) *Confronting Elder Abuse*, Social Services Inspectorate of the Department of Health, HMSO, London.

Tomlin, S. (1989) *Abuse of Elderly People: an unnecessary and preventable problem*. British Geriatrics Society, 1 St Andrews Place, London, NW1 4LB.

USEFUL ADDRESSES

Action On Elder Abuse, Astral House, 1268 London Road, London, SW16 4ER. Telephone: 081-679 2648, for details and membership forms.

Alzheimer's Disease Society, Gordon House, 10 Greencoat Place, London, SW1P 1PH. Telephone: 071-306 0606.

Carers' National Association, 29 Chilworth Mews, London, W2 3RG. Telephone: 071-724 7776.

4

Caring for carers: understanding the process that leads to abuse

Elizabeth Hocking

Abusing carers have lost control of the situation, themselves and their emotions. Amid the chaos, they feel frustrated, embarrassed, angry and powerless.

Discussion of old age abuse is still hampered by the lack of an agreed definition. Each professional discipline that serves elderly people sees a different section of that group, so that experiences vary and no correlation is possible.

Abuse is the result of the complex interaction of a number of factors. I believe that disability and disease are essential components, but many planners and managers in the NHS, who have to juggle the conflicting demands of costly medical developments, still regard abuse as a peripheral issue. It is still not clear whose responsibility it is to care for vulnerable adults and their estates, however small (Homer, 1992), or even what basic services should be provided.

During their lifetimes, elderly people have experienced a unique series of events that have shaped their current situation. While they remain active, they and their relatives can express themselves in any way they choose, reflecting their own, individual personalities. When elderly people begin to need assistance, care-givers take on the role with a mixture of emotions such as love, duty and apprehension, conscious of the need to conform to society's expectations, irrespective of their personal aptitude for care-giving. Once begun, the support of the elderly person continues, in the majority of cases, until the dependent's death, despite the financial, emotional and health costs to the care-givers. Although up to 10% of elderly people may be at risk, abuse actually occurs in only 2–4% of cases.

Chance rather than choice often determines the eventual constitution of a household. Unexpected accidents, death, unemployment and other such events may disrupt carefully made plans and force different family members into living together, the circumstances overriding their incompatibility. A household may become overcrowded so that the frailer member(s) are marginalized and may even become the scapegoats for other problems. Alternatively, there may be only one care-giver, leaving the dependant in a socially, if not physically, isolated household where there is no outside support and therefore no check if abuse is occuring (Hocking, 1988). If abuse is suspected by a rare visitor, such as a GP, but no solutions seem possible, suspicions may be forced to the back of the mind, almost condoning the abuse by inaction.

Chronicity is characteristic of nearly every case (being measured in years). We age at different rates, so a relationship that was rewarding may become unbalanced and under strain.

When the whole community is under stress, for example due to bad weather, influenza epidemics or even official holidays, the households already under greatest stress may break down. Even if the unspectacular problems of the dependant are presented to health care professionals, they are unlikely to be dealt with, being overshadowed by more therapeutically rewarding acute cases.

THEORIES EXPLAINING ASPECTS OF ABUSE

Several professions have recognized abuse among their clients; social workers, psychiatrists, nurses, lawyers and workers for voluntary organizations have all contributed their insights (O'Malley *et al.*, 1983). The findings can be summarized as:

- Violence is seen as a learned behaviour;
- some victims have similar characteristics;

- the considerable stresses on the care-givers have been discussed, and recent work (Pillemer and Finkelhor, 1989; Homer and Gilleard, 1990) has investigated maladaptive or pathological abuses;
- studies into the balance of control and how it is achieved may offer a unifying explanation (Phillips, 1988; Phillips and Rempusheski, 1986).

It is primarily through the family that attitudes to violence are formed, and in some households nurturing and violence are intermingled (Dickstein, 1988). A child brought up in such a setting is much more likely to use violence at a later date when adult and caring for a parent. Just 1:400 children reared non-violently attacked their parents later, compared with 1:2 children who had been mistreated by their parents (Soule and Bennett, 1987). The unloved baby cries and is irritable because it is unloved. Similarly the attention-seeking adult is searching for reassurance. If children were brought up strictly, with high expectations but distant love, they may in turn wish to punish their elderly parents for embarrassing, socially unacceptable behaviour. Sometimes the abused elderly woman who has spent a lifetime caring for others, seeking to please, suppressing her own desires, continues to attempt to please, despite the abuse.

Elderly people may be more vulnerable because of particular characteristics. Their ability to communicate as sentient human beings preserves their identity, and if that is lost a great deal more than function goes as well. Abuse is rarely seen as unprovoked, and may involve environmental as well as physical and emotional aspects.

Communication between humans is essential for a sense of well-being. The carer has to allow extra time for the older person to process given information. Deafness, blindness and dysphasia further restrict a victim's world, and may well be underestimated, so that insufficient imagination and time are spent in communication. Speech is seen as a very human attribute and a speechless person is seen as less than human. For example, a woman said, referring to her husband: 'Look, he's just a cabbage; he can't even say "hello" when I come into the room [in hospital] ... I'll have him home when he can say "hello"'. Her husband's comprehension was intact; his hopes of returning home gone as she refused to accept any explanation. His subsequent deep depression continued until his death.

In a series of geriatric cases (Hocking, 1988) I found one-third of the patients to be aphasic or dysphasic, and one-third to be Parkinsonian. Medication postpones deterioration in this condition but does not cure the disease. Eventually many patients present immobile faces, rarely laughing or even smiling, so the carer receives little feedback, little approval and little satisfaction.

Cancer is perceived to be painful and so elicits sympathy. Furthermore, it is still regarded as a terminal illness so the care-giver can foresee a possible end to the stress. Not one patient in 49 cases (Hocking, 1988) had cancer, but at least three of the care-givers had unrecognized cancer at the time of the abuse.

In contrast, dementia is seen as reducing not only the memory and intelligence but also the personality and worth of the dependant. Following a stroke, up to 20% of patients may become disinhibited and violent towards their carers, especially if frustrated. Fluctuations in function may be misinterpreted as 'not trying'.

A variable and unpredictable amount of help may be needed by patients with multi-infarct dementia, multiple sclerosis, arthritis or Parkinson's disease. Early in the disease Parkinsonian patients may have difficulty turning in bed, causing nocturnal disturbances. Their persistence is saddening yet irritating, and they may also become excessively careful, suspicious, even paranoid. They may have difficulty talking, swallowing and eliminating. If dementia supervenes, not only are they forgetful, but they may also have frightening nightmares. Loss of balance, from whatever cause, is invisible but terrifying to the sufferer and worrying to the carer.

When non-abusive care-givers were questioned (Sandford, 1975), they admitted that nocturnal disturbances due to wandering, noise or the need for toileting was the most difficult problem to tolerate. Urinary incontinence could be contained but faecal incontinence (at once more difficult to control, malodorous and infective) could not. Heavy lifting was a problem for which a solution could usually be found, whereas behavioural problems, such as variability, dangerous behaviour and aggression, were the areas of greatest difficulty.

In a comparison of abusing and non-abusing households Godkin, Worth and Pillemer (1989) (also Homer and Gilleard, 1990; Ogg, 1992) found that the level of physical function may not be an important indicator of abuse. Physical and intellectual impairments were predictors of neglect, but more physical abuse occurred where there was less physical illness.

Elderly people may try to manipulate the situation to retain their previous position in the household. The arrival of a new baby is likely to capture the family's interest, drawing it away from the older generation and dividing the care-givers' loyalties and time. Frail people are particularly vulnerable if they have made over their homes in exchange for care. Elderly people's attempts at manipulation may become so obvious (and unsuccessful) that both they and their influence are diminished and this may be reflected back on to the care-giver.

It may be easier to identify with care-givers. In a recent series of geriatric patients (Piper, cited in Tomlin, 1988), 60% of non-abusing main carers were over 65 years old, and 20% were over 80. They may lack the energy to make decisions or change. Sleeping may have become more difficult with ageing. In longstanding illnesses, the objective burden normally increases with the duration of the illness, but the subjective burden (i.e. that felt by the family) levels off. They may have to cope with between two and six behavioural disorders (Levin, Gorback and Sinclair, 1989), any one of which triggers abuse. The continuous and continuing presence of the dependant is a common provocation: 'I know I shouldn't hit him, but he's always there'. Feelings of guilt may inhibit us from confronting violence.

Several studies suggest that abuse is associated with the care-givers' problems rather than those of the victims (Godkin, Worth and Pillemer, 1989; Ogg, 1992), especially if the care-giver is dependent on the older person for housing and finance as well as for emotional support. Mental illness, such as schizophrenia, and alcohol/drug related problems are significantly over-represented among care-givers.

Personality problems have been found in those who have abused the elderly sexually (Holt, 1993); these victims are often extremely old and unable to resist.

Some children have never left the parental home and as the health of their elderly parent fails they have to take on the responsibility for not one but two lives, rapidly changing their role. Of those children who do leave home, the less adventurous and those with deeper emotional attachments will tend to stay nearer the parental home and will eventually take the heaviest responsibility for their ageing parents.

Deep resentment may build up when one is left to care, although some people escape from unpleasant work to make a job of caring and men may find a new role, and talk of love. They receive relatively more help than women, who are expected to have learnt how to care while bringing up children and are now expected to use their skills and do their duty.

The history of the relationship is important. By entering into a rescue situation care-givers themselves become victims as their opportunities for self-expression become limited. 'Everything that happens in the house happens to my mother as well as me, and I have to take care of it for both of us.'

All care-givers try to reconcile their image of the older person with reality (Phillips and Rempusheski, 1986). Those whose perceptions correlate well are comfortable, but those who see the elderly person in a more negative light, i.e. whose image has been 'spoiled', suffer stress. They may 'punish' embarrassing, senile behaviour and abuse the dependant to restore the present image to its previous level.

Caring remains dynamic in response to feedback. Coping strategies may be positive, neutral or negative. Positive care-givers have insight and sensitivity, accepting the old person as a fellow human being and attending to his or her comfort with love, care and respect. Care-givers with more negative feelings may have been brought up with high expectations rather than close relationships. Their attitude remains rigid while the old person is observed and protected, and more negative strategies are used. Abusing carers have lost control of the situation, themselves and their emotions. Amid the chaos, they feel frustrated, embarrassed, angry and powerless. They have been overwhelmed by their sense of responsibility for their dependants with no relief in sight. Change requires effort and energy, and they have none.

The nearer one gets to personal functions the more the intrusion is resented. Care-givers often defuse the anxiety engendered by close proximity by the withdrawal of emotion. Tiredness itself can produce a sense of unreality, and in this state carers can feel less guilty about abusing elderly people than they would about putting them into care. They feel the shame of failure and may turn their own frustrations on to the nurses or attendants and blame them .

Even in care institutions elderly people may not receive the appropriate treatment, for reasons similar to those that operate at home. Extra guilt is felt by everyone if the abuser is in the caring professions or is remunerated. Staff who abuse have little self-esteem, are likely to have personal problems and would like to escape (Pillemer and Moore, 1989). In this negative atmosphere only feeding and public 'batch' toileting may punctuate the otherwise absolutely blank, empty days. Time is pressing on a few staff, and lack of understanding and supervision may lead to negative controlling strategies and inhumanity. Too few have advice on coping strategies, which have to be learnt.

After satisfying their basic needs people tend to have a deep desire to express themselves, and to do this one must have some control over one's own life and be able to plan for the future; people also expect to have absolute control over their personal functions, although control over events on the periphery of their lives may be negotiable. Dependency and interdependency threaten this control.

Caring may be divided into three phases (Phillips, 1988). In **semi-care** both care-giver and recipient still have control over their own lives; they can express themselves. The care-giver helps significantly but the lifestyle of both is not altered fundamentally and both parties find satisfaction in the giving and receiving of help.

At some point the elderly person's function deteriorates and then **full care** is required; as the needs become so absolutely important they overwhelm the care-giver's needs and indeed all other commitments; yet the carer is developing power over the vulnerable person. Both adults now face a period when the rewards are few but escape more difficult. They face ambiguity as neither is in complete control of the situation and constraints limit their ability to express themselves. There may be uncomfortable proximity or even overlap of areas needed for personal functions. Big decisions are important but it is the little things that matter because normally one has complete control over them. Confrontations with an inordinate amount of anger and emotion erupt over minor matters, and the very pettiness of the episode is demeaning.

In the third phase – **total care** – dependants can no longer help themselves so their care-givers resume the controlling role. They may receive more sympathy and material help and, despite increased physical work, there is less stress: an end may be in view.

A carer who has become accustomed to giving semi-care over a long period may suffer more stress than is at first appreciated when full care becomes necessary: there may have been a crisis for which he or she was not prepared; or the dependant's function may fluctuate, so that semi-care is appropriate one day but full care is needed the next. If the essence of good integration is the setting of appropriate and agreed boundaries, when should the decisions be made? And is help immediately available at this delicate stage?

Semi-care may slip into full care when a situation has developed without full preparation, objective advice, discussion or full agreement. If the relationship is not very close and the dependant enters an institution, the situation reverts to one of semi-care, where both parties regain some freedom within the relationship and stress is reduced. Again, there may be less stress when the dependant is severely demented and the recognizable elderly person has 'gone'; there is less competition for control.

The critical point is when semi-care becomes full care, yet this point may pass without recognition. If so, there is confusion over the balance of control; boundaries are shifting, so everyone feels insecure and emotions are disturbed. It is difficult to contend with unless plans have been discussed and agreed during the semi-care period, before most people are prepared to contemplate deterioration and loss of control. If the carers now lack sufficient support, they may feel out of control and diminished, and resort to negative controlling strategies ending in abuse.

REJECTION AND ABUSE

Rejection is already taking place before it is realized. It may occur in three ways:

- Each time there is a problem the carer makes allowances, adapts a little, but also loses some options and control of the situation. Peace is maintained, but at a cost, and the carer continues 'to cope' until such resentment has built up that, suddenly, at some slight provocation, all control is lost, completely and irrevocably, sometimes murderously.
- The more common pattern is one where little confrontations and emotional outbursts release the tension for the time being. Outside help may be accepted and the situation then returns to nearly normal, but slight resentment may linger. Gradually this base-line of resentment builds up until total rejection occurs. Once this has occurred it is very difficult to reverse.
- Financial, material and even sexual abuse is more likely to be calculated as the victim is regarded as of little worth. Legal steps may have to be taken.

Deep-rooted inhibitions deter animals, including humans, from killing others of their own species while they still have value (as such behaviour would be detrimental to the continuation of that species); alcohol, tiredness or illness may loosen them, however. Relationships formed by schizophrenic people are often brittle and in all these cases the dependant is no longer recognized as a human being. The person becomes simply a problem. As control is lost the emotions become intense but confused, without any moral direction. The ambivalence makes it easier for the abusers to excuse themselves: 'I was helping her and pushed her just a little'. Assistance becomes cruder; the helping hand becomes the pushing, shoving, hitting hand as rejection seeps out through the fingertips – the hands expressing what the voice may hesitate to say. Sometimes children express the family's rejection, by throwing toys at the elderly person, for example. The intensity of the uncontrolled emotion at the time of the abuse contrasts with the rationalization when recalling the event at a later date.

Usually abuse starts verbally, in private. This leaves no visible scar but can be devastating as the victim may recognize the partial truth of what is being said while realizing their own impotence; for example, 'You're no good, not even in bed,' one man said to his Parkinsonian wife. If there is no check the verbal abuse may become habitual and may be said in public.

Physical abuse tends to be directed towards the focus of irritation. Immobility provides both the aggravation and a ready target for hitting, kicking and shoving; one tries to knock or shake sense into a 'silly' head; difficulty in speaking (or talking too much) attracts attention to the throat resulting in mock suffocation, strangulation or submersion in water; incontinence is eventually ignored; aggression retaliated against; wandering, painfully restrained; and food is thrown at the face or head if not eaten. In the USA the abandoning of elderly people in a hospital casualty department or even in another state without identification is becoming increasingly common. Because of their physical attributes, women are more commonly beaten, men neglected or over-sedated to regain control over them. Sexual abuse is relatively rarely reported but very elderly women appear vulnerable and are greatly demeaned by it. Although only one form of abuse may have come to official attention, it is likely that other forms will be admitted to during subsequent discussions.

CARING FOR THE CARE-GIVERS

Elderly people can retain economic power and, even if incapacitated, can give love and approval, thus rewarding the care-giver. Resilient carers manage to cope with the problems of uncertainty, incontinence, aggression and frustration as well as the restriction of their own self-expression and, perhaps, reduced income. They remain realistic and manage to retain a sense of humour to release tension. They do speak of their heavy obligations and occasional satisfaction, but can look forward to another way of life.

If care-givers hang on to the identity of the older people as they knew them in the past, they leave themselves open to suffering a continued, prolonged grieving process over the loss of the people they used to be (Beck and Phillips, 1983). Not only are 50% of non-abusing carers at risk of psychiatric illness, but 50% of daughters who had cared for their mothers without abuse were left with negative feelings (Lewis and Meredith, 1987). They were still bitter about the paucity of support they had received.

Carers need recognition of the work they do, adequate financial recompense, appropriate information on the medical, financial and housing prospects and sensible, sensitive services, available after consultation, and which include opportunities for a regular break so that the care-givers can retain their own identities. As the needs fluctuate, so the available services should be flexible in their response.

During the period of semi-care, care-givers should be made aware of their rights, those of the dependant and the services available. Kosberg's Cost of Care Index (1986) is a useful tool as it indicates the less well-known, as well as the more obvious, pitfalls in caring: 'There are no right or wrong answers, only honest ones'. The carer should have a choice about employment. Decisions about where and who should do what should be discussed openly and agreements made. Regular respite and relief are more effective when arranged earlier than may seem necessary, before rejection has started. A definite date for readmission of the elderly dependant acts as a beacon for the carer. Two or three regular admissions may be necessary before the dependent person trusts the arrangement. Continuing contact and support from someone outside the situation is valuable as carers or practitioners may hesitate to recontact services for extra help.

During full care a full medical examination may disclose a treatable illness or a disability that can be helped. If there are difficulties, a case conference is worthwhile as it formalizes the discussion. Decisions may be written down as a form of 'contract'. The dependant is included and may have an advocate, but the carers must continue to feel in control, at least of themselves. Coping strategies and assertiveness can be taught, such as, 'Don't worry, no one ever died of the sulks', but this may take time. There are no short cuts. Officers should not be afraid to use authority if necessary, such as referral to the police to check abuse, especially if financial.

Separation of the abuser and the abused is often considered initially, but the dependant may be reluctant to leave a home where he or she still expects to have some rights, and the carer may not wish to relinquish all responsibility. Separation can have an unintended negative outcome, such as alienation of the family or nursing home, or retribution. Regular intermittent admissions share the care and support the situation. When the dependant is admitted, it should be emphasized that the carer still has the important task of providing emotional support.

The physical problems in total care are easier to solve than interpersonal tensions. The end may be in sight and reconciliation can occur. One home nurse reported: 'No, do not admit her now. Now he can see that she is dying he has quite changed and is looking after her. It would be wrong to disturb the family now.' However, the cost of caring should not be minimized, especially if the care-giver has become immersed in caring (Lewis and Meredith, 1987).

Voluntary and statutory bodies are beginning to recognize the volume of work done by unpaid carers. Interested professional and self-help organizations, such as the Carers' National Association, have been formed, but if the carer cannot get out, useful booklets and advice are available from them. Experience is highlighting the need for support early in the course of illness before rejection has occurred.

In the future the pattern of care may change. The advent of smaller family units, more purpose-built dwellings for elderly people, the shift of work done by and for social services towards more domiciliary personal care in elderly people's homes may mean that the period of semi-care is extended. The hope is that there will be a corresponding reduction in the periods of full care and total care. Hospital records suggest, however, that longevity is being increased, rather than these periods being shortened. If they do not stay in a hospital setting, more elderly disabled people are likely to enter 'homes'.

Sub-optimal care, neglect and even abuse is a potential risk in single rooms. Effective supervision must include standards of care as well as the facilities. With increasing financial pressures on all sides there is a need for a clear, objective system to safeguard the care of the vulnerable and their estates, but above all we must ensure that there are sufficient staff, who are properly trained and have adequate facilities, continuing advice and respect.

REFERENCES

Beck, C.M. and Phillips, L.R. (1983) Abuse of the elderly. *Journal of Gerontological Nursing,* **9**(2), 96–101.
Dickstein, L. (1988) Spouse Abuse and other Domestic Violence. *Psychiatric Clinics of North America* **11**(4).

Godkin, M.A., Worth, R.S. and Pillemer, K.D. (1989) A case comparison analysis of elder abuse and neglect. *International Journal of Ageing and Human Development*, **28**(3), 207–25.

Hocking, E.D. (1988) Miscare – a form of abuse in the elderly. *Hospital Update*, 15 May, 2411–19.

Holt, M. (1993) Elder Sexual Abuse in Great Britain, in *Elder Abuse: New Findings and Policy Guidelines* (ed. C. McCreadie), Age Concern Institute of Gerontology, London, pp. 16–18.

Homer, A.G. (1992) Letter in *British Medical Journal*, 28 November, **305**(6685), 1363.

Homer, A.G. and Gilleard, C. (1990) Abuse of elderly people by their carers. *British Medical Journal*, **301**, 1359–63.

Kosberg, J. and Cairl, R. (1986) The Cost of Care Index: a case management tool for screening informal care providers. *The Gerontologist*, **26**(3) 273–8.

Levin, E., Gorback, P. and Sinclair, I. (1989) *Family Services and Confusion in Old Age*, Avebury, Aldershot, pp. 93–7.

Lewis, J. and Meredith, B. (1987) Supporting and Supporter. *Community Care*, 17 September, 24–5.

Ogg, J. (1992) Elder sexual abuse – the last taboo. *Geriatric Medicine*, **22**(7), 10.

O'Malley, A., Everitt, E., O'Malley, H.C. and Campion, E.W. (1983) Identifying and preventing family mediated abuse and neglect of elderly persons. *Annals of Internal Medicine*, **98**, 998–1005.

Phillips, L.R. (1988) The fit of elder abuse with the family violence paradigm and the implications of a paradigm shift for clinical practice. *Public Health Nursing*, **5**(4), 22–9.

Phillips, L.R. and Rempusheski, V.F. (1986) Caring for the frail elderly at home: towards a theoretical explanation of the dynamics of poor quality family care-giving. *Advances in Nursing Science*, **8**(4), 62–84.

Pillemer, K. and Finkelhor, D. (1989) Causes of Elder Abuse. *American Journal of Orthopsychiatry*, April, **59**(2), 179–87.

Pillemer, K. and Moore, D. (1989) Abuse of patients in nursing homes: findings from a survey of staff. *The Gerontologist*, **29**(3), 314–20.

Sandford, J.R.A. (1975) Tolerance of debility in elderly dependants by supporters at home: its significance for hospital practice. *British Medical Journal*, **3**, 471–3.

Soule, D.J. and Bennett, J.M. (1987) Elder abuse in South Dakota, Part I: the who, how and why of abuse. *Medical Journal of South Dakota*, October, 7–11.

Tomlin, S. (1988) *Abuse of Elderly People*, Public Information Report, British Geriatrics Society, London, p. 7.

Part Two

Older People, Home and Away

5

Dependency or interdependency? Is the concept of 'dependent-abuse' helpful?

Mervyn Eastman

In the late 1970s there was a reluctance to accept the notion of abuse. In the 1980s that reluctance was transferred to admitting the extent of abuse.

Some years ago, when I first started examining the problems of older people in a domestic setting, there was a number of difficulties. There was a belief that older people were being abandoned by their families in hospitals and residential homes, or simply left unsupported by their families in the community. And, although social policy makers understood the issue of child protection, largely through the original work of the Kemps (1978) and the impact of the National Society for the Protection of Children (NSPCC), nobody (certainly in the UK) had examined domestic violence outside child care or marital relationships.

These factors had a number of consequences:

- There was a resistance on the part of social policy makers to look seriously at violence between specific other family members, e.g. teenage children against parents, wives against husbands, grown-up children against siblings, and parents against grown-up children with disabilities. Within this category, of course, were grown-up children against ageing parents.

- My first notion (Eastman, 1979), which was to link in some way the causal factors of old age abuse with those so called predisposing factors in child protection, was totally rejected in certain quarters (Cloke, 1983).
- There was a total rejection of the notion that old age abuse was anything other than a minority social pathology, limited to a very small number of families (Murphy, 1986; Traynor and Hasnip, 1984).
- A professional and personal hostility erupted against me, for which I was totally unprepared. This attitude was partly responsible for my subsequently being interviewed by senior police officers from Scotland Yard.
- The national media has occasionally shown an interest in old age abuse but I was recently reminded that certain television companies and newspapers are still reluctant (with the exception of Channel 4's *Dispatches*) to explore in any depth abuse that falls outside the recognizable, and therefore acceptable, categories of child protection, marital relationships and, more recently, the problems of care in private residential and nursing homes.

More than a decade on these difficulties are still with us, although my present employers are far more sympathetic, and indeed encouraged Enfield to be one of the first local authorities to produce policy and practice guidelines.

Over the past few years, however, there have inevitably been both subtle and dramatic changes in social work, child protection and the ways in which local authorities assess people for services. These changes have resulted from an increased awareness of the power base of certain interest groups of users/carers. The learning difficulties (mental handicap) and disabled people's lobby has rightly increased its demands and expectations of a society that normally seeks to marginalize.

What are these changes? How have they effected the concept of abuse in a domestic setting? More specifically, how have I come to view the notion of child protection, old age abuse and domestic violence more sceptically, questioning as I now do the whole concept? Should domestic violence be compartmentalized? Separating child protection from the abuse of vulnerable adults may be useful in terms of legislative requirements, but in real terms what is the difference between a parent suffering physical abuse from a middle-aged daughter or son, and a 35-year-old man with learning difficulties suffering abuse from his older sibling or parent?

Beckford and Cleveland, Rochdale and Orkney, the realignment away from the provision by local authorities of residential care to a mixed economy of service, needs led assessments, care planning and management, quality assurance and arms-length inspections have all caused us to question and re-evaluate not only **how** we deliver service, but **what** we deliver!

I wish here to take a liberty! To question and re-evaluate abuse. To examine the concept within a generic family framework that does not differentiate an older parent from a child, a vulnerable adult from a husband who attacks his wife following a row over whether EastEnders or Coronation Street is the best television soap! Is there, in terms of causal factors, a difference between the sexual abuse of a small child and the abuse of an adult with learning difficulties or mental health problems by a sibling, parent or carer?

DEPENDENT-ABUSE?

When I voiced this notion with a friend and colleague some years ago, I hung the concept on the hook of dependency, that somehow it seemed to offer a key to unlock my understanding. In that discussion Dr Mike Bender coined the phrase 'dependent-abuse', and it is this idea that I now wish to explore.

Reports on investigations into the management of old people's homes where physical abuse has occurred are numerous (Gibbs, Evans and Rodway, 1987), and although I had originally excluded institutions from old age abuse, the concept of dependent-abuse brought these settings within the framework. I had never been happy with their exclusion but now institutional abuse can be seen as interrelated, part of the same issues, the same pathology. Therefore, it seemed that interventions that had proved successful in reducing abuse in residential environments could be used in the context of the family setting.

There is, however, a potential problem: morality. In examining abuse we are in the realms of value judgements, what society (and the law) considers to be acceptable or unacceptable, and which issues should be ignored or denied (sexual

abuse of elderly people?) In the late 1970s there was a reluctance to accept the notion of abuse. In the 1980s that reluctance
was transferred to admitting the extent of abuse.

We have already touched on some fundamental concepts
and raised questions about relationships, dependency, denial,
rejection and morality. We have also considered the concep-
tual frameworks used by social workers and policy makers to
understand and deal with social pathology. Researchers are
also not objective: each brings to his or her statistics and
analysis a set of values and assumptions that may influence
the outcome and conclusions of a particular study.

At the 1987 Conservative Party Conference John Moore,
then Secretary of State for Health and Social Services, was criticized by some political commentators for failing to announce
new political initiatives in the field of health and social services
provision. What Moore did do, however, was to outline the
philosophy and principles on which State intervention should
be based. Having spent more than 25 years in local authority
social work, I am particularly interested in the philosophy and
principles on which such action is determined. I totally support
the philosophy and principles behind the NHS and Community Care Act, 1990, the main principles being caring for
people in the community and increasing user and carer choice
and participation. The translation of the theory of the Act into
professional and managerial practice may prove more difficult.
The point I am making, is that to work effectively in the arena
of dependent-abuse we must first be clear of our philosophy.

WHAT LIES BEHIND THE CONCEPT?

First must be a belief in the individuality of each human being;
a belief that we each have our own personal identity, as unique,
separate and distinguishable as a fingerprint. Only with such
a foundation, which may be rooted in religious beliefs or
entirely secular, can the child, the vulnerable adult or the older
person be perceived as uniquely different and, above all, equal
to everyone else.

History testifies to the fact that when people are perceived
as 'sub-human' or less than equal in terms of integrity, they
are turned into scapegoats, exploited and abused; the slavery
of the mid-18th century has given way to the racism of the

20th century. Children, older people, people with disabilities and the mentally disadvantaged are frequently perceived in a negative light; as different, less equal, to be cherished on the one hand, but exploited and abused on the other.

Secondly, we need to examine personal and public morality, the latter consisting of political morality as determined by what is perceived as public opinion. Politicians talk of having a mandate, and it is this notion of authority to act that requires further investigation.

Thirdly, how far does social work practice reflect the public morality of our times? Social work compartmentalizes (specialisms) and colludes in protecting individual pathology, society's myths, and therefore fails to challenge the very constructions of a society that seeks to protect those myths. For example, the notion that old age is a process of deterioration and that the focus of intervention should be the individual's pathology within a family, fails to grasp the fact that this society is ageist; that the rights of older people are determined by nothing more or less than their age. So we build our disposal units and call them residential and nursing care homes. Or am I being unfair? Rather than examine and expose society's inequalities in terms of income, we find other reasons for the dependency of older people on their families.

Several contributors to this book have rightly challenged the concept of dependency, but if dependency is to be understood it perhaps needs to be taken outside the medical model of abnormality and treatability. How far is the issue one of interdependency rather than simply one individual being dependent on another? How far is the issue the interdependence of the individual and the state rather than the dependence of the individual on the state? Children, people with disabilities or mental health problems and older people are all perceived as dependent; they are all equal members of society yet are often perceived as unequal partners by those who are considered 'normal' and productive. The value of children is based on potential, of older people on debt, and of the vulnerable in between on pity! Potential debt and pity cannot possibly be substitutes for the collaboration and co-operation that lead to empowerment.

The philosophy and principles behind the Community Care legislation implemented in the UK in 1993 do at least recognize the rhetoric of empowerment. However, it should be appreciated that the assessment and care planning processes can, if allowed to become too complicated and bureaucratic, even further disempower users and carers. If vulnerable children and adults are perceived as needing experts and professional intervention they remain powerless, at the mercy of the powerful whether that power is invested in a neighbourhood, State agencies or family members – the carers.

A couple of years ago I sat in on a local authority planning committee meeting to advise on an application to convert a large house in a north London residential area into a residential home for people with severe learning difficulties. The label 'mental handicap' was, in the public's mind, inevitably confused with mental ill health, which in turn was confused with criminality. Thus, a sizeable number of local house owners petitioned the authority against approving the proposal on the grounds that their families and children would be at risk from assault and abuse. Well over 100 people were in the public gallery for the meeting, the majority demonstrating a morality that exploited the labels: the powerful over the powerless on the grounds that what was in the interests of one section of the community was at odds with another. After the meeting I talked to a few of the protesters. They were all at great pains to demonstrate their pity for the 'mentally handicapped', their indebtedness to those in the caring professions for 'looking after them' and their acknowledgement of the 'potential of the handicapped if given adequate teaching and care'. But of course none of them wanted such laudable work carried out in 'their backyard'!

FURTHER THINKING?

Dependent-abuse can only be understood within a philosophy that values all individuals as equals, that is, without the trappings of the socialization of vested interests. The principles of understanding are:

- a specific morality;
- social work practice that does not collude with that socialization;
- interdependence rather than dependence.

Next we have to ask further questions related to abuse. How far is the accepted wisdom of our present understanding of child abuse related more to denying the prevalence or incidence of abuse than the abuse itself? How far is the morality of society, as demonstrated by public opinion, dependent on denying our own abuse of children, older people, women and those in society whom we have classified as dependent? How far has social work depended on legislation that reinforces the immorality of society's betrayal of the child (Miller, 1985)? How far has social work depended on the medical/individual pathology of older people in their families rather than society's ageist approach to old age?

In considering these questions readers will, I am sure, have in mind, not only the writings of Miller, but also Parton (1985), French (1986) and Phillipson (1982). The concept, therefore, is not new, but attempting to apply it to assist our understanding of dependent-abuse is challenging.

A recurring theme of many of the contributors to this book is that of defining old age abuse. Some progress has been made with child abuse, but few researchers have investigated children in non-abusing families, perhaps because, as Miller (1985) believes, there are no non-abused children. To recognize this possibility is to recognize the abuse in our own families, rather than that going on next door, in the next street, borough or county!

The morality expressed by the media in understanding or coming to terms with the child abuse cases in Cleveland and Rochdale and that of Jasmine Beckford, was in fact the public morality. In old age abuse society tends to blame 'evil', uncaring families or proprietors of old people's nursing homes – it must project the guilt of ageism onto those in society paid to take that burden. The betrayal so convincingly portrayed in *Thou Shalt Not Be Aware* (Miller, 1985) is equally applicable to the betrayal of older people, people with learning difficulties and other vulnerable adults.

Two key factors would seem to emerge from studies of abuse in families and residential homes: dependency and the carer's (paid or otherwise) perception of that dependency.

DEPENDENCY REVISITED

Within a structured framework of support dependency can be coped with. Ask hundreds of carers, and time and again they will see the most important factor as support. The opportunity to 'get away' from the dependent relative. Single parents of small, dependent children are often considered to be among the most 'depressed'. Carers of ageing relatives talk about needing 'time to be themselves'.

The entrapment caused by being responsible seems to cause a 'fight or flight' response. Many fathers flee from the day to day responsibilities of child rearing, by working late, for example.

Once a child, dependent relative or older person is perceived as a burden, responsible for ruining the independence of the carer, there is a high probability that that dependent individual will become a scapegoat, the focus of all the difficulties within the family (or old people's home). Once the dependant is turned into an object or viewed as sub-human or even non-human, it becomes only a matter of time before 'it' is physically abused, even killed.

Dependent-abuse focuses on the dependency and its inter-relation with both the carer and family, and one thus gets rid of the trappings of moral judgement about potential, debt and pity owed or owing! Dependency clearly brings into considera-tion other family members, the abused partner, the disabled spouse or child.

Does this concept help us in our search for a better under-standing of elder abuse?

Throughout childhood we are 'conditioned to be obedient and dependent' (Miller, 1985); sanctions are brought into play if a child transgresses these rules. Furthermore, we are all subjected in childhood to humiliation, rejection and mistreat-ment. According to Miller, these experiences have a profound effect on our adult feelings, which are normally suppressed. Thus, the dependency we have as children, maintained through childhood into adulthood, is carried through to later years and old age. Miller uses a psychoanalytical model, but equally such dependency can be viewed in the context of the child, adult and parent Ego states used in Transactional Analysis. It is no accident that those early feelings surface when we take on the role of carer for dependent relatives or paid provider. For example, an elderly 85-year-old mother 'sans' teeth, ears and eyes, chairbound and suffering from demen-tia is perceived by the carer as a child.

Indeed, the methods employed in many residential care homes are based on the parent–child interactions of infancy. A 33-year-old adult with severe learning difficulties may well be perceived as no more than an infant, his or her behaviour interpreted as naughty or bad because his or her feelings are perceived as the sulking of a 10-year-old.

How is rage, hatred and indignation acknowledged? By whom and in what situations? Miller suggests the couch be used for patients addressing their feelings. But most of us do not go near a couch and our feelings are for the most part managed. Is it wrong to feel rage, hatred or indignation against an adult figure whether it be one's parent, another adult, a child or one's employer? How we control those feelings is the issue.

Here we begin to understand the seeds of dependent-abuse. It is the carer's perception of the dependency (real or otherwise). Thus, children, people with disabilities and older people become victims for no other reason than that they are perceived and maintained in a state of dependency, powerlessness and disempowerment; but (Miller again) what is important is that the individual perception they have of themselves 'has an effect on those around them, particularly those dependent on him/her'.

Feelings of contempt, dismissiveness, seduction, shame or fear are common to us all, but it is where those feelings come from that needs to be identified. I am increasingly warming to the view that they come from childhood experiences and derive from the power that parents (or authority figures) have over the powerless. The methods of child-rearing that include humiliation, seduction and contempt as a matter of routine are carried over into the role of carer for a 'dependent' relative and into the arena of employment. As senior managers, the way we treat our employees, clients, patients or residents can be perceived as our being the 'parent' (powerful and authoritative) to their being the 'child'. One care assistant in a residential care home perceived himself as the 'parent' of the elderly residents (children). Society maintains that power, indeed pays for it through taxation. Why? Because the old are dependent and need to be cared for, and therefore the roles of child and parent must apply, including their respective ages!

In the following chapter Raymond Jack explores in more depth the issues of dependence, power and violation, developing a new perspective and arguing that mutually shared dependency, powerlessness and violation foster the abuse of older people.

REFERENCES

Cloke, C. (1983) *Old Age Abuse in the Domestic Setting – A Review*, Age Concern, Mitcham.

Eastman, M.L. (1979) *The battering of Mrs Scarffe. New Age*, summer.

French, M. (1986) *Beyond Power – on women, men and morals*, Abacus, London.

Gibbs, J., Evans, M. and Rodway, S. (1987) *Report of the Inquiry into Nye Bevan Lodge*, Southwark Social Services Department, London.

Kemp, R.S. and Kemp, C.H. (1978) *Child Abuse – The Developing Child*, Fontana, London.

Miller, A. (1985) *Thou Shalt Not be Aware: Society's Betrayal of the Child*, Pluto Press, London and Sydney.

Murphy, E. (1986) *Dementia and Mental Illness in the Old*, Papermac, London and Basingstoke.

Parton, N. (1985) *The Politics of Child Abuse*, Macmillan, London and Basingstoke.

Phillipson, C. (1982) *Capitalism and the Construction of Old Age*, Macmillan, London and Basingstoke.

Traynor, J. and Hasnip, J. (1984) Sometimes she makes me want to hit her. *Community Care*, August.

6

Dependence, power and violation: gender issues in abuse of elderly people by formal carers

Raymond Jack

The recognition of the powerlessness shared by old women and their female carers as a result of the combination of ageism and sexism within the professionalization of welfare, leads to new perspectives on abuse by formal carers.

Abuse of the elderly has been defined as '. . .the physical, emotional or psychological abuse of an older person by formal or informal carers. The abuse is repeated and is the violation of a person's human and civil rights by a person or persons who have power over the life of a dependant' (Eastman, 1984).

In this chapter the issues of dependence, power and violation will be discussed as being central to an understanding of elder abuse by formal carers. However, rather than adopting the commonly-held view – as in the definition above – that these apply to either abuser or abused, a new perspective will be developed which views dependence, power and violation as the currency of relationships rather than the property of individuals. Within the 'exchange relationship' of formal care, care-giver and cared for share the currency of dependency, power and violation, albeit in unequal quantities, but it will be suggested that it is the fact of this mutual dependency, powerlessness and violation that fosters the abuse of elderly people by their formal carers (Jack, 1987).

If the term 'old' means people aged over 65, the majority of old people are women. Similarly, the vast majority of formal (i.e. paid) carers for old people are women. The formal care of elderly people is therefore a markedly female environment, and any discussion of the nature of power, dependency and violation involving old people and their formal carers must recognize the importance of age and gender.

Age is a major form of division in our society. Old people are subject to stereotyping that characterizes them as incompetent and increasingly dependent, and ageism – structured, institutionalized discrimination against older people based on these mainly negative stereotypes – deprives older people of control over their own lives in numerous ways, forcing dependent status on them and therefore inevitably violating their 'human and civil rights' (Phillipson, 1982; Midwinter, 1987).

Gender is another major division within our society, and negative stereotypes of women are also pervasive – including the belief that women are physically delicate, over-emotional and more feeling than thinking. These stereotypical qualities combined with womens' biological role in bearing and nurturing infants, mean that women are assumed to be 'naturally' suited to caring for others. Sexism – structured, institutionalized discrimination based on these stereotypes – underpins gender divisions in the distribution of power in society, which disadvantages women in organizations and relationships and forces dependent status on them. This, in turn, promotes the numerous forms of social, psychological and physical violation inflicted on them (Warren, 1985; Peace, 1986; Fennell, Phillipson and Evers, 1988).

The function of caring for dependent people in industrial societies has been professionalized in health and welfare bureaucracies. A hierarchy of skills, knowledge and expertise has been constructed within which caring for old people is doubly devalued. Firstly because it is perceived to be 'women's work', and as such unskilled and not requiring specific, professional expertise. Secondly, since old people are perceived to be dependent and in irreversible mental and physical decline, their needs are assumed to be for 'care' rather than 'cure', for 'maintenance' rather than 'treatment'. Since care and maintenance are considered less demanding in terms of specific expert knowledge and skills than treatment and cure, their formal care is relegated within the professionalization of welfare to a low status occupation, rather than a high status profession. In social services departments the low status, low pay and poor career prospects of mainly unqualified and female residential and domiciliary care assistants working with old people may be compared with the high status of mostly qualified field social workers, a larger proportion of whom are men, who work mainly with children (Borsay, 1989; Winner, 1992).

Thus, within such organizations, the predominantly female, frequently part-time, formal carers for old people are subject to a socially-constructed dependent status in which they have little control over their working lives, their patterns, policies and forms of practice, and in retirement they become economically dependent as a result of a lifetime of low earnings, interrupted employment due to child-rearing and poor occupational pensions.

While old women are in double jeopardy from the adverse effects of ageism and sexism accumulated over their lifespan, their female paid carers share their powerlessness, socially-constructed dependency and violation of rights because of the sex discrimination they encounter within the professionalization of welfare (Finch and Groves, 1985; Social Services Inspectorate, 1991; Phillipson, 1992).

The recognition of the powerlessness shared by old women and their female carers as a result of the combination of ageism and sexism within the professionalization of welfare, leads to new perspectives on abuse by formal carers, perceiving abuser and abused as powerless socially, organizationally and personally, locked together in a relationship of mutual, enforced dependency. The medium through which this socially-constructed powerlessness becomes the individual and collective abuse of elderly people takes place is the 'exchange relationship' of formal care.

Exchange theory proposes that power is central to all relationships and that in their interactions individuals will act according to the real and perceived benefits and costs to themselves of continuing that relationship. Each will strive to maximize benefits while minimizing inputs (Dowd, 1975). The person who is most dependent on the relationship for the satisfaction of their needs is the least powerful, and the level of his or her compliance may be the only currency he or she has to mediate the exchange. In interdependent relationships between people rendered mutually powerless by the effects of age and sex discrimination and the process of professionalization – where there exist minimal potential gains for both carers and cared for – the least powerless participants will seek to minimize their contributions and maximize their gains. In such situations the cared for may come to be perceived as an inconvenience, and a sub-culture of abuse arises, within which the previously unacceptable becomes the norm.

The possible contribution of such a combination of ageism, sexism and the professionalization of welfare to the abuse of elderly people by their formal carers has received comparatively little attention in the elder abuse literature. This neglect may be because the dominant paradigm employed in the analysis of elder abuse has been that of pathology. This reflects the influence of social work and medicine in discourse on abuse of elderly people – the theory and practice of both professions being informed by individualistic, pathology-oriented conceptions of problems rather than by social, structural forms of explanation. Perhaps understandably, the concern with description, identification and treatment of individual cases of abuse within domestic settings has led to an emphasis on individual pathology and family dynamics at the expense of the recognition of abuse by formal carers and its possible social structural origins.

New perspectives can only be achieved once this perspective is complemented by structural analysis that can embrace the social facts of ageism, sexism and professionalization. As the persistence of institutional abuse despite its repeated disclosure suggests, other perspectives are needed if change is to be achieved in our understanding of elder abuse by formal carers.

THE NEGLECT OF AGEISM

The pervasive existence of ageist attitudes in society is well documented and repeatedly shown through social surveys.

A recent survey in the UK has confirmed the continued existence of negative stereotypes of old age and old people, and a fear of ageing and the debility it is commonly assumed to bring (McEwen, 1992).

Ageism is institutionalized in professional health and welfare practice. In the USA, Solomon (1983) identified 29 separate studies that disclosed ageist attitudes among a wide range of professionals, leading to discriminatory practices against older people ranging from their exclusion from psychotherapy on the stereotypic assumption that old people are incapable of change, to the denial by medical students of life-saving treatment to old people in hypothetical situations. In the UK, Borsay (1989) described evidence of ageist stereotypes among social workers, including the belief that old people's needs are purely practical and that therefore they do not require counselling, and institutionalized discrimination based on these stereotypes, such as old people being routinely allocated to less skilled workers, and work with old people being accorded a low status.

Ageist discrimination is institutionalized in training where lower status vocational qualifications are seen as appropriate for residential and domiciliary workers with old people, but not for field social workers, who work predominantly with children. Two recent reports have reaffirmed these findings and condemned widespread discrimination against elderly people in social services departments (Allen, Hogg and Peace, 1992; Winner, 1992). Winner specifically claims that institutionalized ageism has been instrumental in preventing these departments from responding with any urgency to the growing evidence of elder abuse.

Despite this evidence of ageist discrimination among professional carers, there has been remarkably little theoretical analysis of its contribution to elder abuse. Thus, Roger Clough, in a review of reports on institutional abuse over 30 years, identifies the low status of work with older people and the attitudes and behaviour of staff as commonly offered explanations, however, he does not discuss ageism as a possible contributory factor (Clough, 1988). There is a similar neglect in four recent British reports on elder abuse which, as in Clough's work, identify several factors related to ageist attitudes and discrimination among professionals, but do not discuss ageism *per se* or attempt any theoretical analysis of its possible role in abuse of elderly people by formal carers (Tomlin, 1989; British Association of Services for the Elderly, 1991; McCreadie, 1991; Social Services Inspectorate, 1992).

Nonetheless, there is a literature in which ageism has been shown to affect elderly people and their carers in ways that could contribute to the creation of abusive sub-cultures within formal care settings.

Martin Seligman – an influential American social psychologist – suggests that ageist stereotypes of elderly people as dependent and increasingly incompetent lead, within the context of formal care, to the erosion of personal control (1975). He proposes that the persistent inability to control outcomes in one's own life leads to 'learned helplessness', the symptoms of which range from depression and inertia to death. He asserts:

> The mediocre lifespan of Americans . . . may be a testimony not to mediocre medical care, but to the way we treat our aged psychologically. We force them to retire . . . we place them in old people's homes . . . we are a nation that deprives old persons of control over the most meaningful events in their lives. We kill them.

Susan Mercer reviewed numerous studies of the effects of loss of control among institutionalized elderly people. She described them as inhabiting an 'environment which is essentially decision-free and control-free', where too much 'care' is just as damaging as none at all. Referring to a year-long study of residents' perceptions of institutional life, she reported that they considered: ' . . . certain institutional practices were arbitrary, and the end results were feelings of frustration, helplessness, hopelessness and powerlessness' (Mercer, 1983).

Mercer found considerable evidence that the hopelessness, inertia and withdrawal characteristic of many residents could be counteracted by basic measures to return some sense of control, or even the illusion of control – such as being able to decide on the frequency and duration of visits from volunteers. The loss of personal control by recipients of care may be seen as a product of the combination of ageist stereotypes and the professionalization of welfare within organizations.

Thus, the stereotype of the older person as 'incompetent' leads to whole groups being perceived as 'at risk'. Within the professional hierarchy of welfare bureaucracies formal carers are seen to be accountable for the safety of such groups; however, due to their low status within the hierarchy, this responsibility is unaccompanied by authority. In such situations care may easily become control, and dependency lead to subordination (Peace, 1986).

A recent British survey of the use of restraint in residential homes provides chilling evidence of this, reporting that, regardless of their individual needs, residents were 'regularly subject to a degree of restraint which significantly and unacceptably limits their freedom. The use of restraint in various forms gives cause for serious concern' (Counsel and Care, 1992). Methods of restraint ranged from tying residents to chairs, beds and commodes, to attaching them to makeshift harnesses and simply drugging them into immobility. This is clearly abuse constituting the violation of a person's human and civil rights as defined by Eastman (1984), and leading to the loss of control, powerlessness and 'helplessness' described by Mercer and Seligman. Such measures were justified by staff as being for the residents' own safety, protecting them from the risk of wandering and falling. The title of the report, *What if they hurt themselves?*, points to the conflict of responsibilities faced by formal carers who have gone beyond care to control and abuse.

Solomon (1983) describes the origins of this form of abuse within ageist stereotypes:

> By stereotyping the aged person as dependent, senile, incompetent and chronically disordered with a poor prognosis, the health worker does not respond to the older person's behaviour and needs but responds to the patient's custodial or maintenance needs, as perceived by the worker. These perceptions are frequently different from the patient's own perceptions of his needs . . . the older patient's individuality and individual needs become lost to the provider.

This leads to the patient experiencing the helplessness described by Seligman and being rendered powerless. However, Solomon asserts that negative attitudes, such as the belief that older people do not respond to treatment, also lead to a sense of futility among staff, a decline in morale and a consequent reduction in the quality of service. This is a view supported by a study carried out by Carol Martin (1985) of staff attitudes in a psychogeriatric service. This shows that, largely due to ageist assumptions about the unlikelihood of improvement in elderly patients, staff frequently feel powerless and helpless to affect situations. Martin found that:

. . . improvement in patients is (perceived to be) uncontrollable or even impossible because of physical disability and personality problems within this group. These staff see their contribution as unlikely to affect change given these limits.

Staff, it seems, felt similarly unable to alter institutional regimes and in these circumstances, Martin continues:

. . . the first choice of intervention considered (for dealing with problem patients) was in the majority of cases one to inhibit or constrain the behaviour of the difficult patient.

Thus, a combination of ageist stereotypes and the professionalization of welfare within hierarchies where accountability is unaccompanied by authority may lead to helplessness and powerlessness among carers and cared for alike. It is in this situation of mutual powerlessness that exchange theory can illuminate the development of abusive sub-cultures within formal care.

Solomon (1983) asserts:

Health professionals perceive long-term outcome to be negative and the costs to the provider in terms of both emotional and physical energy to be high. Therefore, they are unlikely to invest much energy to minimise cost and maximise the few benefits to be gained from working with the elderly. Their behaviour becomes responsive to their own needs to optimise their own 'cost-benefit ratio', and may become unresponsive to the elderly patient.

This is reminiscent of the description of the behaviour of staff in Clough's review of reports on abuse in institutions. In one home, where a sub-culture of abuse thrived, residents were left for hours in pools of urine, punished for requesting help and frequently humiliated if incontinent, including on several occasions having faeces pushed in their mouths. Residents' care needs were resented, and Clough (1988) continues:

> The most important objective for care assistants seems to have been finding time for socialising with each other, either in the staff room or in the lounge; but always at a distance from the residents. When looking at television, especially the afternoon soap operas, the residents were considered to be an inconvenience to be got out of the way as quickly as possible.

While Clough, and to a lesser extent Solomon, emphasize the power of the formal carer within the exchange relationship, it is clear from the examples they give, and those of Martin that feelings of powerlessness are equally involved. Thus Pillemer, in a paper exploring the 'dangers of dependency' in relation to elder abuse in the domestic setting (1985) lends support to this view:

> In elder abuse the perceived power deficit may be a more important factor than the notion that the abuser holds more power in the relationship. In such a situation the abusive individual feels that he or she lacks control and seeks to restore power. Having few resources with which to do so, the person then resorts to violence.

Pillemer and others (Homer and Gilleard, 1990) have concluded in relation to abuse in the domestic setting that the relative powerlessness of the abuser stems from his or her financial dependency on the abused, or psychological problems such as alcoholism. My own application of exchange theory to elder abuse by formal carers suggests that the powerlessness of the carer originates not in their individual psychopathology, but in the dependency socially-constructed through the ageist and sexist discrimination they encounter within the professionalization of welfare. This deprives them of the caring resources and organizational authority they require to meet the dependency needs of clients while simultaneously making them accountable for their care.

The powerlessness of formal carers and their lack of occupational resources and professional authority is clearly implicated in Clough's findings, where the most common explanations for abuse in institutions included: confusion and lack of knowledge about guidelines; the attitudes and behaviour of staff; staff capacity and lack of training; low staff morale; and the low status ascribed to the work (Clough, 1988). He concludes: 'Good practice demands authority for those living and working in the home'.

In the USA Pillemer presents similar findings. He found that staff are more likely to maltreat patients if they are poorly educated, comparatively young, unqualified and less experienced in nursing home work (Pillemer, 1988). These attributes may be seen as directly stemming from the low status, poor pay and poor prospects of work with older people which leads to a lack of training and high staff turnover – all products of the combination of ageist and sexist discrimination shown to exist within the professionalization of welfare. They are also a measure of the powerlessness of such staff and their comparative lack of occupational resources with which to meet the needs of dependent clients. As we have seen, it is the lack of such resources which, within the exchange relationship, may lead to violence and other forms of abuse in an attempt to restore power and control.

THE NEGLECT OF SEXISM

One of the earliest papers in the UK on elder abuse described it as 'granny battering' (Eastman, 1982). However, gender has been among the most neglected aspects of the study of elder abuse, both in the UK and the USA. In two comprehensive reviews of the literature, Giordano described seven theories of elder abuse (Giordano and Giordano, 1984), and Pillemer and Suitor (1988) described five – none, in either case, includes any analysis of gender issues. Four recent British reviews similarly fail to discuss gender as an influential factor (Tomlin, 1989; British Association of Services for the Elderly, 1991; McCreadie, 1991; Social Services Inspectorate, 1992). This gender blindness is puzzling when numerous studies have suggested that most of the victims of abuse in domestic situations are women (Social Services Inspectorate, 1992; McCreadie, 1991; Wolf and Pillemer, 1989; Giordano and Giordano, 1984; Zdorkowski and Galbraith, 1985; Tomlin, 1989).

Nonetheless, there is ample support from other sources for the belief that gender and sexism should occupy a central position in the understanding of elder abuse, particularly where it involves formal carers. Sex discrimination pervades social policy and professional practice, affecting older women and their predominantly female carers, both formal and informal. Caring is seen as 'women's work' and the public policy of care in the community effectively reinforces this private duty: community care in reality being care by women. Sexist stereotypes relating to the assumed skills of men and women underpin the professional practice which results in female carers being less likely to receive service support than male, and when they do it is often provided at a much later stage of dependency (Henwood, 1990); old men living alone receive more domestic and personal health services than women (Arber, Gilbert and Evandrou, 1988); and different packages of care are provided for the dependants of male and female informal carers (Charlesworth, Wilkin and Durie, 1984).

Research on institutional care has found that old women are more often perceived as 'problem patients' by nurses (Rosenthal, et al., 1980) and that they suffer 'depersonalization' more than men, i.e. less is known about their personal biographies and they are 'more obviously regarded as a non-adult or even a non-person' (Evers, 1981). This depersonalization and discrimination stems from sexist stereotypes of women's work and women's lives as domestically-oriented and therefore essentially unremarkable, and is confounded by the perception that in receiving care instead of giving it, old women 'become not only incompetent, but doubly incompetent' (Evers, 1981).

The predominantly female formal carers of old people within welfare bureaucracies also suffer the effects of sex discrimination. The 'feminization' of care work has lead to its devaluation within the professionalization of welfare for a number of reasons. Because women's work is perceived as 'natural' it is not felt to require particular skills, and therefore its practitioners require no specific training. Such work is therefore by definition unskilled, unprofessional and of low status. Perhaps a more subtle, but nonetheless damaging, effect is that care work is seen as essentially endless and lacking in discrete objectives – 'success' is therefore harder to identify.

This is especially true in relation to the long-term care of old people where the end result will inevitably be death. Thus care work is perceived as goalless and ultimately unsuccessful.

Through the professionalization of welfare a hierarchy of knowledge and skills has been constructed based on ageist and sexist definitions of which knowledge and skills are most valuable, and this legitimates and perpetuates the dominance within these organizations of certain occupational groups that are ascribed professional status (Borsay, 1989). This institutionalized sex and age discrimination is evident in social services departments where, although most of the carers for old people are women and 86.5% of the employees of social services departments are female, domiciliary and residential care assistants are among the lowest paid and most undertrained workers and less than 20% of senior managers are women (Social Services Inspectorate, 1991; Phillipson, 1992).

Despite the virtually total neglect of gender in the elder abuse literature – which may itself be seen as evidence of sexism among practitioners and researchers – there is evidence that women are the victims of sex discrimination both as carers and cared for. Such discrimination itself constitutes an abuse of human and civil rights, and may also lead to forms of conflict more commonly recognized as abuse.

As we have shown, formal carers in low status occupations within professional welfare hierarchies have few occupational resources with which to empower themselves within relationships and organizations. In this situation, the only source of status available to female carers may be that deriving from their social role as the 'nurturing woman'. In order to maintain her self-image and self-respect both as a woman and as a carer within professional hierarchies that threaten to deny her both, the carer must protect her claims to competence in the caring role. This may lead to conflict within the exchange relationship of formal care between old women – who have similarly limited claims to status – and their female carers.

'The role of the old woman . . . has been usurped by female care staff . . . the professionalisation of the caring role within service provision, whether this be the home help, the care assistant or geriatric nurse, often brings women into direct conflict with each other' (Peace, 1986).

Thus, in order to ensure her dependency-needs are met, the old woman is compelled to surrender her claim to adult status to the female carer, whose limited status within the organization depends on her complete possession of the caring role. In Evers' study of long-term geriatric patients there is poignant evidence of this struggle among the powerless. Old women who criticized the care given by nurses were treated more severely than were men who complained. Such old women were avoided, ignored, secluded and publicly rebuked for being demanding. Nurses' strategies 'often incorporated a "punishment" ethos' and consequently '"Awkward Alices" manifested various forms of suffering over and above whatever physical suffering they experienced' (Evers, 1981). In contrast, protest from men, 'Churlish Charlies', was perceived as more in keeping with their male role and hence experienced as less of a threat to the nurses' occupational 'caring' role.

Once again, for the elderly woman and her carer dependency entails subordination within the exchange relationship of formal care. The multiple forms of abuse that this may entail will meet with little resistance from the abused, whose only currency within the exchange is the level of their compliance.

BEYOND THE PATHOLOGY PARADIGM

While the effects of ageism within the exchange relationship of formal care have been explored by a very few theorists, the injurious combination of ageism and sexism within the professionalization of welfare has received little attention. If the 'passive abuse on a massive scale' (Tomlin, 1989) that has been so amply documented within residential care is at last to be confronted, and if the juggernaut of 'community care' is not similarly to violate and consume its recipients, new perspectives are urgently needed.

The search for pathology in the literature on domestic abuse has both neglected abuse by formal carers and offered little to its theoretical understanding. As the origins of abuse lie beyond the exchange relationship of formal care, so too do the solutions. In this chapter we have begun to explore this relationship and how, in reflecting the age and sex discrimination of wider society, it becomes corrupted.

At a recent conference a speaker on institutional abuse warned: 'Once power and authority move away from the management team to a faction within the staff of domestics, you are in trouble' (Morris, 1992). Everything we have described in this chapter suggests that the opposite is true – that powerlessness among carers and cared for is the lock confining them within a relationship of dependency and violation, and that their mutual empowerment is the key to interdependency without subordination.

REFERENCES

Allen, I., Hogg, D. and Peace, S. (1992) *Elderly People: Choice, Participation and Satisfaction*, Policy Studies Institute, London.

Arber, S., Gilbert, N.G. and Evandrou, M. (1988) Gender, household composition and receipt of domiciliary care services by elderly disabled people. *Journal of Social Policy*, **17**(2), 153–75.

Borsay, A. (1989) First child care, second mental health, third the elderly. *Research Policy and Practice*, **7**(2), 27–30.

British Association of Services for the Elderly. (1991) *Old Age Abuse: Lifting the Lid. A West Midlands Perspective*. BASE, Birmingham.

Charlesworth, A., Wilkin, D. and Durie, A. (1984) *Carers and Services: A Comparison of Men and Women Caring for Dependent Elderly People*, Equal Opportunities Commission, Manchester.

Clough, R. (1988) Scandal in residential centres – a report to the Wagner Committee. (Unpublished paper.)

Counsel and Care. (1992) *What if they hurt themselves?* Counsel and Care, London, p. 31.

Dowd, J.J. (1975) Ageing and exchange: a preface to theory. *Journal of Gerontology*, **30**, 584–94.

Eastman, M. (1982) 'Granny battering' – a hidden problem. *Community Care*, 27 May, 12–13.

Eastman, M. (1984) *Old Age Abuse*, Age Concern, London.

Evers, H. (1981) Care or Custody? The Experiences of Women Patients in Long Stay Geriatric Wards, in *Controlling Women – The Normal and the Deviant* (eds B. Hutter and G. Williams), Croom Helm, London, pp. 108–30.

Fennell, G., Phillipson, C. and Evers, H. (1988) *The Sociology of Old Age*, Open University Press, Milton Keynes.

Finch, J. and Groves, D. (1985) Old Boys, Old Girls: Gender Divisions in Social Work with the Elderly, In *Women the Family and Social Work* (eds E. Brook and A. Davis), Tavistock, London and New York, pp. 92–111.

Giordano, N.H. and Giordano, J.A. (1984) Elder abuse: a review of the literature. *Social Work*, **29**(May–June), 232–6.

Henwood, M. (1990) *Community Care and Elderly People*, Family Policy Studies Centre, p. 27.

Homer, A.C. and Gilleard, C. (1990) Abuse of elderly people by their carers. *British Medical Journal*, **301**, 1359–62.

Jack, R.L. (1987) Women in Care – The Submerged Issue of Feminism in the Residential Care of Elderly Women. *Social Services Insight*, **2**(12), 18–20.

Martin, C. (1985) Attributions of Staff Working with the Elderly: A Pilot Study, in *Ageing: Recent Advances and Creative Responses* (ed. A. Butler) Croom Helm, pp. 278–86.

McCreadie, C. (1991) *Elder Abuse: An Exploratory Study*. Age Concern/ Institute of Gerontology, London.

McEwen, E. (ed) (1992) *Dependence: The Ultimate Discrimination*, Age Concern, London.

Mercer, S.O. (1983) Consequences of Institutionalisation of the Aged, in *Abuse and Maltreatment of the Elderly – Causes and Interventions* (ed. J. Kosberg), John Wright PSG Inc., Boston, Bristol and London.

Midwinter, E. (1987) *Redefining Old Age*, Centre for Policy on Ageing, London.

Morris, P. (1992) *Community Care*, April, 4.

Peace, S. (1986) The Forgotten Female: Social Policy and Older Women, in *Ageing and Social Policy: A Critical Assessment* (eds C. Phillipson and A. Walker), Gower, Aldershot.

Phillipson, C. (1982) *Capitalism and the Construction of Old Age*, Macmillan, London and Basingstoke.

Phillipson, J. (1992) *Practising Equality – Women, Men and Social Work*, Central Council for Education and Training in Social Work, London.

Pillemer, K. (1985) The dangers of dependency: new findings on domestic violence against the elderly. *Social Problems*, **33**(2), 146–58.

Pillemer, K. (1988) Maltreatment of patients in nursing homes: overview and research agenda. *Journal of Health and Social Behaviour*, **29** (September), 227–38.

Pillemer, K. and Suitor, J. (1988) Elder Abuse, in *Handbook of Family Violence* (eds V. Van Hasselt *et al.*), Plenum, New York.

Rosenthal, C.J., Marshall, V.W., Macpherson, A.S. and French, S.E., (1980) *Nurses, Patients and Families*, Croom Helm, London.

Seligman, M.E.P. (1975) *Helplessness: on Depression, Development and Death*, Freeman Press, San Francisco.

Social Services Inspectorate (1991) *Women in Social Services – A Neglected Resource*, HMSO, London.

Social Services Inspectorate (1992) *Confronting Elder Abuse*, HMSO, London.

Solomon, K. (1983) Victimization by Health Professionals and the Psychologic Response of the Elderly, in *Abuse and Maltreatment of the Elderly: Causes and Interventions* (ed. J. Kosberg), John Wright PSG Inc., Massachusetts and Bristol, pp. 150–71.

Tomlin, S. (1989) *Abuse of Elderly People: An Unnecessary and Preventable Problem*, British Geriatrics Society, London.

Warren, L. (1985) *Older Women and Social Work Practice*, Warwick Critical Studies, University of Warwick, Warwick.

Winner, M. (1992) *Quality Work with Older People*, Central Council for Education and Training in Social Work, London.

Wolf, R. and Pillemer, K. (1989) *Helping Elderly Victims*, Columbia, New York.

Zdorkowski, R.T. and Galbraith, M.W. (1985) An inductive approach to the investigation of elder abuse. *Ageing and Society*, **5**(4), 413–29.

7

Physical abuse in homes and hospitals

Chris Gilleard

Where physical abuse in institutions has been examined there has been an interesting lack of relationship with characteristics associated with 'quality of care'.

More has been written in the media about abuse of patients in nursing homes and hospitals than has ever appeared in the scientific and professional literature. The reason may be that the professional journals have concentrated on bad practices in care rather than on individual acts of abuse, perhaps because the former are more commonplace and because the need to improve hospitals and home care for infirm elderly patients has been seen chiefly in terms of professional needs – for education and training – rather than personal needs.

Bad practice (in contrast with abusive practice) has in turn been emphasized as the opposite of quality, the antithesis of good quality care. But, of course, we do not know that bad practices and abusive practices represent points along the same single dimension of 'quality of care'. It is perfectly plausible to suggest that incidents of abuse arise as often in high quality care settings as in poor quality care settings. On the other hand, abusive acts may be so infrequent that their significance is minimal for the general planning of quality institutional care for frail elderly patients.

Conceptually, intentional abuse of elderly people by their carers, particularly physical abuse, has been seen as the consequence of pathology within the abuser; it can be contrasted with abuse arising from the stresses of caring and the 'understandable' breakdown of care-giving attitudes, as well as with abuse arising from wilful or unthinking neglect resulting from an unusual failure of carers to care.

The literature on abuse by informal carers has examined individual acts of abuse within a framework that assumes close bonds between kin and a common cultural duty to care. But the context within which domestic abuse occurs may not be appropriate when examining abuse by paid carers. Rather, assumptions about 'professional standards' – of nursing, therapy or medical practice – dominate views of what is or is not acceptable in formal care. The quality of formal care is seen as being determined by standards that are independent of personal/social relationships. Caring badly or not caring at all are seen as failures to meet professional standards, and abuse is viewed as an extreme instance of a more general set of bad (unprofessional) practices.

At the same time, care in homes and hospitals is most frequently given by unqualified, non-professionalized staff whose work is directed by qualified, professional staff. Neglect and abuse by these direct care workers can thus be seen as a breakdown in a professional hierarchy; a failure to obey on the one hand, or a failure to exercise due authority on the other.

From such a perspective, the 'characteristics' of those who are abused seem largely irrelevant to the occurrences of abuse/bad practice. Gripping a particular patient or resident to force food down his or her throat is seen to reflect ignorance about ways of 'coaxing' patients to eat, not the unexpressed feelings of frustration engendered by the patient's utter dependency on the carer; likewise the use of physical restraints for an agitated patient is seen as evidence of ignorance or professional 'backwardness' in managing patients, rather than an attempt to control the frighteningly uncontrollable process of mental and physical deterioration that surrounds the carers. The failure may be one of poor professional management (the failure of officers in charge, ward managers or senior nurses to guide their staff) or one of a lack of 'standards'; the interpersonal significance of abusive or inadequate care is rarely acknowledged.

Most attempts to improve standards in long-term care have emphasized a shift from task-oriented to patient-oriented practices: a deliberate attempt to change the 'culture' of caring to recognize the personal uniqueness, dignity and autonomy of patients/residents. Thus the personal becomes the 'professional' way to care. Task-oriented care is seen as bad practice.

It is legitimate to question whether such a shift in professional-cultural orientation: (a) really does improve the quality of care; (b) is the kind of care patients and residents most value; and (c) serves to reduce the risks of abuse.

If institutionally-based abuse arises from bad (task-oriented, depersonalized) practices, one might expect higher rates of abuse among less qualified staff, in hospitals and homes with absent or poor training programmes, and in settings where there are fewer human and material resources to assist in the care process, and where predominantly task-oriented care models are taught and practised.

If, on the other hand, abuse arises out of the psychopathology of the carer, the competing demands and stresses confronting the carer, or an abnormal dependency between carer and cared-for, then there should be little relationship between the occurrence of abuse and any of the above parameters concerning the organization of the care environment.

In this chapter I shall try to outline some of the extremely limited empirical evidence concerning abuse and its relationship with 'bad practice' in home and hospital care, and in so doing outline potential measures for the development of non-abusive care practices in institutional settings. I shall treat hospitals, nursing and residential homes as largely interchangeable settings in which elderly people will be exposed to varying degrees of supervision and assistance with personal care tasks.

By treating these settings as interchangeable, I realize that I am in danger of ignoring the very real differences between long-term care hospital settings operated within the National Health Service, and private residential and nursing homes. Hospitals are subject to continuous professional scrutiny and function in essentially 'open' environments where abuse is not easily hidden and where practices and standards are subject to continuous monitoring by more senior staff. Nursing homes are subject only to a limited and predictable pattern of inspection, and abuse can occur with only a limited likelihood of its discovery and with staff

working with little expectation that their professional perfor-
mance can be subject to continual monitoring.

THE NATURE AND EXTENT OF ABUSE IN INSTITUTIONS

Nearly every attempt to assess the cause, extent and consequences of abuse of older people must first address the problem
of definition. While some acts, such as punching, slapping,
shouting, swearing or pulling someone's hair, are easily
recognized as abusive, it is not always possible to draw a clear
line between abusive and non-abusive behaviour, even in a
domestic setting. In care settings the problem of definition is
even greater. Identifying when certain dubious care practices
become malpractice (such as the use of restraints, prn ['as
needed'] medications, tube feeding, etc.), or when neglect
reflects a lack of resources rather than a lack of care, can often
seem a matter of personal opinion.

Given the very few studies that have been conducted on
abuse in institutions, it is clear that little headway has been
made in creating a comprehensive taxonomy of forms of abuse.
It is salutary to note, however, that in Baker's (1975) original
article on abuse of old people, among the examples of 'granny
battering' he describes are cases involving polypharmaco-
therapy and the 'unnecessary' treatment of chest infections,
which prolonged the life of an elderly lady with terminal
dementia. Clearly Baker was willing to consider professionally
poor or dubious care practices as abuse. For him the question
of intent was subordinated to the perceived consequences for
the older patient.

The most convenient distinction to be made between types
of abuse committed in homes and hospitals (Figure 7.1) is that
between physical and verbal assaults on an elderly patient
(kicking, slapping, punching, hitting, threatening, shouting
or swearing), abusive practices carried out with some
awareness – if not intent – that they cause unnecessary
hardship (force-feeding, use of physical and chemical
restraints) and humiliating and insulting attitudes consciously
expressed and possessing an evident capacity to harm or
insult. While physical and verbal assaults rarely occur in the
absence of an intent to do harm and are usually reactive, the
last two types of abuse may often occur in the context of

'professional' duties, where the intent to cause suffering may be neither easily established nor readily acknowledged, and the carer may insist that the particular activity was designed to prevent a greater harm arising (to the patient or to other patients) had the action not been carried out.

Abusive/assaultive behaviours:
    punching, hitting, slapping, kicking, dragging hair, pulling, shaking.
Abusive treatments/practices:
    forced feeding, prn sedation/medication, use of restraints/geriatric chairs, group bathing, public toiletting, neglect, financial abuse.
Abusive attitudes/manners:
    belittling or hostile comments and criticisms, neglect of the need for privacy and personal respect, humiliation/infantilization in the face of dependency.

Figure 7.1 Categories of abuse in institutional care settings.

Abusive/assaultive behaviours

Surveys of the extent of potentially abusive care practices, such as tube feeding, use of restraints, sedative medication, 'group' bathing and catheterization of incontinent patients, indicate that these procedures are commonly administered to older patients in hospital and nursing home settings (Gillick, Serrell and Gillick, 1982; Wagnild and Manning, 1985; Frengley and Mion, 1986) with accompanying risks to patients' health and well-being.

At the same time, studies have tended to view these activities as examples of bad practice rather than forms of intentional abuse. As a result, inquiries into the individual causes of such practices have rarely been conducted. Instead, attempts are made to identify those structural or organizational factors that might account for their variation – though rarely with success (cf. Tinetti *et al.*, 1991). In contrast, studies of deliberate assault have been fewer, but these have been conducted with the aim of seeking individual explanations for the abuse.

Pillemer and Moore (1989) conducted one of the few surveys of the prevalence of physical and verbal (psychological) abuse of elderly patients in nursing homes in the USA. In the course of a 30-minute telephone interview, approximately 20% of staff reported having witnessed some form of physical abuse, while 5% reported having carried out physical abuse. When the researchers looked at the rates for 'psychological abuse' (defined as acts carried out with the intention of causing emotional pain to another person), they found an even greater prevalence, with between 50% and 70% of staff having observed an episode of psychological abuse, and between 10% and 33% having carried out such abuse.

There have been no similar studies in the UK. Perhaps one index of the prevalence of abuse can be derived from reports concerning disciplinary action taken against staff in NHS hospitals following patient maltreatment. Only the most serious of such allegations, constituting grounds for professional debarring, are systematically recorded. However, anecdotal accounts from senior nurse managers suggest that few such reports arise in the normal course of events. Rather, matters such as inappropriate sexual contacts, petty pilfering, sleeping on duty and being absent without permission from a clinical area tend to form the majority of routine disciplinary actions.

Despite the absence of any systematic study, it seems likely that physical abuse/assaults on patients are not frequent events in the NHS. Even in the previously cited American study, only 1% of nursing home staff reported any form of physical abuse if one excludes 'excessive use of restraints'.

Data from the disciplinary hearings of the United Kingdom Central Council (UKCC) for nurses, midwives and health visitors, where cases of malpractice are brought forward with a view to the possible striking off of members, indicate that in the financial year ending March 1992, of 771 alleged offences, 186 involved physical or verbal abuse of patients. Fifty per cent of such cases of abuse (which constitute the single largest offence category of cases brought to the UKCC) did involve geriatric wards, nursing homes, or residential homes for the elderly. Although such cases represent small numbers when viewed in the light of the total numbers of staff employed in private, voluntary and NHS homes and hospitals throughout the UK, it is clear that they do represent a significant minority of cases of professional malpractice in nursing (Table 7.1).

Where physical abuse in institutions has been examined there has been an interesting lack of relationship with

Table 7.1 Cases of nursing malpractice in the UK for the financial year 1991/92

All offences	Offences involving abuse	Offences involving abuse in geriatric/nursing homes
771	186	93

characteristics associated with 'quality of care'. In the Pillemer and Moore study cited above, no relationship was observed between the extent of the reported abuse and the size of the nursing home facility, whether the home was a 'for profit' nursing home, whether it was a 'cheap' home, whether the staff were young, poorly educated, nurse aides rather than nurses or staff with limited experience in working with elderly people. The variables they did find predictive of abuse included measures of 'burn-out' and staff–patient conflicts (Pillemer and Bachman-Prehn, 1991).

Abusive treatments/practices

Surveys of abusive practices and treatments have tended to focus particularly on the use of restraints (Tinetti *et al.*, 1991), force-feeding (Norberg *et al.*, 1988) and bathing/self-care activities (Wagnild and Manning, 1985). In each of these areas, however, one can perceive conflicting rather than absent ethical principles. As I shall try and show later, the demonstration of the use of a particular practice, such as force-feeding or the administration of powerful neuroleptics as a means of achieving behavioural control, is rarely sufficient to warrant terming that practice 'abusive'. Much more thought has to go into determining the context in which such potentially harmful procedures are undertaken. Research has not led to any clear empirical guidelines and definitions such as 'rough handling', 'unnecessary' persuasion or 'control' are ambiguous.

Studies on the use of restraints have done little more than document the wide variation in the type and extent of physical restraints with 'an almost complete lack of data concerning the effectiveness of restraints on reducing injury or improving behaviour' (Tinetti *et al.*, 1991). The fact that the use of mechanical restraints is rare in the UK but widespread in the USA indicates non-clinical factors coming into play. At the same time restraints are clearly sources of iatrogenic behaviour disturbance (Werner *et al.*, 1989), as are neuroleptics, used to control agitation and assaultiveness.

Research has not led to any hard evidence that can be used to help care staff reach more informed judgements about the costs and benefits associated with such procedures. Faced with staff shortages and multiple demands on the caring skills of staff it is understandable, if not excusable, that at times patients/residents will be 'locked' into a geriatric chair while staff dash off to deal with another potential emergency. While few care workers would argue that such temporary restraint was for the benefit of the patient/resident, the availability of such restraining devices on geriatric chairs makes it almost inevitable that such events will occur. Moral crusades conducted by the media (such as the *Daily Star* in 1992) to abolish such trappings of geriatric care, fail to acknowledge the daily demands that confront staff in homes and hospitals and the cost implications of replacing restraining furniture with human concern.

The practice of force-feeding older patients who, for one reason or another, refuse to eat is another area of concern, although, again, the issue is hardly one of inflicting deliberate harm. As Norberg has noted in her many pioneering studies in this area (Norberg *et al.*, 1980; Athlin and Norberg, 1987; Ekman and Norberg, 1988; Norberg *et al.*, 1988), the extent to which staff feel obliged to force open patients' mouths with their fingers or spoons, squeeze their nostrils or depress their chin to elicit eating behaviours is determined by the beliefs carers have about the necessity of ensuring their clients eat. Precisely what are acceptable practices in relation to patients who refuse or appear unable to eat must vary considerably. While some centres argue that tube feeding terminally ill older patients is unethical since the practice clearly causes harm to significant numbers of such patients and rarely results in benefits that outweigh the evident risk, others argue that in the absence of clear wishes to the contrary severely demented terminally ill older patients should be nourished by whatever means are available.

Likewise, some settings strenuously seek to avoid the use of p.r.n. sedation and eschew as much as possible the use of neuroleptic or other psychotropic medication as a means of exercising control over the behaviour of older patients with dementia. Others make equally strenuous efforts to demonstrate that clinical control of such 'symptoms' can be achieved using creative and assertive pharmacological regimes, including polypharmacy, and put the case that failing to treat such behavioural symptoms is as negligent as failing to treat an intercurrent infection.

These practices may seem abusive to some, but in other cases they are promoted within the context of a therapeutic commitment that may help instil a belief that older psychiatric patients can be helped no matter how hopeless their condition may appear. Electroconvulsive therapy (ECT) and the use of monoamine oxidase inhibiting (MAOI) antidepressants may be promulgated for 'recalcitrant' depression, and oral and depot neuroleptics for the behavioural disinhibitions of dementia. In such cases, the abuse arises not so much from any particular practice, as from a failure to document in the individual case the assumptions about cause and effect, the positive reasons for pursuing a course of treatment, the fact that the decision was reached within a clinical (multidisciplinary) debate and the fact that active monitoring of the consequences of the chosen practice or treatment was conducted.

The unthinking and unreviewed application of any treatment is perhaps the underlying abuse, which may be thought of as a kind of professional neglect rather than as a form of active assault. Professional depression, authoritarian clinical cultures, emotional exhaustion and dehumanization may be underlying causes for such neglect, just as stress and strain seem to be factors associated with neglect among informal carers (cf. Wolf, 1986).

Abusive attitudes/manners

Surveys of abusive and humiliating attitudes and manners among nursing and other care staff are even less extensive and tend to rely more on open observational studies and accounts derived from participant observation (e.g. Stannard, 1973; Hughes and Wilkin, 1987; Holmes and Johnson, 1988). What is often highlighted is the 'dehumanization' of care, as illustrated in this extract from an observational study of residential care described by Hughes and Wilkin (1987):

> *Resident*: No, no, I don't want a bath. No, don't you dare, I'm perfectly clean.
> *Staff*: [shouting] Behave yourself. [Continues to undress her.]
> *Resident*: No, no, oh dear, no.
> *Staff*: [pushing her towards the bath] It's all right, Emily, I'm not going to bath you.
> *Resident*: I know you're going to bath me.
> *Staff*: No I'm not. [Pushes resident into the upright medical bath and turns on tap – water ejects from the spray.]
> *Resident*: Oh, oh, that's cold. Oh dear, please let me out. This is awful. You won't wash my hair will you? [Attempts to stand up.]
> *Staff*: No, Emily, I won't wash your hair. [Puts shampoo on to resident's head.]

Many of these reports point to the demeaning nature of staff–patient interactions in care settings, but again there is little evidence that such 'ritual' humiliation in long-term care arises out of any hostile intent on the part of care staff. While they may indicate a lack of empathy, more often, as Ekman and Norberg (1988) point out, they reflect the outcome of carers' conflicting ethical principles – respecting autonomy versus avoiding neglect. In the bath-time example, neglect may be thought of in terms of the perceived harm arising from poor hygiene and inadequate skin care, which overrode the care assistant's concern for autonomous decision-making on the part of the resident.

EXPLANATORY MODELS OF INSTITUTIONAL ABUSE

Few models have been proposed as explanations for abuse in institutional settings, in contrast to the relatively rich choice of models to explain abuse by informal carers. This section offers some possible lines of investigation, but is largely speculative since – to the author's knowledge – there have been no attempts to develop and test any aetiological model of institutionally-based abuse. (Figure 7.2).

First and foremost one might suspect that sheer ignorance and lack of education about old age and the needs of older dependent people for care may play a significant part in many forms of abuse. The significance of the institutional setting, its organization and dominant culture might also be thought to play a part. The role of personal psychopathology among care staff should not be ignored, nor should the part played by chronic stress and burn-out. Finally, consideration must be given to those patient characteristics and traits that might predispose them to being victims of abusive acts, practices or attitudes. Each of these factors will be considered in turn.

1. Lack of staff training and education (ignorance).
2. Culture and structure of the organization.
3. Pathological characteristics of care staff.
4. Work-related stress and professional burn-out.
5. Patient characteristics as victims.

Figure 7.2 Aetiological models of institutional abuse.

Staff training and education

Studies examining the relationship between the 'professional' characteristics of staff and abuse are limited. The Pillemer study mentioned earlier found no relationship between either self-reported physical abuse or verbal abuse and the age of staff, their years of education, length of experience or nursing qualifications (nurse aides versus licensed practitioner/registered nurses). Norberg *et al.*, (1988) found no difference between nurse aides and enrolled nurses in their willingness to carry out various 'force-feeding' techniques. Although Astrom *et al.* (1990) found that registered nurses had more positive attitudes towards nursing elderly patients with dementia than did nurse aides, they found no difference between aides, geriatric and psychogeriatric enrolled nurses. This might simply reflect the fact that registered nurses in this study had less direct contact with patients and more autonomous work roles than the other groups that did not differ from each other.

Given the dubious relationship between expressed attitudes and observed behaviours in care settings, it is difficult to know how much weight can be given to staff accounts of what they would or would not do in certain circumstances. In the absence of direct observational data, it is unclear whether any increase in the numbers of qualified staff, or selection of 'experienced' rather than 'inexperienced' care workers, would have any impact on the extent of institutional abuse.

Organizational culture and structure

Working in an environment where the outcomes of one's work are routine, unproductive and frequently end in the death of those one is paid to look after, may call on strategies that sustain esteem and morale among the careworkers, at times emphasizing internal (staff) morale over and above that of the patients. One common result is the development of group cultures that sustain a kind of black (or gallows) humour in which matters that would usually be seen as heart-breaking are used as the subjects of ironic humour. Tragic events become transformed into tragicomic accounts, and the shared release of laughter offers a means of sustaining group support and gives a sense of solidarity that protects individuals from confronting the overwhelming sadness and futility that mark much of the lives of those they care for.

Studies of staff culture and the extent of abusive practices or attitudes are lacking. Most research has focused on the structural, rather than the cultural, features of long-term care. Studies looking at the determinants of such procedures as restraint, excessive p.r.n. medication, high rates of catheterization of incontinent patients or lack of personal belongings, have produced ambiguous results as far as any associations with organizational structure are concerned. Many studies have failed to find clear relationships between structural/organizational factors and abuse or abusive practices (cf. Pillemer and Moore, 1989; Garrard *et al.*, 1991; Tinetti *et al.*, 1991; Mountain and Bowie, 1992).

Research does suggest that nursing homes with higher staff complements, lower staff turnover and lower use of catheters produce improved outcomes for their residents (Spector and Takada, 1991). If one can extrapolate from this that improved resident outcomes are associated with fewer abusive practices, then this study might suggest that institutions that look after their staff and maintain adequate staffing levels do indeed produce better quality care. However, one anomalous finding of this particular American study was the association between 'serious federal citations' and 'improved' outcomes for residents. While the authors argue that this demonstrates the power of policing nursing home care as a means of improving practice, one could cynically argue that it merely serves to demonstrate that bad practice and bad outcomes are not always positively related. This conclusion is reinforced by Booth's (1985) study of old people's homes in the UK, in which he found little relationship between the organizational characteristics of the home and changes in resident status over time.

Pathological professionals

We do not know how widespread psychiatric disorders are among care staff in nursing homes or hospitals, but there is a fair amount of research literature on stress and emotional disorders among nurses. This research does not indicate an unusually high rate of psychopathology within the nursing profession. In a study using the General Health Questionnaire as a measure of psychiatric morbidity, McGrath, Reid and Boore (1989) found the prevalence of possible psychiatric cases no higher than that in the general community and actually lower than that found in other care groups studied (social workers and teachers). Firth *et al.*, (1987) found that while male nurses in long-stay care were more likely to be mildly depressed than males in the general population, there were no differences between female nurses and the general female population.

It would seem reasonable to assume that psychopathology is neither more nor less common among care staff than it is in the general population. The degree of control exercised over care-giving in institutions is much higher than that exercised in the community. Hence it would be surprising if individual psychopathology played a big part in determining abuse in institutional settings. However, newspaper reports of murderous nurses would certainly suggest that occasionally the monitoring of care practices fails to pick up the rare but devastating activities of the mentally disordered carer.

Staff burn-out

While the impact of personal psychopathology in carers on institutional abuse may be minimal, institutional care may lead to a kind of professional pathology, namely 'burn-out'. The importance of staff burn-out in long-term care settings has been recognized in a number of studies, although the clearest link between burn-out and abuse is that demonstrated by Pillemer and Bachman-Prehn (1991).

The extent and significance of burn-out within geriatric and psychogeriatric nursing varies according to the definition employed. Maslack (Maslack and Jackson, 1981; Maslack, 1982) has identified three separate dimensions of burn-out, alluded to above, namely emotional exhaustion, lack of personal achievement and depersonalization. The loss of sensitivity to the 'personal' contact with patients may be particularly significant in relation to abuse; for example, one study showed a significant relationship between nurses' 'extrapunitiveness' (the tendency to direct hostility outwards towards one's environment) and depersonalization or 'hardening' towards clients/patients (Firth *et al.*, 1987).

Investigations of how nurses cope with work-related stress and avoid burn-out suggest that they seek to minimize the emotional demands of patients by setting physical objectives in their work (cf. McGrath, Reid and Boore, 1989), in which case there will clearly be problems with the introduction of more holistic, 'whole person-oriented' approaches in long-term care settings. While such approaches may better reflect the care-giving approaches of patients' kin and enhance the sense of worth of older long-stay patients, one consequence of insisting on a more personally engaging style of nursing may be to increase burn-out and thereby indirectly increase the risk of assaultive abuse. It is important to consider the implications of any policy or procedure that may make formal care-givers 'burn-out' of caring, since it is here that the strongest associations with abuse have been detected.

Patient characteristics

What sort of patient is more likely to be the recipient of abuse, abusive practice or abusive attitudes from staff? Most of the relevant research is confined to studies examining patients at risk of suffering some potentially traumatic or stress-inducing practice such as restraint, major tranquillization, inadequate nutrition or other neglect. The results of these studies (e.g. Robbins *et al.* , 1987; Garrard *et al.*, 1991; Tinnetti *et al.*, 1991; Gillick, Serrell and Gillick, 1982) suggest that the older old patient, who is mentally frail, incontinent, dependent and who has been admitted from another institution, is at higher risk of being restrained, catheterized, receiving 'ineligible' neuroleptic medications and experiencing forced or tube feeding. While these are American findings, there seems little reason to believe they do not also apply in other developed countries such as the UK.

The significance of personality rather than symptomatology as a factor in receipt of potentially abusive practices has not been studied. Whether there are characteristics that contribute to a patient's being someone's 'favourite', and whether such 'favouritism' influences care practices, are questions lacking firm answers. But even if one were to demonstrate such associations it seems unlikely that much good could come of it. It hardly seems appropriate to recommend social skills training to elderly people about to go into hospitals or into care!

The current evidence suggests that the best predictors of abuse and abusive practices centre on patient characteristics and staff burn-out. If certain patients contribute more to burn-out than others this may set up a vicious circle: patients with the greatest mental and physical infirmity are most exhausting to care for; are therefore most likely to induce professional depersonalization in those who care for them; and thus are at increased risk of both individual acts of abuse and more pervasively abusive practices from the staff.

TACKLING INSTITUTIONAL ABUSE

In this final section an attempt is made to suggest some possible approaches to preventing abuse. In particular, the following suggestions are made to reduce the risk of incidents of individual abuse, abusive practices and abusive attitudes in the long-term care of older people. Areas to be considered are:

- staff support and education, including nursing ethics groups, active quality assurance programmes, quality circles, perhaps using discussion documents such as the King's Fund Project Paper *Living Well into Old Age* (1986), accessible counselling for staff, and 'sabbatical leave' after medium- and long-term service;
- formal monitoring of standards of care as part of the contracting process between purchasers and providers and as a nursing management commitment; examples of standard-setting in long-term care have recently been produced by Philp, Mawhinney and Mutch (1991);
- open visiting hours for friends and relatives, introduction of patients' advocates and regular visits to long-term care facilities by Community Health Councils and age-associated voluntary organizations such as Age Concern and the Alzheimer's Disease Society;
- a management commitment to sensible resourcing of quality improvements and priority training;
- a prominently displayed complaints and suggestions box with a response from management that does not seek simply to penalize or make scapegoats of those criticized;
- a distinct reduction in hypocrisy within a culture that recognizes that caring has to be worked at.

No institution can be immune to the blunting of perspective that so easily occurs among those engaged in long-term care of frail elderly people, hence the continual need for staff to be seen to be caring. The more open the care environment, the more open the culture of the care-givers, the less likely it will be that the recipients of care suffer the darker side of insitutional life. The creation of nursing homes affiliated to universities or medical schools would do much to enhance the role of professional long-term care of physically and mentally frail elderly people.

REFERENCES

Astrom, S., Nilson, M., Norberg, A. and Winblad, B. (1990) Empathy, experience of burnout and attitudes towards demented patients among nursing staff in geriatric care. *Journal of Advanced Nursing*, **15**, 1236–44.

Athlin, E. and Norberg, A. (1987) Care-givers' attitudes to and interpretations of the behaviour of severely demented patients during feeding in a patient assignment care system. *International Journal of Nursing Studies*, **24**, 145–53.

Baker, A.A. (1975) Granny battering. *Modern Geriatrics*, August, 20–4.

Booth, T. (1985) *Home Truths: Old People's Homes and the Outcome of Care*, Gower, Aldershot.

Ekman, S.L. and Norberg, A. (1988) The autonomy of demented patients: interviews with care-givers. *Journal of Medical Ethics*, **14**, 184–7.

Firth, H., McKeown, P., McIntee, J. and Britton, P. (1987) Professional depression, 'burnout' and personality in longstay nursing. *International Journal of Nursing Studies*, **24**, 227–37.

Frengley, J. and Mion, L. (1986) Incidence of physical restraints on acute general medical wards. *Journal of the American Geriatrics Society*, **34**, 565–8.

Garrard, J., Makris, L., Dunham, T. *et al.* (1991) Evaluation of neuroleptic drug use by nursing home elderly under proposed Medicare and Medicaid regulations. *Journal of the American Medical Association*, **265**, 463–7.

Gillick, M., Serrell, N. and Gillick, L. (1982) Adverse consequences of hospitalization in the elderly. *Social Science and Medicine*, **16**, 1033–8.

Holmes, B. and Johnson, A. (1988) *Cold Comfort: The Scandal of Private Rest Homes*, Souvenir Press, London.

Hughes, B. and Wilkin, D. (1987) Physical care and the quality of life in residential homes. *Ageing and Society*, **7**, 399–426.

King's Fund Centre (1986) *Living Well into Old Age*, King's Fund Centre, London.

Maslack, C. (1982) *Burnout: The Cost of Caring*, Prentice Hall, Englewood Cliffs, New Jersey.

Maslack, C. and Jackson, S.E. (1981) The measurement of experienced burnout. *Journal of Occupational Behaviour*, **2**, 99–113.

McGrath, A., Reid, N. and Boore, J. (1989) Occupational stress in nursing. *International Journal of Nursing Studies*, **26**, 343–58.

Mountain, G. and Bowie, P. (1992) The possessions owned by long stay psychogeriatric patients. *International Journal of Geriatric Psychiatry*, **7**, 285–90.

Norberg, A., Backstrom, A., Athlin, E. and Norberg, B. (1988) Food refusal amongst nursing home patients as conceptualised by nurses' aids and enrolled nurses: an interview study. *Journal of Advanced Nursing*, **13**, 478–83.

Norberg, A., Norberg, B., Gippet, H. and Bexell, G. (1980) Ethical conflicts in long term care of the aged: nutritional problems and the patient–carer relationship. *British Medical Journal*, **280**, 377–8.

Philp, I., Mawhinney, S. and Mutch, W.J. (1991) Setting standards for long term care of the elderly in hospital. *British Medical Journal*, **303**, 1056.

Pillemer, K. and Bachman-Prehn, R. (1991) Helping and hurting: predictors of maltreatment of patients in nursing homes. *Research on Ageing*, **13**, 74–95.

Pillemer, K. and Moore, D.W. (1989) Abuse of patients in nursing homes: findings from a survey of staff. *The Gerontologist*, **29**, 314–20.

Robbins, L.J., Boyko, E., Lane, J. *et al.* (1987) Binding the elderly: a prospective study of the use of mechanical restraints in an acute care hospital. *Journal of the American Geriatrics Society*, **35**, 290–6.

Spector, W.D. and Takada, H.A. (1991) Characteristics of nursing homes that affect resident outcomes. *Journal of Ageing and Health*, **3**, 427–54.

Stannard, C. (1973) Old folks and dirty work: the social conditions for patient abuse in a nursing home. *Social Problems*, **20**, 329–42.

Tinetti, M.E., Liu, W.L., Marotolli, R.A. and Ginter, S.F. (1991) Mechanical restraint use among residents of skilled nursing facilities: prevalence, patterns and predictors. *Journal of the American Medical Association*, **265**, 468–71.

Wagnild, G. and Manning, R.W. (1985) Convey respect during bathing. *Journal of Gerontological Nursing*, **11**, 6–10.

Werner, P., Cohen-Mansfield, J., Braun, J. and Marx, M.S. (1989) Physical restraints and agitation in nursing home residents. *Journal of the American Geriatrics Society*, **37**, 1122–6.

Wolf, R.S. (1986) Major Findings from Three Model Projects on Elderly Abuse, in *Elder Abuse: Conflict in the Family* (eds K. Pillemer and R. Wolf), Auburn House Publishing Co., Dover, MA.

Part Three

Dealing with Old Age Abuse

8

Clinical diagnosis and treatment

Gerald Bennett

The most sensitive area of questioning is that concerning actual abusive episodes, asking for detailed verbal and physical incidents.

The clinical diagnosis of elder abuse in the UK is still at a very basic level. In cases of physical abuse fairly substantial injuries need to be present before any degree of certainty is reached (Figure 8.1); more subtle features, such as finger-marks resulting from harsh gripping can however be recognized

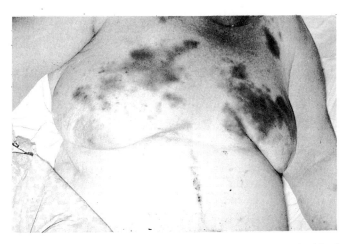

Figure 8.1 Gross physical abuse: an 80-year-old woman assaulted by her grandson (who was later gaoled as a result).

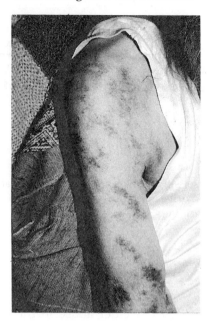

Figure 8.2 Finger-mark bruising.

(Figure 8.2). In the USA, however, some clinicians feel that their knowledge base is sufficiently advanced to allow many physical signs to be accurately diagnosed.

The symptoms and signs of sexual or psychological abuse are still much less well documented for elderly people than for children. Two major reasons account for this.

Until comparatively recently, any form of child abuse was considered rare; sexual abuse was unheard of and not given conscious thought by most clinicians. Gradually case reports began appearing in the medical press of children with fractures and bruises at different stages of healing, which had possibly been caused by parental/carer violence. Awareness slowly grew, and social workers and paediatricians began to climb the long, hard learning curve to the current knowledge base. The initial assessment procedures now seem simple and naive with the benefit of hindsight, research and years of professional–client interaction, but this process has barely begun for elder abuse.

The second reason is more complex. Children have very well-defined and clear developmental stages, thus professionals have their own experience and numerous charts and guidelines to indicate fairly accurately what normal children should be achieving. Children are also seen frequently by many people – health visitors, district nurses, GPs, teachers, etc. – who all have the opportunity to spot abnormal symptoms and signs (failure to thrive, unexplained skin marks, sudden onset bed-wetting, undue fearfulness or precocious sexual behaviour).

This is a very different situation to that of an elderly person, in whom abuse is also much more difficult to establish. The physiological and psychological changes that occur with ageing are not well known even by health care workers dealing with elderly people. Gerontology, the study of ageing, is still a very new science. Normal ageing appears to be a gradual and benign process. A normal fit 80-year-old is mobile, continent and intellectually the match of anyone younger (usually because of the benefit of experience). This differs markedly from the generally held view of elderly people: that they are in a second childhood, are intellectually frail, fall repeatedly, and are incontinent and immobile. These problems do occur, but as a result of disease; they are therefore abnormal not normal ageing.

This distinction between what is normal ageing and what is disease is crucial to the laying down of a knowledge base for the recognition and assessment of cases of elder abuse. A few examples will demonstrate how difficult it can be to draw this distinction.

As we age our skin undergoes subtle changes, mostly at a microscopic level. Most people, however, equate ageing skin with wrinkles, warts and 'liver spots'. This is not normal ageing; these changes are due to the sun's ultraviolet light and are speeded up by sunbathing, leading to wrinkles that are more severe than one's 'family tree' (i.e. genetic inheritance) would have produced. Wrinkles are only cosmetic; other skin changes have a potentially more serious effect.

In most elderly people the unavoidable exposure of their skin to the sun, especially the forearms, results in the skin becoming thinner. A substance called collagen acts as a support for blood vessels just under the surface, and this, too, is affected, so that minor trauma (a knock) can cause a blood vessel to break resulting in a bruise (senile purpura, Figure 8.3). The mechanism for clearing away the effects of bruises is less effective in elderly people, and so the bruises stay for long periods. This situation is made still more complex by the fact that some elderly people are especially affected, and a small group develops the transparent skin syndrome. The skin becomes paper thin with the result that the skin will 'tear' and bruise on even normal contact, i.e. touching and dressing. The results can look appalling and suspicious. Therefore bruising in elderly people is not a straightforward issue and cannot always be used as a definitive sign in elder abuse cases.

Falls and incontinence are two conditions that occur commonly in the very old. They are not part of normal ageing but the signs of an underlying disease process. If this connection is not made, the resulting injuries and poor hygiene can easily be mistaken for evidence of abuse or neglect.

The physiological changes that occur in ageing and disease will thus have a great bearing on the clinical diagnosis procedure. Purely physical signs should be interpreted with great caution until experience and research build up a sound knowledge base. The assessment procedure for an elderly

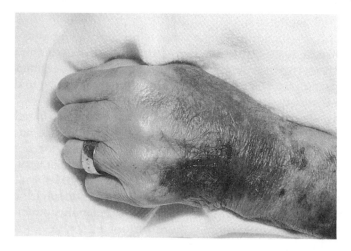

Figure 8.3 Senile purpura.

person suspected of having been abused must be as holistic as possible. The time honoured approach of history-taking and physical examination must be somewhat modified to gain even more information.

In the USA Cochran and Petrose (1987) outlined features that should alert doctors to the possibility of abuse. These include any discrepancy between an injury and the history, inappropriate injuries, conflicting stories, vague explanations or denial. There may be bizarre or inappropriate explanations, or insistence by a patient that an injury is severe when no injury exists (presumably in order to get professional help). A long delay in reporting the injury is also suspicious, as is a story of an elderly person being 'accident prone', histories of previous injuries, untreated old injuries and multiple injuries, especially at various stages of healing. Repeated attendance at accident and emergency departments of elderly people from the same institution should also trigger concern.

Doctors in the USA are also alerted by injuries in areas usually covered by clothing, injuries consistent with the shape of a weapon and of bruising/laceration on the lips (from forced feeding and gagging). Whiplash injuries can occur from shaking; sexual abuse can result in laceration, bruising and bleeding of the rectum and genitalia and the presence of sexually transmitted diseases. Fractures in those who are usually immobile and aloplecia (hair loss) and bleeding from hair-pulling are other suspicious signs. Conditions whose cause is difficult to establish include malnutrition, dehydration, weight loss and pressure sore formation. A history of previous physical abuse of a patient, and occasionally previous suicide attempts, should also alert the doctor.

Fulmer and O'Malley (1987) list the manifestations of 'inadequate care' (their broad definition of elder abuse) for health care professionals (Table 8.1). There are also said to be other physical indicators of abuse not shared with neglect (Table 8.2). The most common presentations of inadequate care usually involve combinations of symptoms and signs, e.g. poor nutrition, poorly-controlled medical problems, frequent falls and confusion. Thus the GP, district nurse, health visitor and casualty officer will often be the first people to be presented with the diagnostic dilemma. Less often, those in the legal

Table 8.1 Manifestations of inadequate care

Abrasions	Dehydration
Lacerations	Malnutrition
Contusions	Inappropriate clothing
Burns	Poor hygiene
Freezing	Over-sedation
Depression	Over- or under-medication
Fractures	Untreated medical problems
Sprains	Behaviour that endangers client or others
Dislocations	Failure to meet legal obligations
Decubiti (pressure sores)	

Table 8.2 Physical indicators of abuse not shared with neglect

Unexplained bruises and welts:

Face, lips and mouth
torso, back, buttocks, thighs

in various stages of healing, clustered, forming regular patterns reflecting the shape of article used (cord, buckles) on several different surface areas, regularly appear after absence, weekend or holidays.

Unexplained burns:

Cigar, cigarette, especially on soles, palms, back and buttocks.

Immersion burns (sock-like on feet, glove-like on hands, doughnut-shaped on buttocks or genitalia).

Patterned burns like electric burner, iron, etc., rope burns on arms, legs, neck or torso.

Unexplained fractures:

To skull, nose, facial structure.

In various stages of healing.

Multiple or spinal fractures.

Unexplained lacerations or abrasions:

To mouth, lips, gums or eyes.

To external genitalia.

Sexual abuse:

Difficulty in walking or sitting.
Torn, stained or bloody underclothing.
Pain or itching in the genital area.
Bruises or bleeding in external genitalia, vaginal or anal areas.
Venereal disease.

profession, social services or the police are the first involved, usually because of housing or financial problems.

The presence of one or more of the items on the list of manifestations of inadequate care obviously does not establish a diagnosis of abuse or neglect: the same findings can occur in frail, ill, elderly people as part of the acute or chronic health process. Nevertheless, the presence of these symptoms and signs should alert the attending professionals to the possibility of inadequate care.

Occasionally elderly people themselves report that they have been abused. This usually happens when they have formed a close relationship with a member of staff and feel able to divulge their worries. Two groups of staff in particular are in a position to form these close bonds: nursing and therapy. The periods of time spent by these two groups in close proximity to their patients, detailed explanation of procedures and a joint striving to reach rehabilitation goals, means that very special relationships can form, which may facilitate discussion of very private concerns.

Fulmer and O'Malley (1987) recommend that the history-taking be expanded and specific questions asked. This will involve enquiring about theft or misappropriation of resources and about possible enforced social isolation or confinement. The patient will need to be asked about any threats or coercion, the use of restraints, any actual episodes of battering, sexual abuse, threats of punishment, being shouted at (chronic verbal aggression) or the withholding of food, clothing or privileges to enforce behaviour.

The social assessment may require many interviews over a period of time and thus the procedure can be very time-consuming. Locally produced guidelines may help with interview techniques. As far as possible only pertinent and appropriate information should be collected, and where possible this should include financial details.

Quinn and Tomita (1986) describe the importance of enquiring about a typical day. This naturally leads into a verbal assessment of the subject's ability to perform the activities of daily living. This may need to be very detailed giving both the old person and carer an opportunity to describe their perceived and actual difficulties. Quinn and Tomita also describe the need to explore the older person's expectations about care, getting information on recent crises in the family as well as the sensitive areas of alcohol problems, drug use/abuse, illness and behaviour problems within the household or family members.

The subject's current mental status should always be ascertained before detailed questioning begins. The reasons and need for this will have to be explained in advance as mentally competent people can get irritated at having their memory assessed. Failure to assess memory can lead to difficulties later. Where there seems to be an indication of some unusual circumstances more in-depth questions should follow, but tact and accuracy should remain paramount.

One quick screening method is the simple 'mental test score' or abbreviated mental test. This consists of 10 questions that test short- and long-term memory, orientation and numeracy. It is a rather crude assessment, and a low score by itself does not imply a permanent impairment, but its value lies in repetition over time, when a rising score indicates resolving acute confusion, whereas a persistently low score shows a more chronic confused state. The 10 questions should be written down as most assessors only remember 9! The questions might include (Hodgkinson, 1972):

- Age
- Date of birth
- Year (current)
- Time (to nearest hour)
- Where do you live? (Town or road)
- Tell subject another address (for recall)
- Name of current Prime Minister or monarch
- Date of start of First World War
- Count back from 20 to 1
- Recognition of two people

This assessment may indicate an obvious problem and further history-taking must be interpreted with caution. A more detailed evaluation of memory is provided by performing a 'mini-mental state' test which involves 20 questions (Folstein, Folstein and McHugh, 1975). A poor score on a mental test obviously does not equate with a blanket lack of capacity to consent or mean that a person is totally lacking in judgement or validity concerning certain situations. It is, however, a difficult area where medicine, law, ethics, morality and professional experience overlap.

The most sensitive area of questioning is that concerning actual abusive episodes, asking for detailed verbal and physical incidents. Specific questions relating to the episodes may need to be asked for greater clarification. Interviewing the care-giver is another emotionally demanding situation. Different interview techniques are used by various professionals, some of whom have developed high levels of skill, especially those in social work.

Many people rely on the use of a formal protocol – an *aidemémoire* to formalize the interview situation. Such protocols, screening instruments for use in suspected cases of elder abuse, are being developed in the USA. They can be very lengthy to complete but are thorough and provide detailed information on which to base reports regarding alleged abuse/inadequate care.

One such protocol is the Elder Assessment Instrument (EAI) (Fulmer, 1984).

It has eight sections and is designed for health care professionals to be able to elicit symptoms and signs, the total forming a small booklet.

Section 1 consists of demographic data (age, sex, address, next of kin). It also includes an assessment of the client's mental state.

Section 2 is concerned with a general assessment (hygiene, nutrition, skin integrity and clothing), scores range from very good to very poor.

Section 3 involves a physical assessment of bruises, contractures, pressure sores, lacerations, and so on, parameters range from definite evidence through to no evidence. Other screening instruments in this section include a human figure chart (back and front) so that location of marks/bruises can be made with estimates of injury dates, etc. In many formats the use of photographs (with written consent) is encouraged.

Section 4 involves an assessment of the elderly person's usual lifestyle, specifically inquiring about medication, ambulation, continence, feeding, hygiene, finances and family involvement, parameters range from totally independent to totally dependent.

Section 5   is a social assessment identifying interactions between client and family, friends and other caregivers. It involves detailed knowledge of social systems and the client's ability to express needs and participate in daily activities (often relying on observational skills). A financial assessment is also made.

Section 6   is the medical assessment, often backed up by laboratory and radiological test results. It can involve assessment of alcohol/substance abuse, dehydration, fractures, excess medication, and so on. Again parameters range from definite evidence to no evidence.

Section 7   summarizes the evidence and states whether there is proof of either financial/possession abuse, physical or psychological abuse or neglect.

Section 8   looks at the outcome, i.e. referral to the elder abuse assessment team (an American concept) or to lawyers, police, etc. It also provides for comment and follow up.

The EAI is proving to be a useful tool in the USA by providing a detailed and standardized assessment of elderly people suspected of being abused/inadequately cared for. The evaluation of such screening instruments (modified for a UK population) is urgently needed.

Elder abuse or inadequate care and neglect may result in physical and psychological trauma that need all the skills of the multidisciplinary team. Physical harm will require expert nursing and medical supervision, and the possible involvement of certain specialties, such as orthopaedics or neurosurgery. The patient may require a nutrition assessment from a dietitian and special equipment such as an alternating pressure air mattress if pressure sores are present or imminent. Sexually abused elderly people may need help from the sexually transmitted diseases team.

The psychological sequelae may require the intervention of a psychiatrist, clinical psychologist, or counselling from a skilled social worker, especially in cases of sexual abuse.

The clinical diagnosis and treatment of cases of elder abuse will form one of the most difficult areas for the multidisciplinary team to confront. Discussion will often involve a case conference where the important information from members of the primary health care team can be fed into the hospital-based process. This also gives an opportunity for other groups to be involved, including the police, clergy and housing representative. It is vital that, where possible, client and carer(s) are given an opportunity to discuss the situation and their wishes for the future.

The clinical findings will often be inconclusive, i.e. it is not possible to be absolutely certain that physical/sexual abuse has occurred. If this is the case the client and carer must continue to feel fully supported by the team. These situations can be grouped under the umbrella of 'inadequate care' so that clinical and social vigilance is continued.

REFERENCES

Cochran, C. and Petrose, S. (1987) Elder abuse: the physicians role in identification and prevention. *Illinois Medical Journal*, **171**, 241–6.

Folstein, M.F., Folstein, S.E. and McHugh, P.R. (1975) Mini-mental method for grading the cognitive state of patients for the clinician. *Journal of Psychological Research*, **12**, 189–98.

Fulmer, T.T. (1984) Elder abuse assessment tool. *Dimensions of Critical Care Nursing*, **10**(12), 16–20.

Fulmer, T.T. and O'Malley, T.A. (1987) *Inadequate Care of the Elderly*, Springer Publishing, New York.

Hodgkinson, H.M. (1972) Evaluation of mental test score for assessment of mental impairment in the elderly. *Age and Ageing*, **1**, 233–8.

Quinn, M.J. and Tomita, S.K. (1986) *Elder Abuse and Neglect: Causes, Diagnoses and Intervention Strategies*, Springer Publishing, New York.

protection cases, which are given priority (although this does depend on how the department is managed!).

The attitude that working with elderly people is 'not real social work' still persists. Workers who are committed to this type of work are seen by many as taking 'the easy option', but in fact working with elderly people can be just as demanding and stressful as working with children and families. Stevenson and Parsloe found in their research study (1978) that 'work with the elderly was perceived in a stereotyped way as tasks which only require practical services and visiting.' This is unrealistic as elderly people, just as any other client group, have a variety of practical and emotional needs. For example, elderly people who have been abused (that is any form of abuse, be it physical, emotional or financial) suffer trauma and other difficulties; therefore, they should be entitled to skilled counselling and therapy as are other clients in younger age groups who have suffered similarly.

A major problem in many social services departments is a lack of awareness that old age abuse even exists: it is not just the general public that does not realize that between 5% and 10% of the elderly population are being abused in some way. I have found that once social workers have been trained or talked to about old age abuse they start thinking about, looking for and finding cases of it and many start recalling cases they may have 'missed'. Therefore, it is crucial that all social services staff are made aware that old age abuse is a very important and live issue. Raising awareness must be the first step in working with abuse and the starting point has to be to define old age abuse. Every one has different values and attitudes and will consequently have different views about what actually constitutes abuse; what may be abusive to one person may not appear to be an abusive situation to another (Pritchard, 1992). This has serious implications for practice as workers may come into conflict with their own colleagues (e.g. care assistants may not have the same ideas about how to approach or speak to a difficult confused client; or a home help may think a carer's manner or attitude towards an elderly person is emotionally abusive, whereas the social worker disagrees).

Raising awareness can be achieved through training, but programmes also need to include recognition of abuse and good social work practice in dealing with abuse. Workers are often uncertain about how to proceed if faced with a clear case of abuse or if they have no concrete evidence. Consequently, it is crucial that all social services departments formulate clear policy and procedures for their staff to follow. Mary Ann Hildrew (1991) found that out of 115 social services departments in England and Wales, 11 had published guidelines, 26 had draft guidelines and 12 had working parties.

Research is also important for the development of good practice in dealing with old age abuse. More needs to be known about the actual incidence of abuse (especially among Black, Asian and ethnic communities, where very little work has been undertaken). Around the UK individuals interested in old age abuse have started their own research projects and small studies. During 1993 Action On Elder Abuse was launched to provide a national network for linking up these people and a central point where information can be collected and disseminated.

Some local authorities have undertaken small projects themselves (Bedford, 1989; Bexley, 1988). During 1993 the Social Services Inspector completed a two stage project whose main objective was to examine how cases of old age abuse in domestic settings were being handled by social services departments (SSI, 1992) and produce guidance for local authorities (SSI, 1993).

CURRENT PRACTICE

When a social services department does not have guidelines to follow, the workers who actually attempt to confront the problems often work in different and imaginative ways because of the lack of support and guidance. I said earlier that many staff do not realize that old age abuse even exists, and this includes managers who should be supporting their workers. It is crucial that all managers who are supervising staff dealing with cases of old age abuse have an understanding and knowledge of the subject. Current expertise is patchy and therefore authorities must train managers as well as practitioners. Dealing with old age abuse can be very stressful and upsetting; managers need to be able to support their staff in a proper and effective manner. So what do social services staff do in dealing with cases of old age abuse?

Some workers may do nothing if they are unsure about what to do, or if they have no hard evidence but are just relying on a 'gut feeling'. Others may try to adapt their knowledge and experience of child protection work if no procedures exist for adults/elderly people at risk. It is important for all social services staff, no matter in which setting they are working, to know who they should go to in dealing with cases of abuse (e.g. a care assistant should know what to do and who to go to if he or she saw one of the domestics slap a resident across the face, and a social worker should know what to do if abuse in a private nursing home was suspected).

Old age abuse has to be confronted; it cannot be ignored. There can be positive outcomes in this area of work and the attitude that 'nothing can be done' must not be adopted. People come into the profession of social work because they believe they can effect change; this must not be forgotten when dealing with old age abuse.

Good practice would ensure an investigation take place with some degree of urgency (as in child abuse cases) every time there is an allegation that abuse is occurring or when an elderly person is thought to be at risk of being abused. In order to protect an elderly person a full assessment needs to be undertaken. Before visiting, workers should try to gather as much information as possible about the person and his/her circumstances. In order to achieve this workers must consult with other agencies. In dealing with old age abuse it is important not to jump too quickly to conclusions, that is, not to diagnose abuse or suggest future treatment/action plans until all the facts have been gathered and discussed in full.

It is important that the elderly person be given the opportunity to talk alone with the workers involved. Abusers should also be interviewed separately, but not necessarily by social services staff because in some cases it may be appropriate to involve the police. This leads us to one of the dilemmas in working with old age abuse: workers know that, sometimes, confronting an abuser might actually make the situation worse for the victim if after the investigation there is no real evidence or no action is taken.

Another dilemma concerns involving the police. Departments need to address this issue in their guidelines. If good working relationships are built up between social workers and the police, they can often work effectively together in cases of old age abuse.

Workers must be trained to look for signs of abuse taking place; that is, not just looking for physical signs of abuse but also for other indicators that a person is being abused, e.g. a change in behaviour/personality. In premeditated cases, abuse is often carried out in a very subtle way, e.g. injuries may be well hidden on the trunk of the body. A social worker who visits for an hour a week is probably never going to see such injuries or notice any change in behaviour. Therefore, it is very important to liaise with the other professionals involved, who may have more frequent contact with the elderly person, in order to share concerns and information.

Professionals can liaise via the telephone, and this can work well, but it is important to ensure that communication takes place between all those involved so that all information is shared and this can best be achieved successfully by convening a case conference. Timing is important as cases should not be left to drift after an investigation has taken place. The purpose of convening a case conference is to share information about an incident and/or an elderly person's situation, assess the degree of risk and finally to make decisions and implement an agreed plan of action when appropriate.

Good practice would mean that victims are monitored while receiving ongoing support so that reviews of the situation can take place at regular intervals. It is important to spend time with elderly clients in the same way as working with children and families. Past history can be a contributing factor to a current abusive situation. For example, a carer may be looking after a relative with whom s/he has had a very bad relationship in the past because of some incident that took place years ago. In other situations, there may be a history of child abuse or marital violence that is relevant. It is helpful, and often enlightening, to know what has happened to the client and other members of the family in the past. Reminiscence work is one effective way of achieving this.

Traditionally, the victim may be seen as 'the client' and the person who needs protecting. What is often so frustrating for workers is that the victim denies that s/he is being abused. If someone is being abused by a member of his/her family it is going to be very painful to admit this to anyone. Trust is an important aspect of working with abuse, and workers need to build up trusting relationships over time in order to facilitate disclosure. Sometimes this can take years rather than weeks or months.

Another frustration is that the victim may not want to be removed from the abusive situation. It has been estimated that 26% of victims choose to stay (Riley, 1989); I actually think the figure is much higher than this, possibly 80–90% (Pritchard, 1992). Social workers are used to protecting children and finding places of safety for them in certain child abuse cases. However, workers have to remember that with old age abuse they are dealing with adults, many of whom can make their own decisions. Social workers are there to facilitate clients, not to tell them what to do. In abuse cases it is important to keep listening and suggesting possible options. Workers also have to respect confidentiality, so if the victim is mentally sound and does not want the worker to take any action this decision must be followed.

Many elderly people accept their 'lot in life' and do not expect anything 'because I'm old'. Some are very private and independent people who do not want to accept 'help or charity' (as they see it) from strangers. It is important for social workers to use their counselling skills in these situations in order to explain that there are options and that they have rights to services available for elderly people.

One of the debates that can occur in this work concerns whether the victim or abuser should be moved from a situation. It is extremely upsetting for someone to have to leave the home where he or she was born or has lived for half a century. And why should the victim leave when s/he has done nothing wrong?

Workers currently offer a range of services to support the victim and/or the abuser in the community, such as day care, short-term care, respite care, family placement schemes and so on.

Permanent care is often a last resort for some victims and it is evident that, because of pressure of work, cases are closed when a person is placed permanently in either a local authority home or in the private sector.

The NHS and Community Care legislation has placed on both housing and social services departments the requirement to explore the accommodation needs of elderly people. This may, at long last, provide for the development of alternative accommodation options for victims rather than simply admission to care. Housing is central to community care and Extra Care Sheltered Housing may prove more appropriate in not only protecting the victims of abuse, but also keeping them within the community. The notion of providing short-term 'refuge' could also be developed.

In many situations it is evident that the abuser needs support. It may be necessary for the social worker involved with the victim to undertake this work, but it may be more appropriate to work the case jointly with another worker, whose work will focus on the abuser. Many abusers have their own personal and/or medical problems which contribute to the abusive situation. For example, if an abuser is an alcoholic s/he may be financially abusing an old person because they need the money. A social worker may be able to offer advice about counselling and help in relation to the alcohol problem, debts, etc.

As well as dealing with practical problems, the social worker needs to help the abuser address the issue of abuse that is still occurring or has taken place previously. It is not enough just to deal with the presenting problem, that is, ensuring the victim's safety by providing care for the victim and/or abuser; the abuser has to be helped in order to prevent further abuse taking place.

DIFFERING ROLES OF STAFF IN SOCIAL SERVICES DEPARTMENTS

So far the discussion has focused on investigation and intervention. This needs to be developed further by considering the role of and communication between staff in social services departments. It is generally accepted that the way forward in working with old age abuse is to adopt the multidisciplinary approach. However, it is also equally important for social services staff to liaise with each other to ensure the safety of elderly people.

Social services departments employ large numbers of staff who perform different roles in providing a quality service. It was stated at the beginning of this chapter that many of these staff will not have given much thought to the issue of old age abuse. However, it is important that they do so as they could have key roles to play in identifying cases of abuse, monitoring and reviewing such cases, and also supporting victims and abusers.

Fieldwork staff include senior managers, team leaders, social workers and social work assistants. These people will be involved in investigations where their skills will be needed to assess situations and, perhaps, to offer practical and emotional support. Managers will be responsible for ensuring that old age abuse cases are investigated properly and that workers are well-supported in dealing with such cases. Where there is continuing involvement it is often useful to identify a key worker so that information is shared regularly and resources co-ordinated. Many people are currently working in isolation because of a lack of knowledge, and work may therefore be duplicated.

Hospital social workers can be important in the same way as fieldworkers, but in addition they can facilitate multi-disciplinary working because they are already functioning in that way in the hospital setting. They may be the first to identify a case of abuse, either because someone keeps reappearing in the casualty department, or because signs are picked up when a patient comes in for respite care on a regular basis. Hospital social workers can be a vital link between field social workers and staff working in the hospital, such as consultants, nurses, physiotherapists, occupational therapists and speech therapists, in order to co-ordinate resources both in the hospital setting and out in the community.

Residential staff may be able to perform a variety of tasks in working with old age abuse (Pritchard, 1991). Firstly, they offer a basic resource, that is, care for an elderly person, whether they be victim or abuser. The different forms of care may be used either in an emergency situation (e.g. where a victim needs to be accommodated in a safe place) or in a planned way (e.g. giving regular respite care to a dependent person to alleviate the stress for his/her carer, or arranging short-term care for someone with Alzheimer's disease who is being physically abused by a spouse).

Residential staff may find themselves in a position where they discover evidence of abuse (e.g. a care assistant may be bathing a resident who has come in for a short-term stay, and discover bruising on a part of the body that would not normally be visible) or a person may disclose to them unexpectedly because he or she feels safe in the unit. Residential staff can also identify abuse that may be taking place within a unit, such as a staff member abusing a resident or abuse taking place between residents.

Day care staff usually build up trusting relationships with clients who regularly attend their centres. It takes a great deal of courage for a victim to disclose abuse and it may be day care staff who hear the disclosure. These staff also have the opportunity to notice any significant changes in people's behaviour/character because they see them regularly and have come to know them well. If the day centre is located within a residential unit, it is important that day care staff liaise with the residential staff so that information is shared. Effective packages of care can then be developed for the victim and/or abuser.

Home care staff, whether wardens or home helps, are another group of staff who build up trusting relationships with elderly people and may be the first people to identify physical injuries or hear disclosure. This is because they see their clients frequently (in some cases three times a day) and perform very personal tasks for them (dressing, undressing, toileting). Home care staff are often the people who identify financial abuse because they deal with clients' money, payment of bills, etc. A very common occurrence is for a home help to discover that an elderly person does not have enough money to buy food because a relative is not leaving enough money; or someone has not been paying the bills and the elderly person is now being threatened with disconnection of the gas or electricity. Home care staff have to be aware that this needs to be reported to their line manager, who can then take further action, either by talking to the people involved in the first instance or referring it on to the duty social worker if a social worker is not already involved.

SOME CONCLUSIONS

Social services departments are going to have to put old age abuse on their agendas. Recognition must be given to the fact that we are an ageing population – people are living longer. More elderly people are going to be living in the community and they are likely to become more dependent, which may increase their risk of being abused. Consequently, there will be a greater need for all social services staff to be equipped to deal with such situations. There needs to be full commitment to working with old age abuse both at directorate and senior management levels. It is not simply a matter of putting the issue on the agenda, appointing a lead person to take responsibility, setting up a working party and producing some guidelines. There has to be recognition that there will be resource implications that need to be planned for if a policy is to be successfully implemented.

The first step must be to raise awareness. This has to be done at all levels from senior management down to the grass roots. This has implications for training: as well as raising awareness, staff need to be trained about definitions of abuse, causal factors and indications of abuse, departmental procedures and intervention. It is vital that training is ongoing, that is, there should be a rolling programme both for experienced workers and new staff, who should undertake an induction course that includes the issue of old age abuse.

Departments need to provide clear policy guidelines on what constitutes abuse, assessment, investigation, legal powers, the use of case conferences, the possible existence of and criteria for an At Risk Register and the monitoring/reviewing process. Once guidelines are implemented as policy they need to be reviewed at regular intervals. In order to do this successfully, consultation must take place with the staff who are dealing with the issue of old age abuse, because they will know what is helpful to them in their work situation. Also, they will be able to identify the resources needed to work effectively in dealing with old age abuse.

REFERENCES

Bedford Social Services Department (1989) *The Abuse of Elderly People: Summary of Workshop and Projects 1987–1988*, Bedfordshire County Council, London.

Bexley, London Borough of (1988) *Abuse of Elderly People: Recognising the Problem*, papers 1–3, London Borough of Bexley, London.

Hildrew, M.A. (1991) New age problem. *Social Work Today*, **22**(49), 15–17.

Pritchard, J.H. (1991) Sufferers in silence. *Care Weekly*, **191**, 10–11.

Pritchard, J.H. (1992) *The Abuse of Elderly People: A Handbook for Professionals*, Jessica Kingsley, London.

Riley, P. (1989) *Professional Dilemmas in Elder Abuse* (unpublished).

Social Services Inspectorate (1992) *Confronting Elder Abuse*, HMSO, London.

Social Services Inspectorate (1993) *No Longer Afraid*, HMSO, London.

Stevenson, O. and Parsloe, P. (1978) *Social Services Teams: The Practitioner's View*, HMSO, London.

10

Considerations for practice

Bridget Penhale

It is evident that procedures in and of themselves are not a solution to the problem . . .

Problems remain in the identification and treatment of both those who are abused and their abusers. This chapter aims to consider some of the barriers to identification and intervention; to look at the similarities and differences between elder abuse and other forms of family violence (particularly child abuse); and to discuss the implications of these for both policy and practice in social work.

In 1975, Baker and Burston both published material in medical journals drawing attention to a phenomenon they termed 'granny battering' and 'granny bashing'. At about the same time, various researchers in the USA were also beginning to report on the abuse of elderly people in domestic settings. A useful review of the American literature from this period can be found in Giordano and Giordano (1984).

Concern and interest in the phenomenon of elder abuse appears to have arisen in the USA in the late 1970s, and there have been fairly steady developments in information, findings and attempts to resolve the problem since then. In particular, the 1980s is viewed as the period where there was a great deal of awareness and action (including legislation) concerning elder abuse. This followed developments in the USA in earlier decades in other areas of family violence, particularly that concerning child abuse (1960s) and spouse abuse (1970s).

In the UK, following the initial concern about the topic raised by Baker in 1975, there appears to have been something of a hiatus for several years. It was not until the early 1980s that there was renewed interest in the topic with the publication of material by Cloke (1983) and Eastman (1984). Since that time there has clearly been an increase in awareness of the subject – especially following the British Geriatric Society Conference, held in London in September 1988 and Tomlin's subsequent (1989) publication – which would appear to be largely due to the efforts of a number of committed individuals from both health and social service fields. However, if the 1990s are to see the development of action on elder abuse (including strategies for prevention as well as intervention), then the potential difficulties and implications for practice must be considered.

I do not intend in this chapter to describe the many forms that elder abuse may take, nor to outline the various theories of causation and predictive factors, for much has already been written on these and related topics elsewhere (Eastman, 1989; Bennett, 1990; McCreadie, 1991; Decalmer and Glendenning, 1993 are the best UK examples).

What is necessary here is to consider some of the barriers to the identification and treatment of abuse; to look at the similarities and differences between abuse of elderly people and other forms of family violence (in particular child abuse); and to discuss the implications of these for social work practice and policy.

BARRIERS TO IDENTIFICATION

As previously stated, there has recently been an increase in awareness and a recognition that the problem exists, particularly over the last six years, together with an increase in published material and a number of conferences at a national level. Nevertheless, many professionals and their agencies still appear to be rather uncertain about how best to proceed. This would seem to be due to a number of different but related factors. It is useful to consider these and some more general barriers to the identification of abuse in more detail.

In 1983, Cloke listed the following factors as causing problems within the field as a whole:

- There is no standard definition of abuse in either the British or American literature.
- Most of the research has been very small scale and uses different definitions, making it difficult to generalize from.

- Claims about the likely incidence of abuse in the UK are difficult to substantiate (due to lack of research).
- The aetiology of abuse is not well understood or developed.
- Simplistic comparisons with child abuse may mask the issues involved.
- The need for formal procedures to deal with abuse has been questioned by some professionals.

Although Cloke was writing some years ago, his perceptions still hold credence, particularly with regard to impediments to the identification of abuse, and are thus of relevance here.

Barriers to the detection of abuse may occur at a number of different levels. It is perhaps useful to consider these levels when looking at the apparent difficulties in identifying elder abuse satisfactorily.

Barriers at the micro-level

At the level of the individual, or micro-level, difficulties in the identification of abuse may arise because of factors such as the comparative isolation of a great many elderly people. Elderly people do not belong to social networks – such as employment or education – and thus there may not be a 'window' to facilitate the detection of abuse that is occurring in private. Wolf and Pillemer (1984) describe elderly people as being 'particularly cut off from the rest of the world'. Unlike children, who come into regular contact with professionals in 'helping roles' more often, elderly people may have few, or even no, contacts with professionals that might be able to assist them.

The ill-health or frailty of a substantial proportion of elderly people (and perhaps particularly those who are victims of abuse) may create an additional restriction on the number of outside contacts they have, thus increasing their isolation and further reducing the likelihood of the abuse being detected. Research cited by Pillemer and Wolf (1986) suggests that victims of elder abuse tend to be more isolated than their non-abused contemporaries. Whether this isolation precedes the onset of abuse is not certain; further research may assist in clarifying the position.

In addition, again at the micro-level, it would appear that access to victims may be limited by the perpetrators of abuse.

The abuser may refuse visits from friends and relatives, may screen letters or prevent telephone calls and may insist on being present throughout any interview with the elderly person. In a study carried out in 1979, O'Malley, Bergman and Segars found that in 40% of cases where further assessment was considered necessary, access proved impossible. Resistance to access may, however, come from the elderly person as well as the informal carer (O'Malley, Bergman and Segars, 1979).

Victims can be very reluctant to report the abuse, which may also make detection problematic. From American research, it would seem that only 24% of known cases of abuse are reported by the victims and 36% of victims did not acknowledge the problems (O'Malley, Bergman and Segars, 1979). There are several reasons for this reluctance to report mistreatment. These include:

- fear of retaliation or of making the situation worse (especially if the elderly person is dependent on the abuser for basic survival needs);
- assumption of blame for the abuser's behaviour (a trait which is also seen in child and spouse abuse victims);
- fear of being removed from home and institutionalized;
- strong bonds of affection that may outweigh any desire to leave the situation;
- guilt and stigma at having raised a child who abuses his/her parents (Steinmetz, 1978);
- concern about jeopardizing the family's status within the community if the victim reports the abuse (Block, quoted in Champlin, 1982);
- widely held views within society about family life and rights to privacy.

It has also been suggested that the lack of widescale public concern or any serious academic interest in elder abuse is due to a denial of both our own ageing and mortality and the possibility of being abused by our own (adult) children (Marshall, 1984).

Barriers at the macro-level

At a broader, societal level, it may be difficult to detect abuse because of the societal views and attitudes surrounding family life. The family is seen as sacrosanct – what happens within it is very much a 'private affair' and should not be subject to interference from the outside world. In addition, the family is seen as a nurturing and protective unit and not as a potentially dangerous environment for some people. This view tends to insulate the family somewhat from receiving (and accepting) assistance, particularly in dealing with conflict.

Moreover, societal views held about violence may be of some relevance here. Violence is very much a part of life, and, in Western culture it seems to be permissible within families so long as it does not go 'too far'. It seems, too, that the intimate nature of family life may make violence more likely (Gelles and Cornell, 1985). All aspects of each member's life are open to the scrutiny of the other members. This may well lead to disagreements between family members and it may be that high levels of concern and involvement can increase the risk of disharmony and conflict (Long, 1981).

The same factors that make family life intimate may also make it prone to conflict and, ultimately, if the conflict is not resolved by negotiation and compromise, to violence. The intimacy and privacy of the family as a unit also tends to exclude and excuse family members from social controls. As Browne (1989) has suggested:

> ... both the law and social policy attempt to discriminate between socially acceptable 'normal' violence and unacceptable 'abusive' violence.

This situation, rather than a condemnation of all forms of violence, tends to complicate most attempts to deal with the problem of abuse.

Additionally, further societal barriers to the identification of abuse may be found within the negative and inappropriate attitudes characterizing the ageism present in our society. A failure to accord our elderly citizens their full rights and responsibilities may mean that abuse is undetected or passed off as 'the confused ramblings of a senile person', for example, if the elderly person actually reports the situation.

What may be far more likely is that abusive situations, or feelings that abuse in some form is occurring, are ignored or denied by professionals or other interested people. It is possible that the strong emotions and taboos surrounding the topic make elder abuse totally abhorrent to professionals (and others) and so it is less likely to be detected. The lack of adequate procedures and interventions to deal with abuse may exacerbate this trend. There may be a tendency, also, to 'by-pass' the elderly person and to attempt to confirm details with relatives (who may, in any case, be involved or colluding in the abusive situation). This may be largely due to inappropriate views held about elderly people and the ageing process.

Professional failure to detect or identify elder abuse can occur for a number of reasons, including:

- a lack of knowledge about abuse;
- a lack of clarity about identification procedures and treatment methods;
- inadequate resources (financial and personnel) for detection and intervention;
- a tendency to give the protection of individual rights (including the right to privacy) a high priority;
- professional's own personal feelings, cultural biases and attitudes about the family, ageing, violence, and abuse;
- professional attitudes and standards about the above topics, generally imbued during training (Bookin and Dunkle, 1989; Hickey and Douglas, 1981; Phillips, 1983; Phillips and Rempusheski, 1986, are examples of these).

It may also be difficult for professionals in the business of caring (who generally have strong protective instincts) to accept that an elderly person has the right, as an adult, to refuse assessment and intervention (particularly if they are referred by a third party). An exception to this right to refuse may arise if the person is either at very grave risk or is severely cognitively impaired.

As has been seen, barriers to the identification of elder abuse occur at a number of different levels. There may be difficulties arising at an individual level for both victims and abusers and, additionally, problems at the level of societal attitudes and culturally-determined views. Further problems can be seen to occur at the professional level: the different responses (or not) of professionals to abusive situations and the reasons for these decisions. Such barriers and associated difficulties are not insurmountable, but they do require both an awareness of their existence and a willingness to address them as fully as possible if abuse is to be successfully tackled or even prevented.

INTERVENTION PROBLEMS

Although, as has been seen, the identification of elder abuse often presents problems for professionals, decisions about intervention can perhaps be even more difficult. There appear to be five main reasons for this.

Firstly, elderly people are adults and as such have the right to be self-determining and autonomous. As long as individuals are not considered mentally incompetent (in a legal sense), their decisions about offers of assistance and intervention are, and should be, final. It is quite possible for professionals to work hard to determine appropriate treatment options and for the elderly person to then refuse such offers. Elderly people can, and do, say no. Generally, they have the right to do so and they frequently exercise that right. Fulmer and O'Malley (1987) found that elderly people favoured autonomy and independence over safety and protection wherever possible. We should not be surprised at such findings. Practitioners have to learn to feel comfortable with these facts. It should not mean, however, that offers of assistance are not made on the basis that they will be rejected by the elderly person anyway.

Secondly, there are at present very few options in terms of proven intervention strategies in this type of work. This is as yet an undeveloped area in the UK and one that will require attention in the near future. It seems that intervention here tends to revolve around the twin elements of provision of practical services (to support care-giving and reduce stress) and therapeutic work to resolve relationship problems (the document recently produced by the Social Services Inspectorate (1992) gives further exposition of this). From work in the USA (and what we know from child protection work) it seems unlikely that ideal, 'once and for all' solutions to elder abuse will be found. It is also unlikely that adequate amounts of money will be forthcoming to improve or even develop techniques of intervention. However, there is clearly a need for what information there is available (about what works and in what circumstances) to be shared between agencies and professionals.

Thirdly, it is important to recognize that some workers, perhaps due to feelings of inadequacy and helplessness, tend to lower their expectations and set low-level objectives for intervention. This seems particularly likely in situations involving patterns of abuse within families that are of a longstanding nature. Other workers, who may not feel capable of dealing with abuse and violence but who want to do something to assist, may offer intervention that is not in fact appropriate to the situation, and perhaps not even related to the cause of the abuse. An example of this would be to focus on care-giving (and providing support with the tasks involved) when the actual reason for the abuse is not (or may not be) due to stress from care-giving (Bookin and Dunkle, 1985; Homer and Gilleard, 1990).

Fourthly, it is possible that the severity of some abusive situations may not be fully evident to professionals at the time of assessment and intervention. This may be due to some of the reasons outlined elsewhere in this article. As Phillips (1989) suggests, however, professionals may tend to see their intervention strategies, particularly those that might be termed therapeutic, as appearing on a continuum from 'least disruptive' to 'most disruptive'. The interventions considered to be most disruptive (e.g. removal from home) tend to be reserved, it is argued, for use as a last resort. Thus, as a result, a situation that might require quite intensive and active intervention in order to adequately protect and safeguard the elderly person may be misconstrued by the professional. The intervention chosen could fail to match the actual or potential gravity of the situation.

Finally, it is necessary to acknowledge that intervention may be a rather uneasy mixture of legal and therapeutic strategies. Most professionals are trained to 'cure' and not to punish, so interventions that invoke the use of legal systems to provide redress or punish abusers tend not to be used. In any case it would appear that legal interventions will only really be considered by professionals if there is incontrovertible evidence that abuse has occurred, which, of course, is rarely the case (Phillips and Rempusheski, 1986, cited in Phillips, 1989). As previously noted, elderly people and their carers have the right to refuse intervention in most situations; it is rarely possible to force people to accept intervention. Use of the legal system may therefore appear to be a rather extreme option, particularly if the evidence about the abuse is inconclusive. Practitioners may not wish to risk making a situation worse for an elderly client and his or her family.

As has been seen, a number of difficulties surround intervention in situations of elder abuse. An appreciation of the nature of these is desirable when attempting to deal with the complexities apparent in many of the situations practitioners are faced with.

SIMILARITIES WITH CHILD ABUSE

Many agencies attempting to deal with elder abuse have looked to the experiences of colleagues in the child abuse/child protection arena for guidance. Indeed, following the 'discovery' of elder abuse in the USA in the mid-1970s, it would seem that in many areas the topic was claimed by experts in family violence. The reasons for this were logical: elder abuse has certain characteristics in common with other forms of abuse, and it is worth looking at these similarities before moving on to consider why the comparisons may not be entirely appropriate. The dissimilarities may, in fact, be more important than the commonalities. What is apparent, however, is that both the ideological and the methodological debates within elder abuse seem to have paralleled those that occurred in the child protection arena.

In its most extreme forms, elder abuse involves physical violence and possibly physical harm to the victim, as occurs in child and spouse abuse. In both child and elder abuse there is abuse of a dependent person by a care-giver (usually a member of the family). Within both situations the dependent person may well be a source of stress (emotional, physical and/or financial) to the care-giver; the pressures on care-givers may be the same. There may also be some comparability in terms of behaviours, with both children and vulnerable, impaired elderly people behaving at times in ways that are challenging and/or difficult to manage (Korbin, Anetzberger and Eckert, 1989).

The theoretical frameworks that have been developed to investigate the possible causes of abuse are similar, and attempts have been made to fit elder abuse into models proposed for other forms of familial violence. These frameworks include such theories as:

- stress theories (internal/external stress for individuals and/or families;
- family dynamics/transgenerational violence theories;
- exchange theories (the abuse continues while the exchange is favourable to the abuser);
- psychopathology of the abuser theories;
- dependency and/or impairment theories.

Additionally, the families in which elder and child abuse occur have been characterized as being socially isolated and having fewer financial and social resources available to them than 'ordinary families' (Pillemer and Wolf, 1986). Roles within families also seem to be somewhat distorted within both types of abusive families and it would appear that role clarity becomes less distinct (Korbin, Anetzberger and Eckert, 1989). Some evidence is beginning to appear suggesting that role reversal and 'generational inversion' occur within some abusive situations in both elder and child abuse (Steele, 1980; Steinmetz and Amsden, 1983). It has also been postulated that unresolved filial crises may be of relevance in this context (Block and Sinott, 1979; Lau and Kosberg, 1979).

Apart from these rather general similarities, there appear to be four specific areas of correspondence between child and elder abuse.

The first is the growing evidence surrounding the transmission of violent responses between generations (Rathbone-McCuan, 1980; Steinmetz, 1983). A person who has been abused in the past (probably in childhood) is more likely to act abusively when adult (Pillemer and Suitor, 1988). In particular, if the abuse was perpetrated by the now elderly parent, then a reversed cycle of violence may be established, perhaps with some suggestion of revenge as an underlying motive for the abuse of the elderly person. There may well be some retaliation for past, or continuing, abuse from elderly parents (Steinmetz, 1981). In addition, since elderly people are often accorded a childlike-status within society, the positions of vulnerable elderly people and children are quite easily equated. And, indeed, both children and elderly people are quite often in relatively powerless positions with regard to their care-givers.

Secondly, gender issues seem to be of importance in abusive situations and are therefore worthy of some examination. In child abuse, it seems that most of the abuse is perpetrated by men, is physical in nature and that the victims are female (Birchall, 1989). A similar situation appears to exist within elder abuse where the majority of victims are also female. The sex of abusers is slightly more complex, however. Many of the early American studies suggested that most abusers were also female and were usually relatives of the victim. A re-examination of this data, separating abuse from neglect, found that men were more likely to be involved in physical violence and women in acts of neglect (Miller and Dodder, 1989). In the original research it seemed that the neglect categories were very large, which may explain why more women than men seemed to be identified as abusers. Additionally, many early studies found there were more female carers of dependent elderly relatives and thus postulated that abuse was therefore more likely to be perpetrated by women. Further research may help to elucidate this issue more fully in future.

The third main area of similarity is as follows. Elder abuse seems to consist of a number of related, but quite distinct, types of abuse that may be compared with different forms of familial violence. For instance, it may be preferable and, indeed, more profitable, to compare abuse occurring between spouses/partners irrespective of the ages of those involved or the length of time the abuse has been going on for (i.e. to compare spouse abuse between elderly people with that occurring beween younger couples). The abuse of vulnerable elderly people by their adult children may perhaps be more comparable to the patterns observed within child abuse. However, as Steinmetz (1990) has suggested, would abuse of adult children by their elderly parents be considered comparable to child abuse (especially if the abusive behaviour was of a longstanding nature, perhaps even dating back to the adult child's childhood)? Research into the extent of such comparability may assist in clarifying these and related issues and is thus of some importance within this context.

The final area of correspondence is that both forms of family violence occur in a society that is very reluctant to acknowledge that abuse actually exists. The societal views concerning the family, outlined above, and associated myths about 'happy families' affect all forms of familial violence equally. The element of taboo within society with regard to admitting that any abuse exists is still strong in many areas, including some professional arenas. Parton's work on child abuse and the stages of recognition of the problem as a problem may be pertinent in this context and may assist in determining the lack of 'moral panic' surrounding elder abuse (Parton, 1981). Additionally, societal stigma surrounds abusers (of all types of abuse) and this could well lead to a reluctance by abusers to seek any help for this problem.

DIFFERENCES BETWEEN ELDER ABUSE AND CHILD ABUSE

Despite the apparent similarities already outlined, there are some important differences between elder abuse and other forms of family violence which should not be overlooked. As with the difficulties in the identification of abuse, these differences appear to occur at different levels, both macro-(societal) and micro-(individual) levels. It is worth examining the nature and extent of these when considering the applicability (or otherwise) of models of family violence to elder abuse.

Societal differences

There does not appear to be any precedent within our society and culture that accounts for elder abuse. In addition to this, while the use of force or restraint of a child is, to an extent, viewed as acceptable in terms of either the maintenance of control or education of the child, a similar act directed towards an elderly person would usually be considered to be at the very least, a violation of rights (Korbin, Anetzberger and Eckert (1989) give a further exposition on this aspect).

Societal expectations of and attitudes towards young and old people also come into the arena here. It is likely that children are viewed as far more vulnerable and in need of protection than older people who are stereotypically seen as being awkward and burdensome. Child abuse is thus considered by many to be the greater crime. And, largely due to the fact that recognition of and intervention in child abuse situations has been with us now for several decades, statutory agencies are far more aware of the problems of child abuse. This means that when possible symptoms are present in a child and family setting, professionals are more likely to suspect abuse and that child abuse is more likely to be accorded a higher priority than elder abuse. The latter situation is, of course, due also to the legislative and statutory responsibilities held in relation to children and the dearth of such systems for the protection of elderly people.

It is also necessary to remember that the social situations of children and elderly people are in fact quite different. Elderly people, as adults, have far more legal, economic and emotional independence than is possible for children. This, as previously stated, also includes the right to refuse offers of assistance and intervention by professionals. The economic independence of many elderly people (their property, possessions and money) may make them particularly vulnerable to a type of exploitation and abuse that is rarely seen in other forms of family violence.

Awareness of elder abuse (in both professional and public arenas) is rather low in the UK. Despite various attempts to put the issue on to the political agenda, there is as yet no coherent, positive action being propounded by central government. However, it is acknowledged that policy decisions to accord the same priority to elder abuse as to child protection matters will not be satisfactorily implemented unless there is a concomitant attitudinal shift on behalf of policy makers, professionals and the general public.

It may not necessarily be particularly expensive to deal satisfactorily with elder abuse. The relatively high costs of many child protection processes can lead to some confounding of the issues if over-simplistic comparisons are drawn between the two forms of familial violence. A further crucial difference between those particular groups that are vulnerable to abuse is that while some protective measures may be necessary, it is important not to treat either elderly people or women who experience abuse like children.

Another reason that the child abuse/family violence model does not entirely fit the experience of elder abuse is because of expectations about the nature of the relationships between the abused and the abuser that seem current within the model. Phillips (1989) has identified four distinct expectations.

These are:

1. The expectation that abuse causes visible harm. If this is not evident, then the situation is 'tolerable'.
2. The expectation that both victims and abusers are readily identifiable.
3. The expectation that victims are not involved (i.e. are innocent) in arousing the abusive behaviour.
4. The expectation that the abuser is motivated by malevolent intent.

From what is known about elder abuse, the realities would seem to challenge the above expectations, albeit to differing degrees. Although Phillips postulates that elder abuse has some very specific qualities that distinguish it from other forms of family violence, the analysis does not seem to be unproblematic in terms of the child abuse model, so caution is clearly advisable.

Individual differences

At the level of the individual a number of significant differences can be found between elder abuse and other forms of family violence. It is worth considering these in some detail.

Firstly, the root causes of the abuse may be quite different. Many victims of elder abuse are mentally and/or physically frail and dependent, while child abuse victims, although dependent, do not necessarily have any disability (although children with disabling conditions have been found to be more at risk of abuse).

Secondly, the abuse of elderly people can be much more difficult to detect. As previously stated, elderly people do not lead such public lives and there may be a lack of contact with external agencies, or indeed, with anyone other than the abuser. They do not attend school or have routine medical examinations. Bennett (1990) has reminded us that, while with young children there are well-established developmental norms and standards (and any undue deviation from these may result in an investigation), with frail elderly people the situation is far more complex.

The differing presentations and extent of acute and chronic illnesses occurring in later life contribute to the lack of comparative norms. It can be very difficult to establish, medically, the difference between an accidental fall and a deliberate injury (Homer and Gilleard, 1990). Thus medical definitions of what constitutes abuse can be misleading and it is therefore generally difficult for doctors to be categorical about situations that are presented to them.

Thirdly, many of the carers of elderly people may themselves be elderly and may also have poor health and/or disabilities. It is not uncommon, given the demographic changes that have been occurring in this part of the century, to find carers in their 70s caring for parents in their 90s, many of whom are in better health than their children whom they may well outlive. It is also necessary to acknowledge that at least some elder abuse is dual-direction in nature. The elderly person may either respond to or even provoke the abuse. Research by Homer and Gilleard (1990) seems to confirm this tendency. Victims of child abuse may not initiate the abuse to the same extent.

Fourthly, with most children (and most child abuse) it is possible for parents or care-givers to envisage a time when dependency and any associated stress ceases and the child attains full independence. The care of elderly people stands in stark contrast to this. As people grow older they are likely to become more dependent and to place more demands on the carer. It is not always possible for a carer to foresee an outcome that is satisfactory, or to have any idea of the time-scale involved. The death of the dependent person may be only a partial resolution if the carer is left with a great deal of unresolved guilt and remorse.

Additionally, in situations involving child abuse, the familial relationships are often comparatively recent in origin, whereas elder abuse encompasses a great many relationships of many years duration. Abusive relationships may arise as the result of longstanding difficulties within a relationship or set of rela-tionships (Fulmer and O'Malley, 1987). It is also possible that the dynamics of power may be different in abusive relationships. Ogg and Bennett (1991) suggest that for abusive carers (within elder abuse) there is a perceived lack of power that may be due to the nature of the caring role itself. The abuser may be more dependent on the elderly person than vice versa. These avenues may well be worth pursuing in future research.

Finally, in connection with the differences between child abuse and elder abuse, Korbin, Anetzberger and Eckert (1989) argue 'against a too-facile linking of the two problems' for a number of different reasons. In a useful article there is an exploration of the commonalities and dissimilarities between these two types of family violence. Included are many of those aspects outlined above: difficult behaviours; levels of dependency; the cycle of violence; expectations of improvement; stress of care-giving; and the social isolation of abusive families. In addition, they suggest two further dissimilarities of some importance.

Levels of violence directed towards elderly people and children may vary in their severity and frequency. It is possible that while children receive more acts of minor violence directed against them, when violence occurs against elderly people it may well be more severe (or be perceived as such, perhaps because it happens less often). It is also possible that, given the frailty of many elderly people, violence directed towards them may have more serious consequences in terms of its effects.

In terms of the 'cycle of violence' theories outlined above, it is useful to look at the differences a little more closely. It is suggested that the dynamics involved are in fact quite different between the two forms of abuse. To state the obvious, perhaps, the child abuser abuses a child, not a former abuser/aggressor. The underlying motive of revenge or retaliation that may be held by abusers within many elder abuse situations is considered to be of crucial importance here.

Having looked at the principal dissimilarities between elder abuse and other forms of family violence it is now necessary to move to a consideration of their implications for both policy and professional practice.

IMPLICATIONS FOR PRACTICE

When thinking about what to do about elder abuse, in a practice setting it does seem relevant to look at the effectiveness of procedures and intervention strategies employed in child abuse. There is some suggestion that the experience gained in recent years in child protection work may provide a useful model for both risk management and for interagency collaboration. The alternative view is that it might be possible to anticipate and avoid some of the pitfalls which have occurred in the child protection sphere.

Organizational issues

It is evident that procedures in and of themselves are not a solution to the problem and that when considering drawing up guidelines for practice agencies must also be mindful of the resource implications involved. It is clearly useless to have guidelines and procedures if these are too restrictive or prescriptive for the staff who have to use them. If this occurs, staff will not 'own' the guidelines, will not be comfortable using them and, perhaps ultimately, will avoid using them. They should always be a tool to improved practice rather than an inhibiting factor.

It is apparent, too, that because of a lack of protective legislation in general with regard to elderly people, there would appear to be a certain amount of permissiveness and freedom in the actions professionals may take. Obviously this should not be read as a reason for inaction by the worker, but it is evident that once professionals begin to feel 'hemmed in' by procedures that seem too tightly drawn a certain amount of creativity and innovation is lost and people are forced to act defensively. Practice thus becomes a vehicle for the self-protection of the worker. As Phillips (1989) has noted, the different sorts of activities connected with self-protective strategies adopted by some workers can include both the inappropriate closing of cases and/or writing copious case records over lengthy periods.

Consideration of the need for additional resources is perhaps paramount here in order to reduce the likelihood of staff experiencing a phenomenon known as post-decisional regret (Janis and Mann, 1973). This is likely to occur when, if no good interventions are available, workers consider that any choice from among the equally bad options available will result in making the situation worse than before the intervention for the elderly person and perhaps also for the carer. Resource implications need to be considered at the strategic planning stage, but must also continue to be raised and addressed following implementation of procedures and strategies for intervention and prevention.

Training issues

It is equally important that proper consideration be given to training for staff. This is important to provide basic knowledge about abuse and recognition of risk factors. Additionally, staff require knowledge about techniques of intervention and continuing work with abusive families. Attention should also be given to the possibilities of using various forms of family therapy as has been suggested by Browne (1989) and also Rathbone-McCuan, Travis and Voyles (1983). There is a growing literature, concerning abuse, albeit largely American, that needs to be disseminated among staff. It is essential that staff should be in the position of knowing how best to act (in terms of strategies for intervention following the identification of abuse).

Senior managers should also be included in training (particularly important if they have little or no direct experience in the field) so that they can assist and support staff as necessary. This should not be construed as a suggestion that managers must be experienced in work with elderly people, but rather that it is desirable for them to have some appreciation and understanding of elder abuse. The need for staff support systems should be addressed and, if necessary, these should be created in order to provide adequate support for staff dealing with what may be very stressful situations. These should be available for all staff that may be involved, including those providing secretarial and administrative support.

A further lesson to be drawn from experiences in the field of child abuse is that it is necessary to ensure that other agencies are involved in planning and training initiatives from an early stage, so that everyone is at the same level of knowledge and understanding about the phenomenon and, equally, that all involved are aware of the courses of action to be taken within a given situation.

Professional issues

There is a clear need for the inclusion of strategy and network meetings in work with abused elderly people and their families. These should include the involvement of clients and their carers. This would seem to be a sensible course of action as at least a proportion of abuse is likely to result from the stress that can occur within the care-giving situation. The importance and centrality of full participation by clients and their carers has been emphasized in a White Paper, *Caring for People*, and in the NHS and Community Care Act, 1990. The involvement of users and carers in the decision-making processes surrounding elder abuse is thus desirable, although as has been seen within the child protection sphere it is not easy to achieve. It can be quite a complicated process, requiring sensitive handling of difficult and delicate situations. There is also a need for careful planning and preliminary work and a real commitment to the principles by everyone involved if participation is to be both full and successful.

Another aspect that may be of some assistance in the development of practice within elder abuse is that of involvement of the police in investigations of abuse. In recent years workers in the child protection field have invested much time in establishing good working relationships with the police and in the development of specialist teams that work together. Although this has not been without its problems, the benefits of co-operative working and the efforts required in maintaining the relationships have been well documented (Thomas (1987) gives a further discussion of these issues).

Shared decision-making by means of the multidisciplinary team approach is likely to help reduce the tendency of individual workers to try to avoid certain situations because of the amount of stress they would cause them. The team approach will lessen the emotional intensity of certain decisions so that the decisions taken are the best possible ones in the circumstances. Responsibility for the decision (and also for any undesirable consequences) is thus shared by a group of people and does not rest solely with one individual.

Implications for practice can also be derived from the demographic changes referred to earlier. Social services departments are now working with older, frailer and more dependent people and this trend, together with changes brought about by the implementation of 'care in the community', will continue for some years. As part of these demographic changes there is a growing number of elderly people in the Black, Asian and ethnic minority communities in the UK, some of whom are likely to need assistance and intervention from social services in connection with abuse. Cross-cultural practice in child protection work has not been problem-free and we should expect similar difficulties in work with the abuse of older people from different racial and cultural backgrounds. Social workers must become more aware of the ways different cultures view ageing, and their attitudes to age, abuse and family life, and practice must be developed in that context. A reminder of this aspect can be found in *Adults at Risk* (ADSS, 1991).

CONCLUSION

It is important that workers are aware of the various issues surrounding elder abuse and know that many other professionals are also trying to resolve them. At present there is no absolute definition of what constitutes abuse and there are no absolute criteria for the identification of abused people and abusive situations. Equally, there are no ideal solutions acceptable to all involved, nor are there necessarily likely to be any in future.

There are valuable lessons to be learnt from experience gained in the child protection field over the last two decades, but there are important differences (legal, cultural and intrinsic) which preclude the simple application of this experience to the context of elder abuse.

The existing guidelines concerning identification of and intervention in situations of elder abuse do not match the complexities of the cases professionals are working with, and the knowledge base is actually quite limited. Nevertheless, it is imperative that professionals are aware of the issues involved and continue to address them as they arise. The knowledge that is available must be used (and in due course updated) in conjunction with a sensitivity to the particular situations that are being dealt with, to the issues involved and to the concomitant practice implications.

REFERENCES

ADSS (1991) *Adults at Risk: Guidance for Directors of Social Services*, Stockport Social Services Division, Metropolitan Borough of Stockport.

Baker, A.A. (1975) Granny bashing. *Modern Geriatrics*, **5**(8), 20–4.

Bennett, G. (1990) Action on elder abuse in the '90s: new definition will help. *Geriatric Medicine*, April, 53–4.

Birchall, E. (1989) The Frequency of Child Abuse – What do we Really Know?, in *Child Abuse: Public Policy and Professional Practice* (ed. O. Stevenson), Harvester Wheatsheaf, London.

Block, M.R. and Sinott, J.D. (1979) *The Battered Elder Syndrome: An Exploratory Study*, University of Maryland Centre on Ageing, College Park, MA.

Bookin, D. and Dunkle, R.E. (1985) Elder abuse: issues for the practitioner. *Social Casework*, January, **66**(1), 3–12.

Bookin, D. and Dunkle, R.E. (1989) Assessment Problems in Cases of Elder Abuse, in *Elder Abuse: Practice and Policy* (eds R. Filinson and S.R. Ingman), Human Sciences Press Inc., New York.

Browne, K. (1989) Family Violence: Elder and Spouse Abuse, in *Clinical Approaches to Violence* (eds K. Howells and C.R. Hollin), John Wiley and Sons, London.

Burston, G.R. (1975) Granny bashing. *British Medical Journal*, **3**, 592.

Champlin, L. (1982) The battered elderly. *Geriatrics*, July, **37**, 115–21.

Cloke, C. (1983) Old Age Abuse in the Domestic Setting – A Review, Age Concern, Portsmouth.

Decalmer, P. and Glendenning, F. (eds) (1993) *Mistreatment of Elderly People*, Sage, London.

Eastman, M. (1984) Old Age Abuse, Age Concern, Mitcham.

Eastman, M. (1989) Studying Old Age Abuse, in *Human Aggression: Naturalistic Approaches* (eds J. Archer and K. Browne), Routledge, London.

Fulmer, T. and O'Malley, T. (1987) *Inadequate Care of the Elderly; A Health Care Perspective on Abuse and Neglect*. Springer, New York.

Gelles, R.J. and Cornell, C.P. (1985) *Intimate Violence in Families*, Sage, Beverley Hills, CA.

Giordano, N.H. and Giordano, J.A. (1984) Elder abuse: a review of the literature. *Social Work*, May–June, **29**, 232–6.

Hickey, T. and Douglas, R.L. (1981) Mistreatment of the elderly in the domestic setting: an exploratory study. *American Journal of Public Health*, **71**(5), 500–7.

Homer, A. and Gilleard, C. (1990) Abuse of elderly people by their carers. *British Medical Journal*, **301**, 1359–62.

Janis, I.L. and Mann, L. (1973) Decision Making: A Psychological Analysis of Conflict, Choice and Commitment, Free Press, New York.

Korbin, J.E., Anetzberger, G.J. and Eckert, J.K. (1989) Elder abuse and child abuse: a consideration of similarities and differences in intergenerational family violence. *Journal of Elder Abuse and Neglect*, **1**(4), 1–14.

Lau, E.E. and Kosberg, J.I. (1979) Abuse of the elderly by informal care providers. *Ageing*, **299**, 10–15.

Long, C. (1981) Geriatric abuse. *Issues in Mental Health Nursing*, **3**, 123–35.

Marshall, M. (1984) Poignancy plus a few pointers. *Social Work Today*, **16**(5), 26.

McCreadie, C. (1991) *Elder Abuse: An Exploratory Study*, Age Concern Institute of Gerontology, London.

Miller, R.B. and Dodder, R.A. (1989) The Abused/Abuser Dyad: Elder Abuse in the State of Florida, in *Elder Abuse: Practice and Policy* (eds R. Filinson and S.R. Ingman), Human Sciences Press, New York.

Ogg, J. and Bennett, G. (1991) Identifying risk factors for elder abuse. *Geriatric Medicine*, **21**(11), 19.

O'Malley, H., Bergman, J. and Segars, H. (1979) *Elder Abuse in Massachusetts: A Survey of Professionals and Para-Professionals*, Legal Research and Services for the Elderly, Boston, MA.

Parton, N. (1981) *The Politics of Child Abuse*, Macmillan, Basingstoke.

Phillips, L.R. (1983) Elder abuse – what is it? Who says so?. *Geriatric Nursing*, May/June, 167–70.

Phillips, L.R. (1989) Issues Involved in Identifying and Intervening in Elder Abuse, in *Elder Abuse: Practice and Policy* (eds R. Filinson and S.R. Ingman), Human Sciences Press, New York.

Phillips, L.R. and Rempusheski, V.F. (1986) Making decisions about elder abuse. *Social Casework*, **67**(3), 31–40.

Pillemer, K.A. and Suitor, J. (1988) Elder Abuse, in *Handbook of Family Violence* (eds V. Van Hasselt, R. Morrison, A. Belack and M. Hensen) Plenum Press, New York.

Pillemer, K.A. and Wolf, S. (eds) (1986) *Elder Abuse: Conflict in the Family*, Auburn House, New York.

Rathbone-McCuan, E. (1980) Elderly victims of family violence and neglect. *Social Casework*, **61**(5) 296–304.

Rathbone-McCuan, E., Travis, A. and Voyles, B. (1983) Family Intervention: The Task-Centred Approach, in *Abuse and Maltreatment of the Elderly: Causes and Interventions* (ed. J.T. Kosberg), J. Wright, Boston, MA.

Social Services Inspectorate (1992) *Confronting Elder Abuse*, HMSO, London.

Steele, R.F. (1980) Psychodynamic Factors in Child Abuse, in *The Battered Child*, 3rd edn, (eds C.H. Kempe and R.E. Helfer), University of Chicago Press, Chicago.

Steinmetz, S.K. (1978) Battered parents. *Society*, **15**(5), 54–5.

Steinmetz, S.K. (1981) Elder abuse. *Ageing*, Jan–Feb, 315–6 and 6–10.

Steinmetz, S.K. (1983) Dependency, Stress and Violence between Middle-Aged Care-Givers and their Elderly Relatives, in *Abuse and Maltreatment of the Elderly: Causes and Interventions* (ed. J.I. Kosberg), J. Wright, Boston, MA.

Steinmetz, S.K. (1990) Elder Abuse: Myth and Reality, in *Family Relationships in Later Life*, 2nd edn (ed. T.H. Brubaker), Sage, Newbury Park.

Steinmetz, S.K. and Amsden, G. (1983) Dependent Elders, Family Stress and Abuse, in *Family Relationships in Later Life*, 1st edn (ed. T.H. Brubaker), Sage, Beverley Hills.

Thomas, T. (1987) *The Police and Social Workers*, Wildwood House, Aldershot.

Tomlin, S. (1989) *Abuse of Elderly People: An Unnecessary and Preventable Problem*, Public Information Report, British Geriatrics Society, London.

Wolf, R.S. and Pillemer, K.A. (1984) *Working with Abused Elders: Assessment, Advocacy and Intervention*, University of Massachusetts Medical Centre, Worcester, MA.

Part Four

Aspects of Abuse

11

Racial aspects of elder abuse

James George

... ethnic elderly people are likely to be at increased risk because of a combination of multiple risk factors not present in the indigenous population.

Old age abuse is a worldwide phenomenon. In India (Hurst, 1992) an old man was left on the streets by his family; passing truck drivers threw him on to a rubbish heap of broken glass to hasten his end! In Florida an old lady was left in casualty with an unsigned note that said: 'Take care of her she is sick'. The worldwide nature of old age abuse parallels the real sense of global shrinking in the latter half of the 20th century. Ease of travel and improved communication systems have both played a part, but a major component has been the migration of people as individuals or groups. This has resulted in an exchange of cultures and the need to be aware of the special needs and characteristics of the different racial and ethnic groups that make up our society.

The study of race and ethnicity in relation to old age abuse is still at a very primitive stage. There are two main hypotheses regarding the interaction of ethnic/racial minority status and old age with regard to old age abuse (Hall, 1987). The first is that ageing somehow diminishes the strength of the adverse racial/ethnic factors and the risk of abuse is consequently decreased. The second hypothesis is that elderly people in ethnic minorities are at an increased risk and are in 'triple jeopardy' due to discrimination and poor health and social status, compounded by lack of access to services. In this chapter the evidence for these two hypotheses will be discussed along with the practical implications for service delivery.

BACKGROUND

The 1991 census was the first in the UK to record information on ethnic origin (Table 11.1). The geographical distribution of each ethnic group has been examined and is very uneven (Balarajan and Raleigh, 1992). Roughly 60% of the Caribbean population and 80% of African people live in London, mostly in Inner London, and about half of the Bangladeshi community resides in London, again mainly in Inner London. In contrast, almost one-third of the Indian community lives in outer London, with only 9% living in Inner London. The Pakistani community lives primarily in the West Midlands (20%) and West Yorkshire (18%), with only 6% in Inner London and 13% in outer London. Thirty-eight percent of Chinese people live in London.

The majority of the ethnic minority groups (especially Afro-Caribbean and South Asian) have a relatively young age structure, with around 5% being of pensionable age compared with around 20% of the general population. The converse of this is that some ethnic minorities contain very few older people, which increases this groups feelings of isolation. There are exceptions, for example Polish refugees who came to the UK in the 1940s now form quite an old population.

The reasons for the migration of people to the UK are many and varied. One useful approach that helps in understanding the background and acts as an explanatory model is the notion of 'pull/push' factors (Young and George, 1991). Characteristic of the 'pushed' group are refugees. They include, for example, Jewish refugees from Russia, and Romanians and Poles, Ukrainians, Czechs, Estonians, Latvians and Yugoslavs following the Second World War. These people may be very vulnerable and feel 'trapped' in that they may be unable to integrate fully and yet no longer feel they belong to their country of origin.

The 'pull' factor operates where an individual or group has been attracted to the UK for self-betterment and the possibility of a more prosperous life. This would include migration of South Asians from the Indian subcontinent and people from

Table 11.1 Ethnic composition of England and Wales from the 1991 census (Balarajan and Raleigh, 1991)

	White (%)	Black Caribbean (%)	Black African (%)	Black other (%)	Indian (%)	Pakistani (%)	Bangladeshi (%)	Chinese (%)	Other (%)
England and Wales (Total population = 49 890 273)	94.1	1.0	0.4	0.4	1.7	0.9	0.3	0.3	1.0

the Caribbean after the Second World War. It was common for one member of the family, usually the son, to migrate and be followed at a later stage by his wife, children and parents. Tensions can potentially develop through a resettlement trap in which the second generation of sons and their wives stand between two cultures. The subsequent third generation children become closely integrated into the British culture and way of life but the first generation parents have great difficulty integrating and remain separate. Competing loyalties may produce latent conflicts that are then stored up to be released at times of ill health.

Religious and cultural factors

As we have seen migrants, whether pushed or pulled, are subjected to increased stress as a result of the migration and this can lead to conflict. However, it is sometimes suggested that strong cultural, religious and family ties offset the stress created by migration. Certainly in all of the cultures of recent migrants, care of and respect for elderly family members, especially one's parents, is expected and is sometimes a religious or filial duty. For example, central to the social and religious philosophy of Islam is the need for children to accept responsibility for elderly relatives, as this extract from the Koran aptly illustrates:

> And that ye be kind to parents. Whether one or both of them attain old age in thy life, say not to them a word of contempt nor repel them, but address them in terms of honour. And out of kindness lower to them the wing of humility and say 'My Lord bestow on them thy mercy even as they cherished me in childhood'.
>
> *Sura VXII, Al-Isra, verse 23–24; Abdullah 1975, 700–701*

Similarly, the Sikh religion embodies a strong tradition of community involvement and family support. There is, however, evidence that the status of elderly people diminishes with increasing modernization and loss of these religious and cultural bonds (Phillips, 1992). Family and cultural ties are easily lost and may be difficult to regain as these two extracts from interviews with a Caribbean woman and an Indian woman illustrate (Schweitzer, 1991).

Caribbean woman:
What I see here and I can't come to it is this, back home
a grandmother looked after her grandchildren and lived in
the house. So when, if a grandmother took sick, the family
is there to look after her. We don't have to send our
grandmothers to homes. Grandchildren grow up to respect
the grandmother, and anything that happens those children
are there to help. You see they support one another . . .
Grandmother plays a vital role as protector of that family.
Grandfathers have their own role to play too, but the grandmother she is the greatest. There is nothing like that here
in England.

Indian woman:
My children were getting older and forgetting the language
that they knew. They were becoming very Westernized and
they were losing touch with my culture and they could
hardly understand when I spoke to them, so my husband
and I decided to take them to India.

When we got to India we got VIP treatment . . . Somehow
my village looked smaller now, but never did I feel that I
didn't belong there. My children didn't like it at first. They
were very frank and forward and not at all like the other
children, but eventually they settled down. I knew deep
down, though, that they were lonesome for England. I think
my daughter missed England the most because she had so
much freedom there, but in India she spent most of the time
with me and the other women. But my purpose was to teach
them Punjabi. Now I am very proud that both my children
speak and write Punjabi fluently and they are in tune with
both cultures equally well. It was a struggle on my part along
with my husband but when I look at our children it all seems
worthwhile.

Adverse health and social factors

Elderly people of ethnic minorities are in a so-called potential
'triple jeopardy': at risk through old age, discrimination and
lack of access to health and social services (Norman, 1985).
The risk factors for old age abuse are listed in Table 11.2.
The problems of conflict between the first, second and third

generations because of different levels of integration and language barriers have already been discussed. Members of ethnic minority groups are more likely to be unemployed or to have manual occupations and to live in inner cities in overcrowded conditions in poor housing (Pearson, 1989). Elderly people from ethnic minority groups may feel isolated and vulnerable, particularly because of language difficulties which can lead to exploitation. Over one-third of Afro-Caribbean old people and 30% of elderly Asians live alone or with only a spouse (Karseras, 1991). Ethnic minorities may face direct racial abuse or indirect discrimination. A major concern of those in ethnic minorities may be the safety of their families in the face of physical threats, which may lead to mental stress (Pearson, 1989).

Table 11.2 Potential risk factors for old age abuse in ethnic minorities

---

- Intergenerational conflict
- Poor housing
- Overcrowding
- Social isolation
- Racial discrimination
- Poor access to health and social services
- Increased incidence of
  stroke
  mental illness   some groups only
  alcoholism

Afro-Caribbean elderly people are much more likely to be victims of stroke (McKeigue, 1991). This can lead to mental and sensory impairment with added communication difficulties, which can all make the elderly person more susceptible to abuse. There is an apparent increase in the incidence of schizophrenia among young Afro-Caribbeans (McGovern, 1989). This finding is controversial and the reasons for it are unknown; it is also not known if it is a risk factor for abuse. Similarly, alcohol-related illness is far more common among some ethnic minority groups, including the Irish and Sikh men (McKeigue, 1991). All these health and social disadvantages are compounded by poor access and low uptake of health and social services (Karseras, 1991), partly because of communication problems and partly because of lack of awareness on the part of health professionals of the need of ethnic minorities.

Implications for service delivery

Health and social professionals must be aware of the particular needs of elderly people in ethnic minority groups (Table 11.3); these are more fully discussed elsewhere (Squires, 1991). Ethnic minority old people may have special religious and dietary needs that should be respected. It is very easy to overlook these needs: for example, serving a devout Muslim an egg for breakfast using an implement also used to serve bacon may cause serious offence. Similarly, a male hospital doctor's failure to recognize the need of an elderly Muslim woman patient to preserve her modesty could also be interpreted as racial old age abuse. Prime (1991) found that Black old people in day care and residential homes were not provided with appropriate food and leisure activities and were subjected to racist abuse from white old people.

Table 11.3 Checklist for provision of services to elderly people in ethnic minorities

- Religious needs
- Dietary needs
- Need to preserve modesty
- Need for reassurance
- Interpreter for good communication
- Explain aims and need for any treatment and follow-up
- Health education advice
- Multilingual leaflets to supplement verbal information
- Consultation with ethnic minority communities concerning service needs

The response of ethnic minorities to illness may be different, particularly with illnesses such as stroke, that occur predominantly in developed countries. This needs to be overcome by good communication (perhaps with an interpreter), and full explanations of treatments and procedures, backed

up with appropriate multilingual written information. In many ethnic communities the first response to illness may be to consult a traditional healer. Primitive medical techniques may, rarely, mistakenly raise the suspicion of abuse. For example, cautery is sometimes used over the site of pain, leaving an obvious burn scar, and the technique of 'cupping' is still sometimes employed, leaving round bruise marks. These are caused by suction from round cups, which are flamed inside with a taper and usually applied to the back. Both cupping and cautery are employed as a powerful counter-irritant to try to relieve severe pain. To avoid misunderstandings, the services of a good interpreter should always be available. The use of other family members, particularly children, as interpreters should be avoided in cases of suspected abuse.

The following case history shows how a different cultural response to ill health, compounded by poor communication on the part of health professionals, can result in a form of old age abuse through neglect.

Case history

An elderly Pakistani man was admitted to hospital as an emergency having suffered a stroke which resulted in severe weakness of his right arm and leg. After three weeks in hospital he made an excellent recovery such that he could walk and dress himself. He was discharged home.

One month later he was visited at home. He was living in very poor conditions in the sparsely furnished attic of a large house. He had become bedridden and was living entirely in the one room with a commode, despite his ability to walk and go downstairs to use a toilet. He gradually became more disabled and dependent because of his inactivity. He felt very isolated and unhappy.

Comment

The patient made a good functional recovery from his stroke and had the potential for a good quality of life. However, his family still perceived him as a 'very sick man' and treated him very much as an invalid. Consequently he had a poor quality of life and quickly became miserable and more disabled. Perhaps this situation could have been avoided if more attention had been given to educating the patient and family about stroke and the principles of rehabilitation before discharging him from hospital.

CONCLUSION

The idea that ethnic minority groups are universally good to their elderly people who are always protected and cared for by their family, is a myth. Most of the evidence would support the second hypothesis – that ethnic elderly people are likely to be at increased risk because of a combination of multiple risk factors not present in the indigenous population. Modernization and the break-up of the traditional extended family, together with the special problems ethnic minority groups face, tend to increase stress and potential conflict. Faced with such pressures we are all likely to act in the same way. Old age abuse seems to be independent of ethnicity and the incidence is remarkably similar among, for example, Hispanic and Black populations in the USA (Hall, 1987). Nevertheless, there seems to be a marked absence of referrals from Black and ethnic minority communities in the UK (SSI, 1992). Obviously further studies are needed to look at different ethnic groups worldwide.

We have very little idea of the true extent of old age abuse in ethnic minority old people in the UK. We know racial old age abuse exists and we have a responsibility to eradicate it, particularly from our institutions and the way services are provided. We also know that, although the actual number of ethnic minority old people is now small, there will be a considerable increase in their numbers over the next two decades. We therefore need to be especially aware of the adverse social and health factors ethnic minority old people face if we are to prevent abuse of all old people whatever their ethnic background. Education in the needs of ethnic minority communities should be a standard part of all professional training.

Consultation with ethnic minority communities, especially ethnic minority carers (Baxter, 1988), is essential in planning appropriate services and ensuring good access to those services. There is still much to achieve in service provision if we are truly to reflect the multiracial nature of our society.

REFERENCES

Balarajan, R. and Raleigh, V.S. (1992) The Ethnic Populations of England and Wales: the Census, *Health Trends*, **24** (4) pp. 113–7.

Baxter, C. (1988) Ethnic minority carers. The invisible carers. *Health and Race*, **15**, 4–8.

Hall, P.A. (1987) Minority elder maltreatment: ethnicity, gender, age and poverty. *Journal of Gerontological Social Work*, **9**(4), 53–72.

Hurst, C. (1992) Granny dumping. *Australian Nurses Journal*, **21**(7), 32.

Karseras, P. (1991) Minorities and access to health care. Part 1; Confronting myths. *Care of the Elderly* 3(9), 429–31.

McGovern, D. (1989) Ethnic Factors in Psychoses: A picture from Birmingham, in *Ethnic Factors in Health and Disease*, (eds D.G. Beevers and J.K. Cruickshank), Wright, London, pp. 190–4.

McKeigue (1991) Patterns of health and disease in the elderly from ethnic minority groups, Multicultural Health Care and Rehabilitation of Older People (ed. A. Squires), Arnold, London, pp. 69–77.

Norman, A. (1985) *Triple Jeopardy: Growing Old in a Second Homeland*, Centre for Policy on Ageing, London.

Pearson, M. (1989) Sociology of Race and Health, in *Ethnic Factors in Health and Disease* (eds J.K. Cruickshank and D.G. Beavers), Wright, London, pp. 71–84.

Phillips, D.R. (ed.) (1992) *Ageing in East and South East Asia*, Arnold, London.

Prime, R. (1991) Social Work with Minority Ethnic Elders, in *Multicultural Health Care and Rehabilitation of Older People* (ed. A. Squires), Arnold, London, pp. 181–92.

Schweitzer, P. (1991) A Place to Stay: Growing Old away from Home, in *Multicultural Health Care and Rehabilitation of Older People* (ed. A. Squires), Arnold, London, pp. 28–41.

Squires, A. (ed.) (1991) *Multicultural Health Care and Rehabilitation of Older People*, Arnold, London.

SSI (1992) *Confronting Elderly Abuse*, HMSO, London.

Young, J. and George, J. (1991) History of Migration to the United Kingdom, in *Multicultural Health Care and Rehabilitation of Older People* (ed. A. Squires), Arnold, London, pp. 17–27.

12

Homicide in elderly couples

Bernard Knight

In all these cases there was no hint of marital discord
according to relatives, friends and neighbours ...

The rate of homicides in the UK is slowly increasing and a
disturbing proportion of those murdered are elderly people.
Many of them are battered to death, often when their dwellings
are broken into by teenage or young adult thieves.

However, there is another class of geriatric homicide that
is intrafamilial and appears to be of a totally different nature
to deaths resulting from opportunist muggings and robbery
with violence. Although the annual crime statistics do not
indicate that this type of murder or manslaughter is increasing,
most forensic pathologists have encountered a steady flow of
such cases over the years.

The killing of an elderly person by his or her spouse should
not be too unexpected as, in spite of the increase in crimes
of violence associated with robbery, at least half the homicides
in the UK every year are committed by 'partners'. Known to
the police and forensic scientists as 'domestics', this husband–
wife–partner situation occurs right across the age range from
the teens onwards. However, the upper end of the age
spectrum seems to have a different aetiology from the younger
and middle-aged groups, the latter usually being concerned
with money disputes, sexual jealousy and catalysed by alcohol.
In the older age groups these factors are less obvious and
the psychological mechanisms more obscure. Although every
instance is different, there appears to be a number of features
common to geriatric homicide that may offer some clues to
the underlying cause.

The fatal assault may be sudden and unexpected, with few apparent warning signs, although with hindsight these may have been obvious. Although little information may be gained about the interpartner relationship before the tragedy, it is unusual for any definite history of longstanding discord to be available. On the contrary, there are often comments from relatives and neighbours along the lines that they were 'a lovely pair'; the term 'Darby and Joan syndrome' has been applied to this situation and those actual words have been used on several occasions by family and friends.

For example, drawing on cases from the author's experience, one homicide characterizes this alleged domestic harmony. An elderly couple, just over the age of 70, lived above a newsagent's shop which they ran together. They were well-known in the district and everyone thought they were senior citizens of impeccable tranquility. One day I was called to the living accommodation over the shop to find the husband sitting in a chair in front of the television set, with severe head injuries of the most gross nature. It transpired that, while he was sitting there, his wife had come up behind him with the heavy iron base of an ice-cream sign from the shop and inflicted such heavy, repeated blows upon his scalp and skull that blood and brain tissue were projected onto the ceiling of the room. No rational explanation was ever obtained from the wife for this attack, and relatives and neighbours used the words 'Darby and Joan' to describe their apparent previous attachment to each other.

As in this case, one of the features of geriatric homicide is the degree of violence often displayed. A forensic pathologist is used to all types and degrees of personal injury, but in some of these geriatric cases he or she may be surprised by the savageness of the attack. It seems as if years of suppressed anger and frustration erupt into one final orgy of hatred, so appalling are some of these attacks. For example, an 85-year-old man suddenly attacked his 79-year-old wife with a heavy claw-ended hammer, inflicting no fewer than 37 wounds to her head, many of which resulted in compound fractures of the skull. Such an attack must have been both strenuous and prolonged, indicating a most determined effort on the part of a very old man to inflict the maximum amount of damage.

Within a few weeks and a few miles of the previous case, another octogenarian attacked his wife with a hammer causing gross head injuries. As with certain other crimes, one cannot help but wonder if reports of incidents in the media have a 'knock-on' effect, by triggering latent intentions or putting ideas into people's heads.

Another factor common to many geriatric homicide cases is that the killer often attempts suicide (and sometimes succeeds) immediately after the killing. This, of course, is a relatively frequent sequel to many murders and it seems to occur just as often in geriatric cases as in others.

For example, a man in his 70s who lived with his wife, of a similar age, in an idyllic thatched cottage in a West Country village, violently strangled her, trussed the body up with dressing gown cord, hid it behind a settee and then hanged himself from the staircase. Another man, aged almost 80, cut his wife's throat as she lay in bed and subsequently successfully hanged himself, again from the bannister of the stairs. A retired butcher of 70 shot his wife at point blank range with a 12-bore shotgun and then transfixed his own heart with a large knife.

Although there is nothing unusual about these instances within the mainstream of homicide, they do contrast with another group, described on page 176, in whom there seems complete inertia following the killing; those who are suicidal afterwards appear to be experiencing remorse and also perhaps the desire to avoid the retribution they know will follow discovery.

In all these cases there was no hint of marital discord according to relatives, friends and neighbours, although two of the men had recently been receiving treatment for depressive illnesses.

On another occasion, the husband died of natural causes within a few hours of strangling, gagging, trussing up and inflicting head injuries on his 70-year-old wife; his own death was attributed to hypertension and heart disease for lack of any other explanation.

Another aspect common to geriatric homicide is the rather bizarre features that sometimes accompany or replace sheer violence. In the last case mentioned, where the husband died soon after the murder, the victim had been trussed up in a chair with complicated bonds of twine and cord, towels and clothes being bound around the face with more twine. The wife strangled in the thatched cottage had been trussed up with the braided cord of her own dressing gown and the body hidden behind the settee, a factor somewhat reminiscent of the 'hide and die syndrome' in old people that is associated with hypothermia.

In another tragedy involving a couple over the age of 70, the man inflicted severe head injuries on his wife with a cricket bat, then drowned her in the bath, the body being found draped over the edge of it with her head under water. The only known motive in this case was that the wife had hidden his tobacco pouch and objected to his visiting the Senior Citizens' Day Centre.

It is difficult to categorize these cases into any pattern as the methods and circumstances are so disparate. The tragic situation of geriatric homicide is almost totally confined to married couples, rarely being seen among other relatives living together. In my experience of 37 years of forensic pathology suicide pacts appear to occur between elderly sisters, but almost never homicide. In geriatric homicide it is much more common for the husband to kill the wife, although the reverse does sometimes occur.

In a number of cases of geriatric homicide the behaviour of the perpetrator after the event may well have some aetiological significance. Although some commit suicide, others become virtually completely mute and unresponsive. In fact, a substantial proportion of these tragedies do not subsequently come to criminal trial because the culprit is deemed unfit to plead as a result of mental abnormality.

After the killing these tragic figures seem to withdraw into themselves and many remain inert and unresponsive. It is probably this group that on retrospective enquiry, were the ones that had shown depressive behaviour before the event. None of the culprits in the cases I have seen had any overt history of serious mental illness, including senile dementia, although immediately after the incidents a number became so obviously abnormal that they were confined to institutions. Of these, most were so affected that they were 'unfit to plead' at a trial and most of the remainder pleaded, or were found, 'guilty with diminished responsibility'. It transpired that some of them had been prescribed medication for endogenous depression before the event, usually by their GPs rather than after referral to psychiatric services.

The unnecessary degree of violence and the sometimes bizarre choice of weapon or accompanying bondage may well have some psychological significance, as perhaps does the usual absence of any history suggesting that previous non-fatal violence had taken place. In none of the cases I have seen has there been any suspicion of previous aggression, rather the reverse. All the deaths occurred in the family home, which invariably seemed comfortable and in good condition, with no evidence of material deprivation or the squalor that sometimes accompanies the fatal end-point of longstanding domestic strife in younger age groups.

In only a few of the cases I have seen was hard evidence of motive available. Several were later alleged by the culprit to be 'mercy killings', the husband alleging that he wished to put his wife out of her misery. However, only a minority of these victims had any serious illness and in several cases it seemed more likely that the husband was tired of waiting on a hypochondriacal or mildly debilitated but demanding wife.

Specific motives were occasionally alleged, but may have been the result of delusion or misunderstanding. The oldest killer, the man of 85 who inflicted 37 hammer wounds on his wife, did so because he claimed she was having an affair with a 70-year-old neighbour and was demanding a divorce.

In younger domestic homicide the strongest precipitating factor seems to be alcohol, which is also almost always a factor in street and public house violence that results in death. In domestic homicide over issues such as jealousy, sex and money, alcohol is often the final trigger, the drug obviously suppressing the inhibitory effects of upper cortical activity, releasing the pre-existing aggressive behaviour. To quote De Quincy, 'Sobriety disguiseth man'!

Although alcohol rarely seems to be a trigger in geriatric domestic homicide, it might be considered that senile changes in the brain may act in the same way, reducing cortical inhibition and releasing the baser emotions of rage and violence, as neurones shrivel with advancing cerebral atrophy or atherosclerotic degeneration.

Irritation, discontent and anger are present in most marriages. If the union remains intact these feelings may be suppressed or rationalized, but if they are cumulative, may not some partners store up their anger for many years, causing the pressure to rise under the lid of cortical inhibition in the absence of a safety valve? When senile changes eventually fail to keep the lid sealed, may it then not suddenly blow off in a single and finally fatal episode of violence? These are matters for psychologists and psychiatrists rather than forensic pathologists, but the pattern of intrafamily homicide in the elderly has so many common features that it is tempting to consider that such a mechanism may exist.

In summary, these cases are presented as a phenomenon arising from forensic medical practice and no claim is made that this is a widespread and specifically identifiable psychiatric syndrome. However, it is suggested that the changing demographic structure of society, with a progressive increase in the number of elderly people, especially those surviving into their 90s and over, may require more attention to be paid to the possibility of sudden, unexpected and often gross violence among aged couples. Given the apparent lack of warning signs and the generally high incidence of mild depressive illness in the community, it is difficult to see what preventive measures could be taken, but perhaps greater awareness of the potential risks might lead geriatricians, psychiatrists and GPs to be more watchful for danger signs in elderly couples when one of them shows signs of depressive illness.

13

Social work and old age abuse: laying down the law

Phil Slater

The law is both the bedrock of social work practice and the touchstone by which its actions must ultimately be judged.

Ball et al., *1988, p. 11*

When social workers come to consider any particular area of practice they need to maintain a dual focus. On the one hand they need to develop an understanding of the area in question in broad terms; and on the other they need to be able to specify in detail their own role within that area.

The particular weight attaching to legal knowledge in this endeavour remains a matter of often heated dispute (Braye and Preston-Shoot, 1990), but nobody has seriously denied that social workers need to know the legal parameters of their professional intervention. Adopting a philosophical turn of phrase, one can conclude that legal knowledge is a 'necessary but not sufficient condition' for competent practice. The following discussion focuses on that particular condition for articulating the parameters of social work intervention in the specific area of old age abuse.

WELFARE LAW AND OLD AGE

An important document on the subject of old age abuse published in early 1992 noted: 'at present there is no protective legislation specific to older people' (DHSSI, 1992, p. 3). This contrasts with the situation in relation to children, in which the Children Act, 1989 incorporates, alongside many other provisions, measures for the protection of children 'suffering or likely to suffer significant harm'. There is no corresponding Elderly People's Act, nor any specific protective provision elsewhere.

However, there is one important legislative provision with direct, explicit and exclusive reference to the welfare of elderly people in general. Under section 45(1) of the Health Services and Public Health Act, 1968, a local authority '**may** with the approval of the Minister of Health, and to such extent as he may direct **shall**, make arrangements for promoting the welfare of old people'.

The accompanying circular helpfully elaborates the services previously sanctioned under other auspices: the provision of home help (section 29 of the National Health Service Act, 1946); the provision of meals and recreation (section 31 of the National Assistance Act, 1948, as amended); the provision of residential accommodation for those in need of care and attention, whether directly (section 21 of the 1948 act) or through voluntary organizations or in private homes (section 44 of the 1968 act); the assistance of voluntary organizations to provide services (section 65 of the 1968 act); further services in respect of substantial and permanent handicap (sections 29 and 30 of the 1948 act); and prospective developments under the Chronically Sick and Disabled Persons Act, 1970.

The circular highlights the novelty of the new provision under the Health Services and Public Health Act, 1968 as enabling authorities to make 'other approved arrangements for services to the elderly who are not substantially and permanently handicapped, and thus to promote the welfare of the elderly generally and so far as possible prevent or postpone personal or social deterioration or breakdown' (DHSS, 1971, para. 2). Old age abuse is not specifically referred to, but would reasonably be encompassed by the concepts of 'social deterioration/breakdown'.

The then Secretary of State declined (as have all his followers) to issue directions, but arrangements for the provision of socal work support were specifically approved. Indeed, in the enthusiastic vision of a multidisciplinary preventive service it was envisaged that 'improved social work services for individuals and groups will play an important part and an adequate complement of social workers will be needed to plan and undertake this task' (DHSS, 1971, para. 7).

REASONABLE CARE VERSUS NEGLIGENCE

With the notable exception of the compulsory powers vested in an approved social worker under the Mental Health Act, 1983 (discussed below), legislation is not considered an appropriate medium for stipulating standards of professional competence. Nonetheless, as professional people social workers owe a duty of care towards their clients, particularly if they are referred as presenting special risks, as in the case of elderly people suffering abuse at the hands of their unpaid carers.

If the social worker's duty of care is breached, with consequent harm to the client, proceedings could be initiated alleging negligence. Three things would then have to be demonstrated: first, what would have been normal practice according to the standard that can reasonably be expected of a person fulfilling a social worker's role or function; second, that the defendant did not follow such practice; and third, that the alternative course, that was in fact followed by the social worker, was one that 'no professional person of that status or experience, displaying reasonable skill and ability, would have taken in acting with reasonable care' (Griffiths, Grimes and Roberts, 1990, p. 260).

To establish such a case, expert witness would be called, and the court would hear an account of the profession's own standards of competent practice. The witness might be the author of a book on the subject, but reference to such literature would almost certainly be made. *Old Age Abuse* (Eastman, 1984) could well be cited, both for its originality and abiding practical relevance as well as in consideration of the fact that it was published by Age Concern, a recognized charity dedicated to promoting the welfare of elderly people.

While not concerned in any detail with specific legislative provisions, this book nonetheless founds its exposition of professional intervention on a basic consideration of the civil liberties normally pertaining to adulthood: 'The most fundamental principle of all is the client's right to determine for him or herself whether to accept intervention and help.' Indeed, 'until it is generally acknowledged by social service agencies that the old have basic human and civil rights', all discussion of a proper framework for professional intervention will remain 'academic' (Eastman, 1984, p. 70).

At the same time, the book acknowledges situations where 'the degree of physical neglect or abuse is felt to be sufficient to warrant **removal from the family**', and envisages convening a case conference 'within 24 hours **after admission to hospital or residential home**' (Eastman, 1984, p. 74, emphasis added). However, no consideration is given to the legal dimension of the possible conflict between the perceived need for 'removal' by the professionals and the supposedly sacrosanct principle of client self-determination propounded earlier.

The same limitation characterizes the *Guidelines for Action* produced by Age Concern in collaboration with several other agencies (Age Concern *et al.* 1990). These envisage the possibility of emergency action in that 'the social worker must take immediate action to prevent or stop abuse'. Unfortunately, no consideration is given to the lawful authority to initiate such action in the face of possible resistance, not least from the 'victim'.

This is remedied somewhat in the 'generically' pitched *Adults at Risk: Procedural Guidelines for Professionals* (ADSS, 1991) which breaks new ground by not merely listing but actually outlining some of the relevant legislative provisions. Unfortunately, the actual coverage of this material (paragraphs 6.3–6.9) is not only uneven, but incomplete. For example, while 'sectioning' under the Mental Health Act, 1983 is covered in some, albeit inadequate, detail no consideration is given to the crucial powers of access under the same act (see below).

Nonetheless, the general message in terms of competent practice is admirably clear, and well worth quoting: if 'a decision is made to exercise compulsory powers of removal of a person from his or her normal environment, the greatest possible effort must be made to ensure that the client understands what is proposed, and the authority's reasons for invoking compulsory powers' (ADSS, 1991, para. 7.1.11).

TORT, CRIME AND PROSECUTION

Before moving on to specify the statutory powers of social workers in detail, it is as well to remember one simple fact:

'physical abuse is a criminal act and, through the existing legal system, if there is sufficient evidence, prosecutions can be initiated' (Greengross, 1986, p. 32).

The more recent and exhaustive work *The Law and Elderly People* (Griffiths, Grimes and Roberts, 1990) elaborates on this as follows:

> Where abuse is alleged, two forms of legal intervention exist. These consist of civil actions in tort alleging some form of trespass to the person, or criminal proceedings for assault.
>
> Trespass to the person consists of battery, assault, or false imprisonment. An assault can arise whenever a person has reasonable cause to fear that direct harm is to be directed at him/her. The tort of battery, however, requires actual, direct, and intentional application of force to the person.
>
> The Offences Against the Person Act 1961 ... sets out a number of criminal assaults ranging in seriousness from common assault to assault with the intention of causing grievous bodily harm.
>
> (*p. 303 et seq.*)

Common assault normally requires the victim, rather than the police, to initiate proceedings, but it has been established at common law that elderly and 'infirm' people are to be treated as exceptions to this rule (Griffiths, Grimes and Roberts, 1990, p. 305).

Age Concern is explicit and unequivocal in its view that this perspective should be an integral part of the social work repertoire, alongside the traditional interpersonal skills: social workers can offer advice, counselling, referral to emergency accommodation for the victim (often financed but not managed by the local authority), or 'referral to a solicitor and/or the police' (Greengross, 1986, p. 33). Experience suggests that the mere suggestion of a referral to 'the law' can sometimes suffice to induce a preparedness to accept help and engage in 'some honest work' (Stevenson, 1989, p. 26), thereby avoiding the need to actually resort to statutory powers.

REMOVAL UNDER THE NATIONAL ASSISTANCE ACT, 1948

Diminishing the need to resort to statutory powers is, of course, not only wholly laudable, but in tune with the basic principles of social policy generally and social work in particular.

Nonetheless, social workers working in the area of old age abuse cannot use this preventive rationale to justify blissful ignorance of the law. Indeed, it may well be that confidence in one's knowledge of the law can actually free up greater energies of creativity precisely with a view to prevention.

One statutory power that social workers need to be aware of concerns removal to 'suitable premises' under section 47 of the National Assistance Act, 1948, including an accelerated procedure in emergency situations as provided by section 1 of the National Assistance (Amendment) Act, 1951.

Under section 47(2), the Medical Officer of Health (Community Physician) must certify that removal is necessary 'in the interests' of the person concerned, or 'for preventing injury to the health of, or serious nuisance to, other persons'. If satisfied, a magistrates' court may order the removal of that person by the officer to a 'suitable hospital or other place', and his or her 'detention and maintenance therein', under section 47(3).

These provisions are not addressed explicitly to cases of old age abuse as such, but could be relevant in cases where abuse is suffered by elderly people who additionally meet the criteria specified in section 47(1), namely that they are 'suffering from grave chronic disease or, being aged, infirm or physically incapacitated, are living in insanitary conditions', and that they are 'unable to devote to themselves, and are not receiving from other persons, proper care and attention'.

Indeed, while the wording of section 47 is such as to provide for compulsory removal of a range of vulnerable people, it seems to be used primarily in relation to elderly people (Griffiths, Grimes and Roberts, 1990, p. 173). This very fact has led to pressure in some quarters for its abolition, or at least drastic reform (Greengross, 1986, p. 39 *et seq.*).

For the moment, however, social workers cannot 'wash their hands' of section 47 since they are in the frontline of preventive work and are thus quite likely to be the first to recognize irretrievable breakdown. Nonetheless, it is important to bear in mind that in this particular legislative provision, 'the social worker is not the one who has the powers to remove a person against their will' (Brayne and Martin, 1991, p. 209).

ACCESS UNDER THE MENTAL HEALTH ACT, 1983

For the possible relevance of statutory powers exercised by social workers directly one has to turn to the Mental Health Act, 1983 relating to 'mentally disordered persons'.

Needless to say, 'there are many old people who are vulnerable through chronic disability or mental or physical infirmity who do not come within the purview of mental health legislation' (Freeman, 1989, p. 747). But this should prompt social workers to clarify carefully in their own minds the provisions of the Mental Health Act, rather than disregard them altogether. This is especially true of social workers appointed to act as approved social workers under the act in accordance with section 114.

Perhaps the most fundamental function of the approved social worker (ASW) is to gain access to people whose mental disorder renders them vulnerable. Under section 115 of the act, an ASW may at all reasonable times, after producing (if asked to do so) some duly authenticated document showing that he or she is such a social worker, enter and inspect any premises (not being a hospital) in which a mentally disordered person is living, if he or she has reasonable cause to believe that the person is 'not under proper care'. It is submitted that physical and/or emotional abuse would be encompassed by the latter phrase.

Under section 129(1), obstruction of the ASW in this line of duty is an offence. However, if this fails to impress the obstructor, the ASW has no power to force entry, and would be obliged to consider an application to a Justice of the Peace under section 135(1). The relevant wording in this case is that there is reasonable cause to suspect that a person believed to be suffering from mental disorder 'has been, or is being, ill-treated, neglected or kept otherwise than under proper control'. If the JP is satisfied, he or she may issue a warrant authorizing the police to enter (if need be by force) the premises specified and, if thought fit, to remove the person concerned to a place of safety, with a view either to 'sectioning' or guardianship, or making any 'other arrangements for his treatment and care'.

'SECTIONING'

'Sectioning' is professional slang for making an application for the detention of a person in hospital under section 2 (admission for assessment, or assessment followed by medical treatment), section 4 (admission for assessment in cases of emergency) or section 3 (admission for treatment).

ASWs have the power/duty to make the application where they consider it right and proper to do so. But their professional brief is much wider than this: in the words of the relevant circular (DHSS, 1986, para. 14), 'their role is to prevent the necessity for compulsory admission to hospital as well as to make application where they decide this is appropriate'.

In a rare example of Parliament legislating for a principle that many would consider to be straightforward competent practice, section 13(2) stipulates that 'before making an application for the admission of a patient to hospital an approved social worker shall interview the patient in a suitable manner and satisfy himself that detention in a hospital is in all the circumstances of the case the most appropriate way of providing the care and medical treatment of which the patient stands in need'.

Specifically included in the DHSS's elaboration of 'all the circumstances of the case' are not only the past history of the person's mental disorder, his or her present condition and medical opinion, but also the social, familial and personal factors bearing on the strictly clinical situation (DHSS, 1983, para. 38). Clearly, actual or suspected abuse would be of direct relevance in this context, possibly rendering impractical a psychiatric care and treatment plan that might otherwise be safely accommodated within the home setting.

However, before the ASW takes the momentous step of 'sectioning' a victim of old age abuse, s/he must remember that under all three sections detention must not only be in the interests of/necessary for the person's 'own health or safety' (or 'for the protection of other persons', which is scarcely likely in this case), but also be warranted by/appropriate in the light of the 'nature or degree' of the mental disorder itself. This greatly restricts the potential reference of these provisions to cases of old age abuse, particularly when compared with the less clinical focus of the 'access' sections 115 and 135, discussed earlier.

GUARDIANSHIP

Last, but not least, consideration of the Mental Health Act in respect of old age abuse must give some regard to the provisions relating to guardianship applications, which ASWs are also under a duty to make where they consider it right and proper to so do.

Section 7(2) of the act lays down that the overriding criterion for invoking guardianship is that such an arrangement must be necessary 'in the interests of the welfare of the patient or for the protection of other persons'. The memorandum explains that 'the purpose of guardianship is therefore primarily to ensure that the patient receives care and protection rather than medical treatment' (DHSS, 1983, para. 45). And the long-delayed Code of Practice (DoH, 1990) argues that guardianship 'enables the establishment of an authoritative framework for working with a patient with a minimum of constraint to achieve as independent a life as possible within the community' (para. 13.1).

However, this generally optimistic account of guardianship needs to be qualified by reference to two quite significant limitations. The first relates to terminology. Whereas for sections 2 and 4 (in parallel with sections 115 and 135) 'mental disorder' is not further specified, section 7(2) follows the pattern of section 3 in stipulating that for guardianship applications the mental disorder in question must be specified as 'mental illness, severe mental impairment, psychopathic disorder or mental impairment'.

As Gostin (1986) explains: 'it is important to appreciate that the four terms of mental disorder specified in the act are legal, not medical, terms'. Helpfully, Gostin refers the reader to the World Health Organization's classification of mental disorders into psychoses, neurotic disorders and personality disorders, and submits that 'psychoses are the clinical forms of mental disorder which most closely correspond with the statutory concept of mental illness' (Gostin, 1986, para. 9.07).

Since there is ample evidence (Tomlin, 1989, p. 5; BASE, 1991, p. 8; DHSSI, 1992, p. 5) that the psychotic mental disorders, and thereby the 'mental illnesses', of old age are a frequent, though obviously not universal, feature of old age abuse situations, the diagnostic criteria for guardianship would seem to be satisfied in a significant number of cases.

But this immediately brings the discussion up against the other problem confronting the implementation of guardianship, not just in cases of old age abuse: in general, its relative lack of 'clout'. The powers conferred on the guardian (normally the local social services authority itself) under section 8(1) comprise: first, the power to require the person to reside at a specified place (but not the power to take them there in the first place); second, the power to require the person to attend at specified places and times for the purpose of medical treatment, occupation, education or training (but not the power to compel treatment); and thirdly, the power to require access to the person to be given to any registered medical practitioner, approved social worker or other specified person (but not the power to force entry).

As the Sweet and Maxwell annotations of the act observe, with the exception of the power to retake a patient under section 18(3), which in any case is not the preserve of the guardian as such, 'the powers given to the guardian under this provision are not capable of enforcement, but rely on the co-operation of the patient' (Jones, 1991, p. 37).

This is not to say that a guardianship arrangement might not have a beneficial effect by seeming to confer greater powers than it does in reality. But this is highly dubious, not only in moral terms, but also in strictly legal terms since it would seem to negate the criterion of guardianship being necessary in its own right under section 7(1). As the Code of Practice emphasizes, if none of the actual powers conferred by section 8(1) are considered necessary for achieving any part of the care plan, 'guardianship is inappropriate' (DoH, 1990, para. 13.4).

It is not surprising, therefore, that authors and campaigners on old age abuse have turned their attention, among other things, to a possible reform of the law in this area. This will be discussd presently. First, however, it is important to identify the overall legislative context within which such discussions are usually, and quite rightly, located.

LIBERTY, PROTECTION AND LEGISLATIVE ANTI-AGEISM

Reviewing the literature on 'elder abuse' in 1991, the author of an exploratory study published by Age Concern's Institute of Gerontology aptly notes that 'the legal questions are extremely complicated, revolving around the balance between protection of a vulnerable individual and respect for adult status and the right to autonomous choice' (McCreadie, 1991, p. 44).

Greengross (1986) put the dilemma fairly and squarely:

There is sometimes a tension between the protection of the welfare and the representation of the interests of this vulnerable group of people in our society. Vulnerable old people are often dependent and ... may need protection and support through outside intervention. Any such intervention by another must inevitably reduce self determination, and can be seen as an infringement of individual liberty.

(p. 18)

In fact, as will be seen shortly, this publication set the agenda for all subsequent debate on the positive value of actually extending statutory powers.

At the same time, Age Concern has remained at the forefront of the critics of legislation, both current and potential, that stigmatizes elderly people. The most significant contribution in this area is the volume entitled *Age: The Unrecognised Discrimination*, which contains the following forceful argument:

The use of the word 'age' in legislation has helped to create age discrimination. Age was put alongside grave chronic disease, infirmity or physical incapacity as a qualifier in the 1948 National Assistance Act, and to this day the word continues to be used in legislation as a blanket term to imply dependence ... To ban the use of the word in legislation would encourage the awareness that age is not an illness or a disability ... It would stress that it is the circumstances and condition of individuals, not their age, that is significant.

McEwen, 1990, p. 26 et seq.

This would suggest that if statutory powers of relevance to cases of old age abuse were to be extended, they should be framed in the 'generic', i.e. non-age specific, terms of the ADSS's guidelines in respect of 'adults at risk', discussed earlier. However, this is not the view taken by campaigners generally, nor even by Age Concern itself, as will become clear in what follows.

THE CASE FOR NEW STATUTORY POWERS

It is perhaps appropriate that if new powers affecting elderly people are to be enacted, they should be framed in the first instance by an organization with a proud record of championing the rights of this group. This is one of the key features of Greengross' *The Law and Vulnerable Elderly People* (published by Age Concern), which has been referred to on several occasions already.

Among other things, this publication argues for a fourfold development in the law: first, that a general power be introduced enabling local authorities to promote the welfare of elderly people, and to advise, guide and assist old people and make available resources as necessary; second, that a specific duty on local authorities be introduced to consider the case of individual vulnerable old people; third, that an Intervention Order be introduced to enable individual old people and/or their carers to oppose or to appeal against a decision of the local authority, and to enable a local authority to oppose or appeal against the decision of an individual; and finally, that the above legislation be backed up by limited Emergency Powers (Greengross, 1986, p. 137).

An Emergency Intervention Order could make the following directions: first, that specific help be brought to the old person where s/he resides, subject to the availability of such help; second, that the old person be removed to a place of safety: and/or thirdly, that named individuals be restrained from assaulting, molesting or otherwise interfering with the old person, or be excluded from the old person's home (*idem*, p. 136).

While there remains a certain equivocation in terms of the elderly person's 'right to refuse any intervention' (*idem*, p. 137), a subsequent publication by Age Concern nails its colours to the mast in favour of compulsion:

> It seems clear that, with certain safeguards, we need some legal machinery, similar to the provision of Place of Safety Orders for children, by which an old person could be received into residential care for their own protection, at least for a limited period of time, which would afford a breathing space for all concerned and enable a proper assessment to be made of the situation – including the wishes of the old person **once they were out of the violent or neglectful environment**.
>
> *Stevenson, 1989, p. 27* (emphasis added)

This, according to the author, is totally distinct from 'unwarrantable intrusion' (*idem*, p. 28).

Other legislative possibilities have been mooted, of course. It has been suggested, for example, that consideration might be given to a 'more flexible approach to guardianship', notably its extension to people not currently covered by the Mental Health Act, 1983, i.e. to 'certain vulnerable old people' (Greengross, 1986, p. 91). An extension of the terms of reference of section 47 of the National Assistance Act, 1948 to cover cases of 'non-accidental injury' has also been considered, though less enthusiastically (Freeman, 1989, p. 749). And an article in *Geriatric Medicine* has attempted to lend credence to the prospect of introducing US-style 'competency hearings' to assess a person's mental competence to refuse help (Bennett, 1990, p. 60).

THE LAW COMMISSION AND 'VULNERABLE ADULTS'

The argument for an extension of statutory powers finds its most forceful expression in the recent work of the Law Commission on 'mental incapacitation'. Its initial overview in 1991, *Mentally Incapacitated Adults and Decision-Making*, included a specific consideration of neglect/abuse as it pertained to 'elderly people with mental infirmity', and came to the early conclusion that in this and related areas the existing law was 'fragmented, complex and in many respects out of date' (Law Commission, 1991, p. 5).

Of the Law Commission's three subsequent consultation papers, all published in 1993, the crucial document in the present context is *Mentally Incapacitated and Other Vulnerable Adults: Public Law Protection*. The extended frame of reference indicated by the title is explicitly argued in the text itself:

> We think it essential to go beyond the narrowly defined group of mentally incapacitated clients with whom this project is principally concerned ... There are other people who are not incapable of taking their own decisions, but are also especially vulnerable to abuse or neglect from which they are unable to protect themselves. Some machinery is needed to protect them and the existing procedures ... are widely believed to be unsatisfactory for this purpose.
>
> (*p. 3*)

As a provisional proposal for further discussion, a definition is offered by virtue of which a person is vulnerable if 'by reason of old age, infirmity or disability (including mental disorder within the meaning of the Mental Health Act, 1983) he is unable to take care of himself or to protect himself from others' (Law Commission, 1993, p. 28).

In its substantive discussions the paper ranges far and wide, and includes recommendations in Part Four for tightening up existing guardianship provisions. But the heart and soul of the paper's recommendations are contained in Part Three, entitled 'Investigation, Assessment and Short Term Intervention'. The first eight recommendations deserve explicit itemization in the present context. As will be readily apparent, they are closely modelled on the Mental Health Act, 1983, with further elaborations inspired by the Children Act, 1989.

The local authority social services authority should be the agency responsible, by way of specific duties, for initiating proceedings in relation to the care and protection of the target group, including the investigation of allegations of neglect or abuse (Recommendations 1–3). An officer of the authority, authorized for the purpose, should have appropriate powers of entry and it should be an offence to obstruct him in the exercise thereof (Recommendations 4 and 5). Authority to enter by force, if necessary, would be conferred by warrant on the police upon application by the local authority officer (Recommendation 6). And additional orders would comprise an assessment order and an emergency protection order, authorizing removal to a place of safety (Recommendations 7 and 8).

Regrettably, the paper's definition of 'vulnerability' rests on an unfortunate association of old age with 'infirmity' and 'disability'. Paradoxically, however, the inclusion of elderly 'vulnerable' people with their non-elderly counterparts means that the former can share in a right to protection **from** statutory powers that is more usually reserved for the latter. For Recommendations 7 and 8, the granting of an order in respect of a person who is 'vulnerable' but not 'mentally incapacitated' or 'mentally disordered' should be dependent on reasonable grounds to believe that the 'victim' would not object to the orders being made. This is also stated as a general principle in the overall argument:

The authorities may not know whether a person is incapacitated or only vulnerable until they have gained access to him and made some inquiries. Once the position has become clear, however, our present view is that a person who is capable of making his own decisions has the right to decline the authorities' help and protection, even if this means that he is left in an environment which is harmful to him. If he is capable of making the choice, that is a choice he must be allowed to make. It follows that longer term decision-making powers will not be justified.

Law Commission, 1993, p. 7

This contrasts with the relative equivocation on the part of Age Concern noted earlier.

A ROLE FOR SOCIAL WORK

In as far as the proposed legislative reforms allocate a central role to local authority social services departments it is safe to assume that social workers would play a part in implementing the new-style social policy. But the existing literature is remarkable for its paucity of direct reference to the specific role that social workers might assume in the prospective scenario. This contrasts markedly with the run-up to the Mental Health (Amendment) Act, 1982, where the greatly enhanced legal standing of the social worker was a major plank in the reform campaign's proposals (Gostin, 1975, p. 36 *et seq.* and p. 144).

The outstanding exception to this reticence comes not, as one might expect, from the British Association of Social Workers, but from the Law Commission, in its overview paper on mentally incapacitated adults and decision-making (1991). In consideration of Age Concern's proposal for an Emergency Intervention Order, it points out that certain matters would require 'particular attention', and lists one such:

There should be a clear allocation of responsibility for invoking the procedure as between health authorities and social services. It might serve to reduce confusion if the model of the Mental Health Act were used, in which the application is made by a social worker on the recommendation of one or two doctors.

Law Commission, 1991, p. 161

This would remedy the current confused situation whereby applications under section 135 of the Mental Health Act are made by approved social workers, while those under section 47 of the National Assistance Act are made by community physicians (see above), with the result that 'responsibility for taking emergency action does not lie clearly in one place' (Law Commission, 1991, p. 77).

The Law Commission's recommendation that the power/ duty to apply for an Emergency Intervention Order should be vested in a social worker, following the model of the Mental Health Act, also raises the prospect of a statutory provision in respect of what would be considered good practice along the lines of section 13(2) of the act. Adapting the wording of the latter, the following formulation would be extremely helpful:

> Before making an application for the removal of an elderly person to suitable accommodation, a social worker shall interview the person in a suitable manner and satisfy her/himself that removal to such accommodation is, in all the circumstances of the case, the most appropriate way of providing the care and protection of which the person stands in need.

This could be reinforced by a corresponding Department of Health Circular. Adapting the wording of the circular in respect of approved social workers (DHSS, 1986, para. 14), the social worker's role and repertoire in cases of old age abuse could be crystallized thus:

> They should have the specialist knowledge and skills to make appropriate decisions in respect of both clients and their relatives and to gain the confidence of colleagues in the health services with whom they are required to collaborate. They must be familiar with the day to day working of an integrated health service and be able to assess what other services may be required and know how to mobilize them ... Their role is to prevent the necessity for compulsory removal as well as to make application where they decide this is appropriate.

Similar adaptations of the relevant *Memorandum* (DHSS, 1983) and *Code of Practice* (DoH, 1990) (see above) would be equally valuable.

14

Lifting the lid on elder abuse: questions and doubts

Jim Traynor

I'm a bit of a doubting Thomas on occasions and elder abuse has been one of those topics that gets me going . . .

The rest of this book is most likely full of erudite and learned writing on detecting, investigating, defining and responding to the topic of abuse of older people. To raise doubts about it may seem a little churlish, but to ask questions about an issue need not weaken it. Indeed, the opposite is often the case. I don't possess the answers, and envy those that do. I'm a bit of a doubting Thomas on occasions and elder abuse has been one of those topics that gets me going, but I hope you will recognize and share some of my genuine concerns regarding this popular subject.

The study and investigation of elder abuse has always, for me, been fraught with difficulty. As a practitioner rather than an academic I have known of elder abuse since my first days in social work, yet I find myself reluctant to join in the pressure to put the issue at the top of our priority list and even more so to join the populist clamour for instruments of intervention similar to those adopted in child protection. As a social gerontologist and practitioner I worry about the degree of importance given to the topic and its place in the struggle for scarce resources.

Over the years I have noted that lectures and discussions on topics relating to abuse, violence, aggression and sexuality are very popular and draw in crowds out of all proportion to the frequency of the occurrence of these behaviours. Trying to get those same people to come to sessions covering incontinence or sensory impairment is a very different story. There is a certain attractiveness or glamour surrounding abuse that holds our attention while repelling us at the same time. This is not exclusive to old age abuse, a similar situation exists in child care.

My scepticism regarding elder abuse relates to its prevalence and nature, not its existence. I am not making a case against intervention, only that such action should have the older person's best interests at heart, even when it may well not be strictly within the legal powers available. I remember listening to Sue Tomita describing her work with abused elderly people in Seattle during which she bravely identified a course of intervention known as UBC, unlawful but courageous.

My interest in elder abuse goes back more than 10 years to a discussion on the topic at a local meeting of the British Society of Gerontology at the London School of Economics. The meeting's organizer knew of my interest and I was asked to speak on the topic. It was noticeable even then that academic interest was secondary to that of the practitioners, a situation that I am not convinced has changed yet in the UK.

I still have my notes from that meeting and, despite the time lapse, I find my views now are little different from then. I was sceptical about the scale of the problem then referred to as 'granny battering', the definitions used, the absence of concern about the violence used by older people towards their carers, the sampling techniques, and the reliability of extrapolating American research straight on to the UK scene.

There seemed to be a danger of a moral panic over the issue and I worried about headlines in the popular press talking of 500 000 to 1 000 000 elderly people at risk; a worry mirrored by Crystal (1986) who commented: 'The impression conveyed to the public and to policy makers – that a million elderly people are beaten up by their children or other care-givers each year – is palpably wrong'.

My concern was exacerbated by muddled use of descriptions and swapping of definitions which resulted in the findings being presented as being about 'physical abuse', a perception then seized on by the general public, when in fact the original figures were often about non-physical abuse.

These concerns have not disappeared over the course of 10 years, indeed some remain as relevant now as then. It is interesting to note that I was able to turn up at that meeting with just a few pages of notes and be confident that I had covered all the relevant research on both sides of the Atlantic. In trying to update myself before writing this chapter I was overwhelmed by the sheer volume of literature on elder abuse. It even has its own journal! In the light of all this, are we any clearer now about how much priority to give it than we were then? The answer is probably yes, but not if the question is where we place it in relation to the multitude of challenges facing our older population.

When people find that I am interested in old age abuse many, even gerontologists, make the assumption that I am in the process of exposing it as a creeping epidemic. The myth is a powerful one that can only be debunked through proper comparative study, and nowhere does it linger more strongly than in the eyes of the media, always on the look out for a good story. Shortly after the widespread reporting of a particularly nasty and brutal assault on a very elderly woman, I was contacted by a journalist doing a piece on abuse of older people. She wanted to interview me about the increased targetting of older people, compared with other age groups, by criminals. When I said I was unaware of any evidence to support this notion and that my understanding was that older people were less likely to be victims of violent assault, she soon lost interest.

Worried lest I had been wrong in saying this, I hastily checked the literature and found that the rates of victimization were indeed lower on both sides of the Atlantic for older people. I mention this because I fear that sensational reporting of cases where older people are the victims runs the risk of increasing old people's fear out of all proportion to the actual threat. This can lead to their taking the decision to remain unhealthily closeted in 'fortress home'.

Despite reassurances at the end of the television programme *Crimewatch UK* to the effect that the crimes featured are not typical, the fear factor of viewers can remain acute. The connection with the topic in hand is that the danger of falsely reporting the incidence of a particular behaviour can lead to its being perceived as normal and perhaps to an acceptance by victims that their suffering is in some way normal, too.

The flip side of this over-reporting coin is the way in which violent behaviour **by** older people is ignored. I have yet to see a headline along the lines of 'Carer bashed by elderly person'! Why is there so little interest in abusive behaviour towards carers? Could it be a fear that we might just have to put in resources to combat it, whereas if we treat it as part and parcel of the caring task we can acknowledge it and ignore it? Ageism cannot even be used as an excuse since many of the carers are themselves elderly people. The fact that abuse is double directional encourages me to focus on the idea of family or relationship abuse, rather than seeing it as an ageist problem that only surfaces with the attainment by the victim of a certain age.

Ten years ago I had four basic objections to the concept of widespread abuse. Firstly, substantial research was lacking in both the USA and the UK. This area has since been the focus of an enormous amount of work at both an academic and a practical level in the USA. According to McCreadie's exploratory study (1991), the Americans have examined all the problems associated with elder abuse and found that their 'research findings could not be compared because the definitions used were unclear and inconsistent'.

My second objection was that the definitions and language used to describe elder abuse were too loose to allow proper comparisons. Unfortunately we do not appear to have progressed particularly far with this since agreed definitions are still frustratingly absent.

My third objection was to the size of research samples and their selectivity. Since then this area has improved with an increase in sample sizes and the welcome addition of control groups. These appear to have already cast doubt on the initial focus, which was exclusively elderly people living with relatives.

My fourth objection was to the apparent ease with which American research findings were applied to the UK. The levels of violence vary between the two countries. I would suggest that there may be inherently more violence in the USA, and that the severity of that violence may well reflect the norms of the community whence it originates. Therefore, there is a need to be cautious about building social policies purely on the basis of research from the USA.

It is noticeable that the focus of attention has tended to be on abuse in domestic settings and has often ignored that occurring in institutions despite well-catalogued incidents culminating in that at Nye Bevan Lodge (Gribbs, Evans and Rodway, 1987). Again, the question must be why we adopt what often seems to be a double-standards approach when it would surely be that much easier to put our own house in order?

It is not as if abuse of older people is a new phenomenon; the pioneering Fabian, Beatrice Webb suggested that a Royal Society for the Protection of Cruelty to the Elderly should be set up. The image of the halcyon days when old age was an honoured and venerated state is a powerful myth that remains firmly rooted in the imagination of both the public and professionals despite evidence to the contrary. A reading of Peter Laslett's (1977) work on the history of ageing or of American accounts of the victimization of older women as witches, might prompt the scales to fall from some eyes. However, nostalgia is strong stuff with an enduring appeal.

There is something comforting in locating the origins of elder abuse in individuals and families: it allows us to pass judgement and abdicate responsibility for its existence. Yet we often turn a blind eye to societal abuse and neglect, passing on the street elderly vagrants, now as much as part of life in the UK as in the USA: we prefer not to consider that they are also abused and neglected and just as worthy of our outrage, because that would mean being outraged at ourselves. If we are serious in our concern about abuse of older people, we need to address as worthy of notice all abuse, not just that part that gets up our comfortable noses. Through the sustenance of inequality and injustice that causes large scale abuse of older people, we all play a part. When are we going to rage against this in a similar manner to that of domestic abuse? To do so, of course, would mean turning the microscope on societal structures, and those interests are often best served in the continuing location of dysfunction within the individual.

An interesting trend, which I perceive to be growing, is the call for us to spend less time seeking definitions of elder

abuse and instead to get on with the job in hand. I find this
all the more worrying because it comes from professionals who
in other areas of practice would question the validity of findings in the absence of agreed definitions. I can understand
the desire to dispense with the difficult and onerous task of
agreeing on terminology, having myself spent fruitless hours
with colleagues searching for the Holy Grail of a complete and
encompassing definition. However, I do not see that a search
for definitional integrity need necessarily prevent us from
tackling the issue in practice. The fact that theory has not kept
up with practice is not, in itself, an argument for abandoning
the search.

Some of the unease expressed by myself and Hasnip in 1984
was related to the vagueness surrounding abuse and the
plethora of actions and terms used to describe it. Perceptions
of abuse were firmly rooted in physical violence, yet the data
was pointing elsewhere in terms of incidence. I was particularly
concerned at the separate inclusion of yelling, partly because
it was included at all as an abusive category, and partly because
this area dwarfed the other categories. It goes without saying
that yelling can be distressing and hurtful, but I'm not sure
that I would include it as a category of abuse worthy *per se*
of intervention in every instance. In my own life, both as a
child and an adult, I regrettably have yelled and been yelled
at and, I would suggest, am not alone in this; in all instances
of this behaviour I would not however, have taken kindly to
finding an agent of the caring services on my doorstep seeking
to intervene!

It is not that I seek to deny the hurt that is caused by
this or other non-physical means, only that the decision to
intervene should not be based on rigid categories of what
constitutes abuse or on the age of the victim. There is a danger
that in our search to help older people we may deny them
the darker side of human relationships and in the process
inadvertently patronize them on account of their advanced
years and devalue them as citizens. It is especially ironic since
the behaviour pattern may well have been present all a
person's life.

I find the use of frequency as a measurement of abuse no
more convincing. It needs, I suggest, a subjective measurement to make any sense of it. An anecdote from my own

practice springs to mind. I remember having great difficulty in making arrangements for an elderly mentally infirm patient to attend her sister's funeral. They had been lifelong companions and had ended up together in a residential home. However, the sister I was involved with had had to enter hospital for treatment and while she was there her sister had died. The general view was that she would not be aware of her sister's death and should be left in ignorance, that I was cruel and unkind to wish to expose her to suffering. In the event I attended the funeral with her, there being no other attendant, and observed a remarkable change in her as she became distressed and lucid in her grief, calling for her sister by name. There was little doubt in my mind that she appreciated what was happening and was hurt by her loss, but I remain convinced to this day that she was accorded only that which all of us seek, the right to live as a human being, warts and all. But some people may view the incident as emotional abuse.

A useful concept that I have only recently come across is that proposed by Gelles and Cornell (1985) in offering the categories of 'normal violence' and 'abuse violence', the suggestion being that certain acts of violence are part and parcel of daily living and can be differentiated from abusive violence of a criminal type. The concept of suffering is introduced to separate out behaviours that may be objectively questionable but viewed subjectively are seen to be integral to normal daily living patterns.

> It is important to keep in mind that what we are experiencing is neither new nor particularly unique to our own society. While we look for causes and solutions in individuals, or families, or even in communities, we should remember that cultural attitudes about violence as a means of self expression and solving problems are at the root of private violence.
>
> *Gelles and Cornell, 1985*

Gelles and Cornell point us to that most violent of social institutions, the family. Family violence is not new, rare or unique to one country. They show that in many homes, and in society at large, violence is the norm rather than the exception and that violent behaviour towards certain groups, such as children, is often approved of. Many people grow up believing that violence and love coexist within the family and that it is acceptable to hit the ones you love. If this is so then it is unlikely that such behaviour will cease upon the attainment of a certain number of years of life.

> The controversy in this definition is that it does not take into account what actually happened to the victims of the violence . . . The reasons for not being concerned about consequences is that research on assault and homicide, which has been carried out by criminologists, has consistently found that things which differentiate injurious violence from violence that causes no harm are typically random phenomena such as aim or luck.
>
> *Gelles and Cornell, 1985*

This approach is, in many ways, supported by those such as Riley (1989) who advocate concentrating on the outcome rather than the specific type of abuse used. For her it matters nought whether the causal actions were intentional or not, deliberately neglectful or ignorant. She feels the important thing to be that intervention is considered and that there be a degree of coterminosity between the relevant agencies. I, however, feel that the question of intent **is** important, especially when considering ongoing work.

We seem to make an assumption in our society that people will automatically know how to care for an older person. This may be contrasted with our approach to child-rearing where organized state health supervision is provided, generally both before and after a baby's birth. So how do people learn to look after ageing relatives? Often by trial and error. The number of ingenious but dubious methods that relatives I have come across, have devised to help them care for their dependants needed to be seen to be believed. I think it does matter whether a person who locks his or her dementing partner in a room does it to protect that partner or to punish him or her for a misdemeanour. It is all too easy as a professional simply to sit in judgement on what should and should not happen, especially if we have nothing to offer in its place.

It may, therefore, be the case that suffering is part of normal family life and the choice of many adults who would objectively be identified as being the subjects of abuse. That free-thinking individuals can choose to return to or remain in an abusive situation is no easier to understand in the case of an older person that it is in that of spouse abuse. The lack of subjective understanding leaves us lost for words and often less tolerant when the behaviour is repeated.

There are arguments about alternatives – the premise being that a range of alternative accommodation is the solution. The answer may be similar to that found in child protection, that the victim's primary concern is that the abuse should stop. There is little interest in, indeed, there is a revulsion towards, the detection and punishment so beloved by the statutory agencies, because of the incarceration and break-up of the family unit that often accompanies such actions. The destruction of the family unit is, for many, too great a price to pay for their unharrowed well-being; and older people often fear residential care more than the abuse they suffer.

Crystal (1986), reporting an early study, pointed out: 'The most significant long term outcome was a higher rate of mortality among those receiving the special intervention.' In other words, those who received help were often moved for their own good to institutional care, with its attendant higher rates of mortality.

Just as Lord Justice Butler-Sloss' report on child abuse in Cleveland (1988) highlighted the move away from automatic removal of the victim, so might we hope for a similar response where older people are concerned. This, of course, requires that the resources are available to ensure alternative support services can be provided. As our American colleagues are keen to point out, legal remedies after the detection of abuse cases are of themselves useless unless the resources to deal with the aftermath are also forthcoming (McCreadie, 1991).

In 1989 Riley listed five types of provision, from marital support to interpreting services, that are required to help combat abusive situations. Without them or similar I suggest the chances of the older victim being left in the home are much reduced.

The issue of removal of older victims can also be usefully compared with the strategies adopted in spouse abuse where the onus is often on the healing of the relationship rather than its automatic cessation. The concept of a refuge may also be helpful. I remember a BBC documentary series on social work a few years ago in which one of the scenarios shown was that of an older couple where there was abuse by the husband. The response was the removal of the wife. The outcome may well have been the correct one but the point was that little was done to consider alternatives, and I had little doubt that had the couple been 30 years younger they might have had difficulty in even having their problems addressed.

In the Pillemer and Finkelhor study on prevalence, spouse abuse accounted for more than double the number of cases of abuse by adult children (quoted by McCreadie, 1991, p. 31). Despite this we still seem to respond to people on the grounds of their age rather than who they are. The right of an individual to be offered help and support should be based on his or her need for it rather than age. The compartmentalizing of people into different age bands may ease administration, but runs the danger of artificially splittng up people in need into competing groups.

This view was clarified for me by Fay Lomax Cook (1982), who offers a framework for considering the efficacy of age-based approaches as opposed to age-neutral ones. Cook suggests that such choice can be aided by the use of a multistep 'decision tree' which offers a logical progression through a number of questions designed to get at the specialness or otherwise of the policy under scrutiny. I found the framework directly applicable to the issue of elder abuse.

The starting point is whether abuse is special for older people or subgroups of older people in particular. Three criteria are offered to help decide this: age discontinuity; age trend; and high levels without age trend. Without repeating Cook's article here, using her framework leads me to conclude that an age-neutral approach is the strategy of choice. To be completely authoritative on this we would, however, need to draw on accurate data, and that is still as elusive now as it was 10 years ago.

A criticism I had of Steinmetz's 1981 figures was that her sample was highly selective with no control group. Yet I noted that in 1988 she was using a non-representative sampling technique so that: 'It is not possible to generalise the results to the population at large'. Writing on the difficulty in finding witnesses for the Congressional Hearings she also pointed to the fact that few had suffered physical abuse, most had suffered financial and resource abuse.

Confusion in categorizing abuse runs throughout the literature. Hudson (1986 and 1989) offered: 'mistreatment, maltreatment, older abuse, elder neglect, active neglect, passive neglect, physical abuse, psychological abuse, sexual abuse, medical abuse, financial abuse, material abuse, isolation of rights, deprivation, exploitation and self neglect and abuse.'

It is surely this very plethora of different descriptions that lie at the heart of much of the confusion surrounding the topic. It is small wonder that practitioners have despaired of their academic colleagues and question Straus' suggested social contract. 'The terms of the contract free the scholar from having to deal with the real work and also place on him or her the obligation to produce insights and knowledge that are unlikely to be produced by those caught up in the day to day demands of the real world' (Straus, 1986).

We are waiting. This failure has created a vacuum into which practitioners, myself included, have stepped with an attendant rise in strategies, not all of which demonstrate the benefit of reasoned thought. The desire is to do something in the face of suffering. Legal redress for many of the problems facing a vulnerable group of elderly people are noticeable by their absence, despite the work of Age Concern, among others, to put the issue on the table. The criticism of the protective services by the US legal profession, which sees mandatory programmes as an intrusion on civil liberties, has yet to be addressed by a wave of action based on well publicized failures of the welfare state. It is to be hoped that we do not throw out the baby with the bathwater in our desire to care.

It is sometimes forgotten that legal options are often available, if somewhat tardy and cumbersome. Some 18 months ago a case of physical abuse came to light in my own area. The social worker, with great determination and effort, worked with the victim getting her legal advice as well as practical help, and tackled the abuser. The case followed the familiar pattern in that at the last minute the elderly woman balked at actually bringing the weight of the law to bear on her daughter. She was, however, fully aware of her position, and with the help of her social worker chose an alternative route. Legal redress could and would have been sufficient if pursued, and although the perpetrator went unpunished this caused no distress to the victim.

One of the queries raised in the Cook approach is whether an age-specific approach is any more effective than a neutral one. I see this as a key point. To date the evidence, even in the USA, seems to suggest that many of the victims are already known and that age is chosen merely as a convenient parameter (McCreadie, 1991).

CONCLUSION

Progress has been made over the last decade in the study of elder abuse and it is worthy of our closest attention. We must, however, be careful to keep it in perspective when comparing it with the many other problems facing our older population. We must be vigilant for its presence and willing to tackle it when discovered. Research in the UK is still required if scaremongering is to be avoided and proper policies developed. Putting our house in order through constant critical inspection of our own residential sector is also required.

As recently as March 1993 *Aging and Society* carried a review symposium on 'Elder Abuse, Education and Training' in which one reviewer was an academic, the other a practitioner. They were reviewing two training manuals, one written by academics, the other by a practitioner. The different opinions of the reviewers on the merits of the books, as well as the different content of the manuals, highlighted for me the gap that still permeates this topic between research and practice. The reviewers each saw and found evidence in support of their perspectives. The practitioner found the practitioner's approach 'sensitive', but the academics' 'overwhelming'; whereas the academic found the practitioner's manual to have 'built-in difficulty', but the academics' to be 'an outstanding contribution'. I believe they were both accurate in their assessment, but until we bridge this gap between theory and practice and bring the two together there is the strong possibility of being ill-served by both.

The last word comes from Chen (1981), whom I quoted at that first LSE meeting: 'Few practitioners actually deal with cases of elder abuse and some have had little direct contact with the abused elderly. Hence, these factors, rather than lack of interest, accounted for the low response rate'.

REFERENCES

Butler-Sloss, Lord Justice E. (1988) *The Report of the Inquiry into Child Abuse in Cleveland 1987*, HMSO, London.

Chen, P.N., Bell, S., Dolinsky, D. *et al.* (1981) Elderly abuse in domestic settings: a pilot study. *Journal of Gerontological Social Work*, **4**(1).

Cook, F.L. (1982) Assessing Age as an Eligibility Criterion, in *Age or Need*, (ed. B. Neugarten), Sage, Beverley Hills.

Crystal, S. (1986) Social Policy and Elder Abuse, in *Elder Abuse: Conflict in the Family* (eds K.A. Pillemer and R.S. Wolf), Auburn House Publishing Company, Massachusetts, pp. 331–40.

Gelles, R.J. and Cornell, C.P. (1985) *Intimate Violence in Families*, Sage Publications, London.

Gibbs, J., Evans, M. and Rodway, S. (1987) *Report of the Inquiry into Nye Bevan Lodge*, Southwark Social Services Department, London.

Hudson, M.F. (1986) Elder Mistreatment: Current Research, in *Elder Abuse: Conflict in the Family* (eds K.A. Pillemer and R.S. Wolf), Auburn House Publishing Company, Massachusetts.

Hudson, M.F. (1989) Analysis of the concept of elder mistreatment. *Journal of Elder Abuse and Neglect*, **1**(1).

Laslett, P. (1977) *Family Life and Illicit Love in Earlier Generations*, Cambridge University Press, Cambridge.

McCreadie, C. (1991) *Elder Abuse: An Explanatory Study*, Age Concern Institute of Gerontology, London.

Riley, P. (1989) Professional Dilemmas in Elder Abuse (unpublished paper).

Steinmetz, S. (1981) Elder abuse. *Ageing*, January–February.

Steinmetz, S. (1988) *Duty Bound: Elder Abuse*, Sage Publications, Newbury Park.

Straus, M.A. (1986) Foreword, in *Elder Abuse: Conflict in the Family* (eds. K.A. Pillemer and R.S. Wolf), Auburn House Publishing Company, Massachusetts.

Traynor, J. and Hasnip, J. (1984) Sometimes she makes me want to hit her. *Community Care*, August.

Part Five

Part Five

Training Issues

15

Elder abuse and neglect: developing training programmes

Simon Biggs and Chris Phillipson

An important principle to convey to workers is that the mistreatment of older people starts from the initial experience of ageism within society.

Training workers in the field of elder abuse is likely in the future to become an important issue for health and social services agencies. This reflects a number of developments that took place in the 1980s and early 1990s and which may be summarized as: first, the growing body of research highlighting both the different types of abuse and their prevalence within the community (Ogg and Bennett, 1992; Wolf, 1992); second, the emergence of guidelines advising workers how to handle problems relating to elder abuse and neglect (Age Concern, 1990); third, the publication of training manuals with a direct focus on the issue of the mistreatment of elderly people (Biggs and Phillipson, 1992; Pritchard, 1992).

The need for training had already been established by American research on abuse carried out in the 1970s and 1980s. Hudson (1989), in a review of this research, notes that several studies recommend better training of professionals, with a strong educational component covering the ageing process as well as advice on detecting potential neglect and abuse. Arising out of this, many of the American research projects generated training manuals and videos targeted at professional health and social workers (McMurray-Anderson and Wolf, 1986).

There has also been some work on developing training pro-grammes aimed at helping people cope with the emotional pressures associated with the role of informal carer (Scogin *et al.* 1989).

British initiatives on training have, in contrast, taken much longer to develop. The reasons for this are, firstly, an over-riding concern with child abuse and child protection, and the concentration of financial resources in this area (especially for courses at post-qualifying levels). Secondly, the limited amount of research on elder abuse, resulting in a lack of awareness about the scale of the problem and limiting the scope of interventions to improve knowledge and expertise in the field (Ogg and Bennett, 1992). Thirdly, the narrow scope of train-ing for work with older people. Evidence from research suggests that the nature of such training is often of variable quality, with traditional approaches to ageing (emphasizing issues relating to sickness, frailty and disability) still prominent in course programmes at qualifying and post-qualifying levels (Phillipson and Strang, 1986).

Despite this environment, it is clear that the factors cited at the beginning of this chapter will promote significant new work in the field of training in mistreatment of elderly people. The aim of this chapter is to assess some of the principles around which this work will need to be developed, to review issues relating to good practice in the conduct of training, and, finally, to consider issues relating to the organization of training initiatives.

KEY PRINCIPLES IN THE DEVELOPMENT OF TRAINING

In order to set out some guiding principles and themes in developing training programmes, the following areas will be covered:

- aims and objectives of training;
- anti-ageist perspectives;
- theoretical perspectives;
- empowering older people.

The first item, aims and objectives, concerns ensuring that workers are sufficiently clear about the purpose of interven-tion in what is a sensitive and difficult area of social work practice. There are at least two issues which training should seek to clarify in terms of intervention work. First, that the goal of work in the field of abuse and neglect should be about enabling people to live their lives free of violence and mistreatment – in all the different settings and relationships the older person may be exposed to. Second, that in attempting to free the person from mistreatment, it should be recognized that distinctive moral and ethical issues may need to be faced. In particular, unlike other types of domestic violence, there may not be a clear victim or perpetrator. Because most elderly adults are legally (and actually) autonomous human beings, it may be difficult to determine who is responsible for mistreatment. This leads, as Linda Philips has pointed out, to difficult questions for professionals working in the field.

> Is it the responsiblity of an adult child to enforce rules of cleanliness on a legally competent elder when the elder does not want to be clean? What is the effect of geographic distance or filial distance on legal and moral responsibilities? Who is the victim and who is the perpetrator in situations where a legally competent elder refuses to act in his or her own best interests? And perhaps even more basic than any of these is the question of how can responsibility be assigned in a society that has yet to establish clear criteria regarding the minimum material and emotional rights to which every individual in society is entitled? (Phillips, 1989).

The issues raised by Phillips will need to be explored in some detail on training courses, with participants developing a clear ethical framework for guiding subsequent interventions within their agencies.

Anti-ageist perspectives

One of the key ethical problems confronting work with older people is the issue of discrimination in society on the basis of age (McEwen, 1990). Arising from this there is a requirement for training to develop within an explicit anti-ageist framework. Work in this area has been developed by Biggs(1989) and Itzin (1986), and this will need to be reviewed before training on abuse is developed (Biggs, 1992). Typically, training would need to consider the impact of ageist attitudes on:

- the personal relationships of older people;
- the workers' own feelings about ageing and potential conflicts arising from this;
- the practices of major social institutions.

An important principle to convey to workers is that the mistreatment of older people starts from the initial experience of ageism within society. Indeed, we can see ageism as a crucial mechanism for producing, sustaining and justifying abusive actions: through infantalizing the older person; through various institutional practices; and through the transmission of negative stereotypes (Biggs and Phillipson, 1992). Confronting ageism is, therefore, central to understanding and confronting abuse and it is consequently important to maintain a clear link between the two on training programmes concerned with the mistreatment of older people.

Theoretical perspectives

Training programmes on elder abuse should be grounded in clear theoretical perspectives that will provide the basis for workers to understand some of the complex issues surrounding this phenomenon. Two such examples are interactionist theory and political economy theory (Phillipson, 1993). The former suggests that the way in which social life is organized arises from within society itself and out of the process of interaction between its members. The theory would suggest that abuse and neglect can be viewed as a consequence of patterns or types of interaction within either families or institutions. More specifically, the theory would predict that processes arising from social and biological ageing might change role definitions within the social groups in which the older person was interacting. Such alterations might challenge hitherto stable identities, causing stress to develop within social relationships. This could be resolved by the negotiation of new self-validating identities. Alternatively, forms of psychological abuse (such as infantalization) could emerge, possibly leading to other forms of abuse and neglect (Phillips, 1986).

Interactionist perspectives focus on the question of how individuals adapt and respond to old age. In contrast, critical, or political economy perspectives examine the impact of society on the lives of older people, with a particular emphasis on the role of dominant social and economic institutions in influencing experiences in old age. Critical perspectives adopt the view that old age is a social as well as a biologically-constructed status (Phillipson, 1992).

In this context many of the experiences affecting older people can be seen as the product of particular divisions of labour and the structure of inequality, rather than as a natural product of the ageing process. Alan Walker (1980) high-lighted this perspective with the notion of the 'social creation of dependency in old age'. Peter Townsend (1981) used a similar term when he described the 'structured dependency' of older people. This dependency is seen to arise from compulsory retirement, poverty and restricted domestic and community roles. Finally, Carroll Estes (1979) coined the term 'the ageing enterprise': ' . . . to call attention to how the aged are often processed and treated as a commodity and to the fact that the age-segregated policies that fuel the ageing enterprise are socially-divisive "solutions" that single-out, stigmatize, and isolate the aged from the rest of society' (Estes, 1979).

The value of a critical approach is that it places the struggles of both carers and older people within a framework of social and political structures and ideologies. The implication of this approach is that abuse may arise from the way in which older people come to be marginalized by society (and by the services they receive). If people are encouraged to abuse the old because of their biological dependency, the likelihood may be said to increase through social forces that discriminate both against the old as well as those involved in their care (McEwen, 1990).

Such a perspective would suggest that the challenge to abuse must be seen as an issue of social policy, in addition to that of interpersonal problems among older people and their informal carers. Moreover, from the standpoint of the 'ageing enterprise' identified by Estes, we should also be concerned with potential and actual mistreatment by formal carers – either in special settings such as residential or nursing homes, or through the failure of professionals to provide adequate levels of care in the provision of services within the community.

Empowering older people

Training must also address different ways in which the power and influence of older people as individuals and in groups may be raised within community settings (Rees, 1991).

Programmes will need to address areas such as promoting advocacy and developing self-help skills. These should be seen as an essential part of developing the basis for a life free of abuse and violence. In other words, it will be important for training to cover, firstly, immediate issues such as how to recognize that abuse is occurring, how to make an assessment and how to devise appropriate measures of intervention. Secondly, however, training will need to move towards establishing that the basis for a life free of violence will be one where older people have regained control over their lives – either through their own actions or through the support of an advocate. For some groups of older people – especially those suffering from dementia – developing effective work in the field of advocacy may be crucial to the development of initiatives in the area of elderly abuse (Biggs and Phillipson, 1992).

GOOD PRACTICE IN THE CONDUCT OF TRAINING PROGRAMMES

Important questions to ask whenever a training programme is being developed centre around issues such as preparation before the training event, process and content during training itself and, finally, follow-up once formal learning has taken place.

Preparation

Biggs and Phillipson (1992) have identified a number of issues that a facilitator should appraise in the period before designing an event in order to add clarity to the intervention. The key questions to explore are:

- Who has asked you to set up the group?
- What are the expressed needs of intended participants?
- What are the similarities and differences between the two agendas?
- What mechanisms have you set up to consult on content?

- What expectations are you arousing?
- What can you offer, how much, and for how long?
- How have participants learned about the course? How accessible is information and to whom?

Answers to these points should provide important indicators about the situation the trainer is preparing for, as well as about how their work will be received and used. The character of sessions will vary considerably depending on who the training is aimed at, for example, a workshop for students who may not have had firsthand experience of working in abusive situations will be very different to one for a specialist team with a history of having worked together with older people.

In the first case, the question of who has asked the trainer to teach is relatively unproblematic as systems for invited training are likely to be routine. Consultation on content would depend on existing curricula together with the knowledge base of students at the particular point they had reached in their training. It will also be important to gain information about course members ahead of the sessions by means of a pre-course questionnaire, this gives the opportunity for an assessment of students' current life-goals, how these might affect their attitudes to older people, and the need for special facilities, such as interpreters or signers.

Questionnaires to participants are also a useful way of communicating the teacher's interest in the learning group. They allow questions of a confidential nature to be asked, such as whether individuals have had personal experience of abusive situations, and the voluntary nature of participation in the course to be underlined.

In the second case, where the trainer is invited to work with an existing team, a different set of problems are raised. Participants will already be embedded in organizational and managerial structures that will have influenced the decision to initiate training on elder abuse. This decision may also be related to specific events in the group's history, such as a particular case that has thrown up difficulties in existing practice. The question of competing agendas around training therefore takes on a higher profile in the minds of participants, even if it is not the explicit reason given for training at this point. Consultation on content can therefore be an important factor in ensuring the commitment of participants and in assessing the most effective means of intervention. Although it is important to achieve a balance between the expressed need of the parties involved, facilitators must also judge whose assessment of training needs the initial request for training or consultation reflects.

A final point about preparation concerns the facilitator's own position with regard to the intervention. Perceptions of the facilitator can be expected to vary depending on whether s/he works for the same agency, a different but related one or has external status. These factors will influence the degree to which trainers are seen as independent of other interested parties and therefore able to act disinterestedly on key issues (Nay, 1978).

Preparing the training event

When preparing training it is important to have a clear idea of the type of intervention required. The preparation period will almost certainly influence the eventual form that an event takes. It is generally helpful to classify types of intervention into two broad categories.

First, there are what may be termed technical interventions. These would focus on a particular skill to be learned and might include assessing elder abuse (Breckman and Adelman, 1988), communication skills with older people (Bender-Dreher, 1987), or methods of working (Biggs and Phillipson, 1992). This type of intervention assumes that the problem of abuse has already been examined by the organization and that a pattern of response has already been agreed. The training requested would attempt to provide answers of the 'this is what you do' variety and rely on finding educators with sufficient specialist knowledge to implement them.

Second, there are interventions that attempt to address the context within which abuse has taken place and to examine the types of response currently adopted. Here, the emphasis would be on facilitating understanding of the processes influencing current practice in order to change them in the service of more effective future functioning. These interventions may take place over a longer period, involve considerable organizational soul-searching and have less tangible results.

Unfortunately, the authors are unaware of any literature that specifically addresses elderly abuse from this perspective, although Dartington (1986) looks at collaboration between services and users in the case of 'elderly mentally infirm people', and Woodhouse and Pengelly (1991) examine anxiety and the dynamics of collaboration, drawing from their experience of child protection.

It is likely that any training intervention that extends over a longer time period will be a hybrid of the two approaches, in which questions affecting service systems feed back into the agencies, while specific technical needs will arise as a deeper understanding of the problem emerges. The rest of this section will look at issues involved in running shorter specified training events as space does not allow a fuller discussion of systems intervention.

The training session

Biggs (1989) has suggested that it is helpful for facilitators to think of any short-term event as being divided into a beginning, a middle and an end. At the beginning, especially if it is the first session of a series, participants, will need time to 'ventilate', to talk about their reasons for coming, their previous experience and their particular views on elder abuse. If this opportunity is not allowed, misunderstandings and resentment may impede learning. It is also an opportunity for the facilitator to find out about the group and communicate that the participants' own experiences and opinions will be taken seriously.

During the beginning period the task at hand can be explained, the trainer's role clarified and boundaries set around the purpose of that exercise. It might, for example, be necessary to clarify whether the purpose of the course is to be personally therapeutic for participants, to focus on problem-solving or to provide a rehearsal of social skills. These considerations are particularly relevant to elder abuse given the strong responses of blame, guilt, impotence, the need of instant solutions or intellectualization that it can evoke.

The task, the use of particular training methods, is addressed in the middle period. During this stage the facilitator has to ensure that participants understand what they have to do and should provide a framework to shape their ideas. Depending on the focus of the session, expectations of participants would vary with respect to the 'rightness' of the practical activity. If, for example, the task addressed the correct use of assessment material, there may be specific procedures that have to be learned. If the task centred on attitudes, such as the different associations evoked by the labels 'abuser' and 'carer' (Biggs and Phillipson, 1992, pp. 99–102), the acceptable latitude of personal opinion is that much broader. Indeed, the success of the exercise may depend on insights gained from some of the more unexpected responses.

At the end of a session participants should have time to reflect on the task and share their insights and conclusions. Facilitators should take care that discussion is not dominated by a few vocal members and may need to intervene to ensure a more representative picture emerges. If the session is part of a series, this period will reveal information on how the group is responding to elder abuse as a subject and the value of the training method being used. This can then inform modifications of intervention or course design, and also gives an indication of how far responses have changed across a series of sessions.

It is important to bear in mind (sometimes simply in order to retain a modicum of self-worth as a facilitator!) that elder abuse can evoke a need to find the right solution quickly; alternatively, it may generate feelings that the problem is insoluble. Both of these reactions place the trainer under considerable pressure not to allow space for constructive reflection, either because it is not seen as directly relevant or, as in the second case, because it brings participants closer to tackling a difficult and emotionally-demanding situation. This is a particular difficulty when skill-learning is addressed as it lends itself to the 'technical fix', which seems to offer a relatively undemanding solution in the short-term, while leaving other issues – such as the process of interaction between a worker and an abused older person, their carer or abusing paid worker – unexamined.

Given that the atmosphere in the learning group will also affect the facilitator/trainer, it is important to assess the meaning of feedback. This will reflect group processes and attitudes to the subject, rather than that the whole programme needs to be thoroughly rethought. Undue flight into the latter can easily reproduce anxieties emerging from the group within the trainer's own planning. Reflection on those feelings that the facilitator is left with can, on the other hand, considerably deepen his/her understanding of the issues raised by abuse itself, and thereby improve future sessions.

Follow-up

Different training formats allow different possibilities for follow-up, that is the degree to which learning can be consolidated after the formal input has finished. Follow-up is important because it will influence whether learning is generalized to other settings and sustained over time. Developing strategies for follow-up is easier if work has taken place with a committed team that continues to work together in the setting where learning took place. It is most difficult if participants have attended a short course away from their work setting as isolated individuals who then have to return to an environment that is either unaware of or unwilling to recognize their new learning.

A particular problem of working with older people and abuse is the low institutional priority that is often given to this area. Both groups of former participants may find that mechanisms for responding are underdeveloped and subject to ageist assumptions. There is, therefore, a need to ensure that time is allotted in which workers can regularly review progress made, refresh knowledge and understanding and find support from peers. In the case of isolated short course attenders it may be necessary for consenting participants to exchange work addresses and telephone numbers. Training can also build follow-up days into the conditions of registration to facilitate support and sharing practice experience.

CONCLUSION: ORGANIZATION ISSUES IN THE DEVELOPMENT OF TRAINING PROGRAMMES

An additional consideration in the development of training programmes concerns that of multidisciplinary working. Elder abuse invariably involves a range of professional groups, whether at the level of assessment, the organization of case conferences, or developing specific forms of service delivery (Eastman, 1984; Breckman and Adelman, 1988;

DoH/SSI, 1993). Based on the American experience, it seems unlikely (as well as undesirable) that the response to abuse (whether in terms of training or service organization) should be exclusively an intra-organizational matter. Wolf (1992), in a review of research and practice in the field of elder abuse, notes that a major achievement of the American scene has been the development of community task forces to improve service delivery to abused and neglected older people. She writes:

> These interorganizational structures bring together representatives of many different sectors of society including law, medicine, nursing, social services, mental health, ageing, religion, criminal justice, law enforcement, financial management and adult protective services. They have been responsible for identifying service gaps, establishing new programmes, educating the public and professionals, and advocating for legislative changes to the system.

Forums such as these clearly provide the basis for developing training on an inter-agency basis, with the sharing of financial resources, skills and levels of professional expertise. Some moves in this direction have been made in the UK, notably under the influence of Bennett and his colleagues in the London Borough of Tower Hamlets. In theory, such work should be facilitated by the National Health Service and Community Care Act, 1990 and its development of locally-based community care plans.

The way forward for work in the area of elder abuse, and for training initiatives in particular, must lie in improved service co-ordination within neighbourhoods, especially between primary health care on the one hand, and social services departments on the other. Whether this can emerge through goodwill alone remains doubtful. It may require positive moves in the direction of inter-agency training (along the lines adopted in the field of child protection) with the provision of financial resources to stimulate appropriate seminars and workshops. Given the increased attention and concern being given to the area of abuse and neglect, it is hoped that a substantial initiative will emerge along these lines.

REFERENCES

Age Concern (1990) *Abuse of Elderly People: Guidelines for Action*, Age Concern, London.

Bender-Dreher, B. (1987) *Communication Skills for Working with Elders*, Springer, New York.

Biggs, S.J. (1989) *Confronting Ageing*, Central Council for Education and Training in Social Work, London.

Biggs, S. (1992) Groupwork and Professional Attitudes to Old Age, in *Gerontology: responding to an ageing society* (ed. K. Morgan), Jessica Kingsley, London.

Biggs, S.J. and Phillipson, C. (1992) *Understanding Elder Abuse*, Longmans, Harlow.

Breckman, R. and Adelman, R. (1988) *Strategies for Helping Victims of Elder Mistreatment*, Sage Books, London.

Dartington, T. (1986) *The Limits to Altruism*, King's Fund, London.

Department of Health/Social Services Inspectorate (1993) *No Longer Afraid: Practice Guidelines to Safeguard Older People in Domestic Settings*, HMSO, London.

Eastman, M. (1984) *Old Age Abuse*, Age Concern (England), Mitcham.

Estes, C. (1979) *The Aging Enterprise*, Josey Bass, San Francisco.

Hudson, M. (1989) Analyses of the concerns of elder mistreatment: abuse and neglect. *Journal of Elder Abuse and Neglect*, **1**, 5–26.

Itzin, C. (1986) Ageism Awareness Training, in *Dependence and Interdependence in Old Age* (eds C. Phillipson, M. Bernard and P. Strang), Croom Helm, London.

McEwen, E. (1990) *Age: The Unrecognised Discrimination*, Age Concern (England), London.

McMurray-Anderson, S. and Wolf, R.A. (1986) *Elder Abuse and Neglect in the Family: Training Guidelines*, University Center on Aging, University of Massachusetts Medical Center, Massachusetts.

Nay, W.R. (1978) Intra-institutional roadblocks to Behaviour Modification Programming, in *Child Behaviour Therapy* (ed. D. Marholin), Gardner, New York.

Ogg, J. and Bennett, G. (1992) Elder abuse in Britain, *British Medical Journal*, **305**, 998–9.

Phillips, L. (1986) Theoretical Explanations of Elder Abuse: Competing Hypotheses and Unresolved Issues, in *Elder Abuse: Conflict in the Family* (eds K. Pillemer and R. Wolf), Auburn House Publishing Company, Massachusetts, pp. 197–217.

Phillips, L. (1989) Issues in Identifying and Intervening in Elder Abuse, in *Elder Abuse: Practice and Policy* (eds R. Filinson and S. Ingman), Human Sciences Press, New York pp. 86–93.

Phillipson, C. (1992) The social construction of old age: perspectives from political economy, *Clinical Gerontology*, **1**, 403–10.

Phillipson, C. (1993) Abuse of Older People: Sociological Perspectives, in *Mistreatment of Older People* (eds P. Decalmer and F. Glendenning), Sage Books, London.

Phillipson, C. and Strang, P. (1986) *Training and Education for an*

Ageing Society, Health Education Council (London) in association with the University of Keele.

Pritchard, J. (1992) *The Abuse of Elderly People: A Handbook for Professionals*, Jessica Kingsley, London.

Rees, S. (1991) *Achieving Power*, Allen and Unwin, London.

Scogin, F., Beall, C., Bynum, J. *et al.* (1989) Training for abusive caregivers: an unconventional approach to an intervention dilemma. *Journal of Elder Abuse and Neglect*, **1**(4), 73–86.

Townsend, P. (1981) The structured dependency of the elderly. *Ageing and Society*, **1**(1), 5–28.

Walker, A. (1980) The social creation of poverty and dependency in old age. *Journal of Social Policy*, **9**, 49–75.

Wolf, R. (1992) Victimization of the elderly: elder abuse and neglect. *Clinical Gerontology*, **2**, 269–76.

Woodhouse, D. and Pengelly, P. (1991) *Anxiety and the Dynamics of Collaboration*, Aberdeen University Press, Aberdeen.

16

Perspectives in training: assessment and intervention issues in old age abuse

Fiona Goudie and Drew Alcott

Participants with extensive knowledge of old age abuse from one particular professional or theoretical orientation were sometimes completely unaware of the existence of other models and theories.

INTRODUCTION

This chapter is based largely on our personal experience of running a series of training workshops on old age abuse. We ran 10 two-day workshops for a number of different agencies between 1989 and 1992. In most cases this involved running 'in-house' courses for health authorities or social services departments, where participants came from the same background (for example, nursing or social work) with a variety of experience and qualifications (for instance, care assistants with no formal qualifications and social workers with CQSWs). Five of the courses were run for a training agency, and participants on each course came from a variety of backgrounds (housing associations, nursing homes, voluntary sector agencies, health authorities and social services departments). Most participants on these courses were professionally qualified in their respective fields.

BACKGROUND OF TRAINERS

We are both chartered clinical psychologists and at the time of developing and running the courses we were working within a multidisciplinary community support team for elderly people with mental health problems. In our clinical work we had both been involved in cases where abuse was either suspected or confirmed. Alongside this developing clinical interest we were involved in the development and implementation of a training programme called 'Working with Dementia'. Feedback from participants in this programme suggested that interest in the topic of abuse was increasing and there was a number of requests for us to run workshops on old age abuse.

The training programme

The development of the programme was based on:

1. a review of topics highlighted in existing literature;
2. areas of interest expressed by those requesting workshops;
3. our own interests and experience of working with those at risk of/experiencing abuse.

We aimed to provide a framework within which participants could explore current issues related to the identification, assessment and intervention in old age abuse from a theoretical and practical perspective. We used case study material to encourge participants to explore these items based on their own experiences.

ISSUES ARISING FROM THE TRAINING COURSES

The issues outlined below include those raised by individual participants in formal and informal feedback to us or the agency involved in organizing the training courses. They also incorporate our own retrospective views of the issues that emerged repeatedly in various courses over the three-year period. We acknowledge that the content is subjective and influenced by our own background as psychologists and our position as trainers on the courses.

Level of interest

Although it may seem an obvious point, we believe it is worth highlighting the fact that interest in the topic of old age abuse seemed to increase considerably during the period we were involved in running the workshops. In particular, there was a rise in the number of health service professionals showing an interest in attending or commissioning workshops. This increasing level of interest seems to have been reflected elsewhere. McCreadie's (1991) exploratory study of old age abuse suggests that there was only a trickle of published work on the topic in the UK in the 1970s and early 1980s (Baker, 1975; Burston, 1975; Clark, 1975; Eastman, 1980, 1982, 1984; Cloke, 1983), but that this had become a steady stream by the turn of the decade (Kingston, 1990; Pritchard, 1989, 1990, 1991, 1992; Pugh, 1990; Homer and Gilleard, 1990; Bennett, 1990). In addition, a number of professionals and statutory agencies began to produce practice guidelines (British Geriatric Society, 1990; British Association of Social Workers, 1990; Law Commission, 1991; London Borough of Bexley, 1988; Enfield Social Services Department, 1989; Kent Social Services Department, 1987; Rochdale Social Services Department, 1989).

The diversity of interest and points of view expressed suggested a wide range of theoretical and practical knowledge. However, participants with extensive knowledge of old age abuse from one particular professional or theoretical orientation were sometimes completely unaware of the existence of other models and theories.

Controversy over the definition of old age abuse

Discussions about appropriate terminology generated heated discussion in some workshops. Some participants felt that the term 'inadequate care' (Fulmer and O'Malley, 1987) was less stigmatizing than 'mistreatment' (Johnson, 1986) or 'elder abuse' (Eastman, 1984; Pillemer and Finkelhor, 1988; Wolf, 1988) in relation to carers who may abuse through ignorance or the strain of caring for a dependent relative 'around the clock'. Others felt that 'inadequate care' encompassed neither the abuse of a carer by the person being cared for, nor deliberate or malevolent abuse of older people in the absence of a caring relationship.

Belief and disbelief in the existence of some types of old age abuse

Although it could be argued that concerns about definitions are semantic, or that different definitions are needed for research or practical purposes (McCreadie, 1991), preferred definitions in the context of the workshops seemed to relate to the extent to which participants believed in the existence of certain types of abuse. The majority of participants were concerned about abuse arising as a result of carer strain, or as a result of the impact of abuse of a carer by an older person being cared for. Some participants were sceptical about the existence of intentional physical, sexual or institutional abuse by carers or strangers, even when other participants mentioned examples from their own clinical practice. It appeared that direct experience of clients who had experienced a particular form of abuse had the most impact on participants' beliefs in particular types of abuse and on their preferred definitions.

Lack of co-ordinated UK research

Large scale research studies have almost exclusively been carried out in the USA. We included presentations of the work of Pillemer and Wolf (1986), Pillemer and Finkelhor (1988), Kosberg (1988) and Wolf (1988) among others. Participants were, quite understandably, concerned about the extent to which incidence and prevalence figures could be extrapolated from the USA to the UK and were keen for information on research being conducted in the UK. Apart from the published work of Eastman (1984) other ongoing but unpublished work (for example that of Kingtson, 1990) was sometimes known only to participants in certain professional fields or geographical areas. McCreadie's collation of known UK sources in one volume has played an important part in beginning the exercise of co-ordination.

Statutory frameworks: models and philosophies

The model that appeared to be favoured by the majority of participants was one based on the protective framework originating from child abuse work. Other participants held the view that elder abuse should be viewed in the same way as other types of adult abuse depending on the circumstances (spouse abuse, for instance). Considerable concern was expressed about the lack of statutory regulations empowering social services departments to intervene.

Participants were keen to see clear guidelines and procedures developed, although there were mixed feelings about the creation of 'at risk registers' or 'place of safety orders' for vulnerable older adults. There was an acknowledgement that the evaluation of risk by older people themselves needed to be taken into account, and that sometimes people would choose to remain in potentially abusive situations in order to remain in their own homes.

Mental health professionals, familiar with situations where older adults were strongly 'persuaded' to come into hospital by professional collegues reluctant to make use of existing legislation under the Mental Health Act, were concerned about this and other forms of restraint (such as *de facto* detention or the use of locked doors). It was felt that these procedures could themselves be 'abusive' because they were not carried out under strict guidelines and there was no official right of review or appeal.

During the period we were giving our training workshops the Law Commission (1991) produced its consultation document on mentally incapacitated adults and decision making. This was discussed with interest in some of the later workshops. It was felt that the differences in philosophy behind a protective framework governed by the principle of acting 'in the best interests of' an individual, compared with a framework governed by the concept of 'substituted judgement', would have an impact on the development of professional guidelines.

The 'substituted judgement' principle has relevance when an individual has expressed views or judgements about particular events or circumstances at some point in the past, but is no longer able to do so. Thus, for instance, if an older person has expressed the view that he or she would never wish to be cared for in a nursing home but then develops a dementing illness that means he or she requires some care and is no longer able to express a preference, the 'substituted judgement' principle would give weight to his or her previously expressed view. The 'best interests' principle would be based on the notion of what an 'average citizen' would consider to be the best course of action, whether or not this coincided with the previous wishes of the individual, even if the 'best interests' judgement could itself be viewed as 'abusive'.

Participants seemed most comfortable with guidelines based on the notions of 'best interests', particularly where people with dementia or other cognitive impairment were concerned. However, there was interest in the concept of 'substituted judgement' among those working in the voluntary sector and those with an interest in advocacy.

Counselling and therapeutic issues

There was a great deal of interest expressed in the development of appropriate counselling and therapeutic tech- niques for carers under strain and at risk of abusing those they cared for. This included an identified need for appropriate counselling and support aimed at formal carers, particularly those working in institutional settings who may be particularly vulnerable to stress and potential burn-out.

During the workshops we introduced Breckman and Adelman's (1988) work on strategies for helping victims of elder abuse. This model conceptualized the process of moving in a stepwise fashion from a life of being abused to one in which abuse is absent. The work of the therapist is to help the abuse survivor move from denial to an acknowledgement that abuse is taking place, and ultimately to take steps to stop the abuse.

It was of interest to us that the majority of course participants were interested in protective or statutory methods by which abuse could be prevented if carers could not be helped by counselling or therapy to modify their actions, rather than considering the value of therapy to empower the victim. This may, in part, have been due to a greater degree of concern about cognitively-impaired individuals, despite the evidence that a large number of those suffering abuse are cognitively intact.

Differences in skill level and ability of workers to undertake assessment and intervention work

Running workshops with participants from a wide variety of backgrounds and experience suggested that while most people could develop the knowledge necessary to identify suspected abuse, not everyone had the necessary skills to undertake the complexity of the task of assessment and intervention. Familiarity with interviewing people in a non-directive fashion about sensitive issues, being able to tolerate ambiguity and use counselling skills are necessary prerequisites to assessment and intervention in this area, as is an awareness of how our own personal values and beliefs about ageing and abuse can effect our judgement – not always in the best interests of the abused client or patient.

LESSONS LEARNED: CONCLUSIONS AND RECOMMENDATIONS FOR THE FUTURE DEVELOPMENT OF TRAINING WORKSHOPS ON ELDER ABUSE

Participants will have different perspectives on what constitutes elder abuse whether courses are run 'in-house' or are open to a range of agencies. We have found it helpful to acknowledge and reflect on these at the start of a course and to emphasize the acknowledgement of differences rather than trying to present a uniform definition.

It is important to consider the context of abuse with which participants are concerned. We differentiated abuse from formal and informal carers and abuse within the home from abuse in residential settings. Participants were, on the whole, keen to consider abuse in different settings through discussions and exercises split up into different sessions. A number of participants wanted to split considerations about abuse of cognitively-impaired individuals from abuse of those who were unimpaired, although we had not incorporated this into the design of our workshops.

Although splitting sessions in this way allowed participants to address the different assessment and intervention strategies that might be needed, in retrospect it also encouraged and reinforced a compartmentalized view of old age abuse. For instance, some participants held the view that the 'most important' area for us to be concerned with was institutional abuse or abuse by informal carers, and felt sessions that focused on these topics were sometimes too short and other topics were less relevant.

In retrospect this problem could have been addressed by exploring the similarities between abuse in different contexts and by looking at similarities between participants' views. Indeed this seems to be a matter for urgent consideration by those involved in training as well as those involved in policy development. On the one hand, as has been pointed out by

McCreadie (1991), 'Different kinds of abuse in different family contexts appear to have different explanations and require different kinds of intervention'. On the other hand, compartmentalizing elder abuse and developing special strategies for intervention that differ from those for abuse against all adults, could itself be abusive. We know of situations that suggest that 'Guidelines On Elder Abuse' may not be acceptable to those they seek to protect; local authority Part III homes being offered as a place of safety instead of a women's refuge to a woman who has been physically abused by her husband, would be one example of this.

Participants on most courses were keen to learn about guidelines and any relevant developments in the politico-legal framework (for instance, the Law Commission's consultation document). Overall, the development of local guidelines seemed to be a positive move, representing increased awareness of the issue of old age abuse. We were concerned that the UK was in danger of repeating some aspects of the American experience, the danger of focusing on developing guidelines as an end in itself rather than developing appropriate preventive and intervention strategies. The introduction of mandatory reporting in 43 of the states in the USA does not appear to have reduced the incidence of elder abuse. A report by the United States House of Representatives (1990) claimed that 42 of the 49 states that responded to the enquiries of the committee, replied that elder abuse was increasing. It has been suggested that this reflects an imbalance between reporting laws and the provision of services. There are also suggestions that investigations may themselves be abusive if no abuse has in fact taken place (Fulmer and O'Malley, 1987). Likewise, the interventions may expose the older person to an increased likelihood of subsequent abuse. Outcome data collected in the wake of mandatory reporting laws in the USA identify that of the cases of elder abuse brought to diagnosis and intervention, 50% of the victims were placed in institutional settings, 25% received various home supports and another 25% declined any assistance at all (O'Malley *et al.*, 1983, cited by Staats and Koin, 1989).

In relation to the points made above there is a need for co-ordinated UK research to determine whether extrapolation from the American studies is valid. What have been the outcomes, for instance, in areas where guidelines exist? As mentioned earlier there may be a need to involve staff with advanced training in assessment and intervention after possible abuse has been identified. Is the use of residential care as an intervention something that tends to occur in a crisis or with workers less skilled in counselling or therapy? It may not be possible to gain answers to these questions from American research, but ongoing evaluation of work being done in the UK will help us to establish more clearly what is effective and what is not.

In-house training was, in our experience, more successful since participants either had the same professional background or were interested in the same sorts of issues based on common work experiences. However, we acknowledge that this could lead to piecemeal, uncoordinated local policy if inter-agency training and development does not occur subsequently. We would recommend that in-house training is the first phase of a co-ordinated strategy helping to build confidence, clarify issues of concern common to participants and introduce them to different views and the perspectives of other agencies in a 'safe' environment. The second phase should involve inter-agency work run in a sensitive way by facilitators or trainers who are familiar with likely differences and who can use these in a positive way to build up a good multidisciplinary resource rather than letting differences become destructive.

We believe there would be merit in the development of a basic syllabus for post-qualification training of specialists that takes into account the pooled experience of trainers who have been involved in this sort of work to date.

We think that training course and workshop organizers should pay attention to the issues from workers' own backgrounds that may affect their objectivity in working with the survivors and perpetrators of elder abuse. Intense emotions can be aroused in work of this nature, which may relate to the worker's own experience rather than being an empathetic response to that of the client. For instance, feelings of strain, being undervalued and overburdened in one's own work or personal life may mean it is easier to identify with the situation of an apparently overburdened carer and harder to identify with a needy, dependent person who may be experiencing neglect or abuse.

Being aware of the presence of such feelings can be important in evaluating difficulties and blocks one might be having with a particular case. One of us (Goudie) used a case study in one of our courses that involved the disclosure of details in five stages. Initial information encouraged identification with a carer who appeared to be under strain, later information suggested the perpetrator may have had malevolent motives or a significant mental health problem. Participants reported that they found it useful to reflect in a non-threatening workshop setting on how positive identification with a particular individual would affect their strategy for intervention.

Appropriate, sensitive supervision for those involved in on-going abuse work is crucial to ensuring that workers have the opportunity to reflect on the impact of their own experiences of working with older clients. Acknowledging that some of our own views and work practices may be ageist, and thus potentially abusive themselves, should be a feature of such supervision.

In conclusion, we feel there is a useful role for short, inter-disciplinary courses that introduce concepts and practical issues related to working with elder abuse. Such courses can be a starting point for skills development and initiatives in service planning. They need to be part of a comprehensive range of training courses that includes more extensive training for people who are likely to be involved extensively in assessment and intervention work with survivors and perpetrators.

REFERENCES

Baker, A.A. (1975) Granny battering. *Modern Geriatrics*, **5**(8), 20–4.
Bennett, G. (1990) Assessing abuse in the elderly. *Geriatric Medicine*, **20**(7), 49–51.
Bexley, London Borough of (1988) *Report of a Working Party and Seminar on Abuse of Elderly People*, London Borough of Bexley, Kent.
Breckman, R.S. and Adelman, R.D. (1988) *Strategies for Helping Victims of Elder Mistreatment*, Sage, California.
British Association of Social Workers (1990) *Abuse of Elderly People – Guidelines for Action*, BASW, Birmingham
British Geriatric Society (1990) *Abuse of Elderly People: Guidelines for Action for those Working with Elderly People*, Age Concern (England), Mitcham.
Burston, G.R. (1975) Granny battering. *British Medical Journal*, **3**, 592–3.
Clark, A.N.G. (1975) The diogenes syndrome. *Nursing Times*, **71**(21), 800–2.
Cloke, C. (1983) *Old Age Abuse in the Domestic Setting – A Review*, Age Concern (England), Mitcham.
Eastman, M. (1980) The Battering of Mrs Scarfe. *New Age*, Winter 1980/1981.

Eastman, M. (1982) Granny battering, a hidden problem. *Community Care*, **413**, 27.

Eastman, M. (1984) *Old Age Abuse*, Age Concern, Mitcham.

Enfield Social Services Department (1989) *Notes of Guidance (practice and procedure): abuse of vulnerable adults*, London Borough of Enfield, London.

Fulmer, T. and O'Malley, T. (1987) *Inadequate Care of the Elderly*, Springer, New York.

Homer, A.C. and Gilleard, C. (1990) Abuse of elderly people by their carers. *British Medical Journal*, **301**, 1359–62.

Johnson, T. (1986) Critical issues in the definition of elder abuse, in *Elder Abuse: Conflict in the Family* (eds V.A. Pillemer and R. Wolf), Auburn House, Dover, Massachusetts.

Kent Social Services Department (1987) *Practice Guidelines for Dealing with Elder Abuse*, Kent County Council, Maidstone.

Kingston, P. (1990) Elder Abuse. University of Keele masters degree in gerontology dissertation.

Kosberg, J. (1988) Preventing elder abuse. *The Gerontologist*, **28**, 1.

Law Commission (1991) *Law Commission Consultation Paper 119: Mentally Incapacitated Adults and Decision Making*, HMSO, London.

McCreadie, C. (1991) *Elder Abuse: An Exploratory Study*, Age Concern Institute of Gerontology, London.

Pillemer, K.A. and Finkelhor, D. (1988) The prevalence of elder abuse: A random sample survey. *The Gerontologist*, **28**(1), 51–7.

Pillemer, K.A. and Wolf, R.S. (eds) (1986) *Elder Abuse: Conflict in the Family*, Auburn House, Dover, Massachussets.

Pritchard, J.H. (1989) Confronting the taboo of the abuse of elderly people. *Social Work Today*, 5 October, 12–13.

Pritchard, J.H. (1990) Charting the hits. *Care Weekly*, 19 October, 10–11.

Pritchard, J.H. (1991) Sufferers in silence. *Care Weekly*, 9 August, 10–11.

Pritchard, J.H. (1992) *The abuse of elderly people: a handbook for professionals*, Jessica Kingsley, London.

Pugh, S. (1990) *Adult Abuse: Decision Making*, Tameside Metropolitan Borough Council Social Services Department, Tameside.

Rochdale Social Services Department (1989) *Adult Abuse – Practice Guidelines*, Rochdale Metropolitan Borough Council, Rochdale.

Staats, D. and Koin, D. (1989) Elder Abuse, in *Geriatric Medicine: Fundamentals of Geriatric Care*, 2nd edn (eds C.K. Cassell and J.R. Walsh), Springer Verlag, New York.

US House of Representatives (1990) *Elder Abuse: a decade of shame and inaction*, Select Committee on Aging, Subcommittee on Health and Long Term Care, Government Printing Office, Washington DC.

Wolf, R.S. (1988) Elder abuse: ten years later. *Journal of the American Geriatrics Society*, **36**(8), 758–62.

Appendix

A summary and commentary on *No Longer Afraid: Practice Guidelines to Safeguard Older People in Domestic Settings*, SSI CI (93/23), Department of Health, 1993.

This book was in press when the Department of Health published *No Longer Afraid*, which is therefore not discussed in the text. The *No Longer Afraid* guidelines are such an important development in the old age abuse arena, however, that I thought it only fitting that a review of them be included. What follows is a short, personal consideration of the main issues they cover.

In 1990, concern about the reports of abuse of older people in their own homes led the Social Services Inspectorate to examine the problem in two London boroughs. I was fortunate enough to be part of that survey, the findings of which were published in a report that recommended the Department of Health to produce some guidelines. *No Longer Afraid* is the result and it deals with the issues local authority social services department managers and practitioners need to consider in undertaking work with abused older people.

David Tomlinson, a Social Services Inspector and the author of the guidelines, has been working to raise awareness of elder abuse for many years long before it was even on the social services agenda. His leadership and commitment to the needs of older people have culminated in these practice guidelines.

No Longer Afraid puts forward a definition of abuse that focuses on the type of abuse and its effect. Sexual abuse is included, as are comments that many definitions leave out neglect, while others make no reference to time factors.

People's rights and the power one person can exercise over another do not, unfortunately, feature in the recommended definition, despite being mentioned in the main body of the guidelines.

PREVALENCE AND INCIDENCE

Local authorities are encouraged to record quantitative information, including ethnicity data, but Tomlinson acknowledges the fact that there is no accepted way of recording reported cases, let alone unreported or undetected cases.

It is to be hoped that as both health and local authorities monitor and identify unmet need through assessment and care planning processes, a clearer picture of prevalence may be obtained.

CAUSES AND INDICATORS

It is pleasing to note that the guidelines recognize carer stress, inadequate caring skills and poor family relationships as being among the causal factors of abuse. Some researchers and academics are beginning to question the relevance of these factors, but I remain convinced that stress is an important aspect. Appendix One of the guidelines suggests there can be no comprehensive check-list of indicators that may lead to abuse, but attempts to give as detailed a list as our present knowledge allows. The danger is that as agencies draw up their own guidance notes from this framework, workers might use it as a check-list rather than as an aid to professional judgement.

POLICY AND STRATEGY

It is satisfying to note the recognition that a policy must include management responsibility. Strategies developed for the management of child protection have given agencies expertise in this area, and the guidelines take the precaution of including, in an appendix, specific details on the difference between child and elder abuse.

TRAINING AND SUPPORT

The guidance will encourage agencies to adopt an integrated multi-agency approach to training and staff development. Professionals from both social work and health care should find them invaluable in framing sessions on causes and awareness to heighten responsiveness to elder abuse.

ACCESS TO ASSISTANCE

The racial or ethnic background of many victims of abuse precludes them either from being identified or, having been identified, from experiencing the appropriate or relevant intervention. Agencies are urged to ensure information leaflets are translated into languages appropriate for the local ethnic profile and interpreting services that are available from trained interpreters.

ASSESSMENT, CARE PLANNING AND CARE PACKAGES

There is a useful guide to ensure that agencies maintain their needs-led rather than service-led approach to the assessment process. The holistic approach is rightly seen as the most appropriate, with the care plan designed to meet particular needs rather than determined by what service has traditionally been available. One point which, although mentioned, gets a little buried, is that of the contribution of the abused and abuser to the design of the care plan.

The publication of *No Longer Afraid* was a milestone event after years of inactivity on the part of many statutory agencies. The Community Care legislation has proved to be a useful spur by making explicit the principles of assessment and care management, and stressing the importance of assisting vulnerable older people.

It may be appropriate for agencies to develop guidelines for vulnerable adults, an approach taken by the London Borough of Enfield. However, the guidelines address the specific issue inherent in elder abuse: the changing burden for relatives/carers as the people on whom they were once dependent now depend on them. The guidelines also emphasize the importance of racial and cultural issues and the need to take these fully into account when assessing cases and planning intervention.

No Longer Afraid is a valuable document that is not only timely but crucial if agencies are to meet the challenge of an ageing population and the diminishing number of carers available to support their relatives.

Mervyn Eastman

Index

Page numbers appearing in **bold** refer to figures and page numbers appearing in *italic* refer to tables.